Perennials All Season

Planning and Planting an Ever-Blooming Garden

Douglas Green

Contemporary Books

Chicago   New York   San Francisco   Lisbon   London   Madrid   Mexico City
Milan   New Delhi   San Juan   Seoul   Singapore   Sydney   Toronto

The McGraw-Hill Companies

Library of Congress Cataloging-in-Publication Data

Green, Douglas.
    Perennials all season : planning and planting an ever-blooming garden / Douglas Green.
       p.   cm.
    ISBN 0-8092-9988-7
    1. Perennials.   I. Title.

  SB434 .G68   2003
  635.9′32—dc21   2001052967

Interior design by Nick Panos
Interior illustrations by Dan Krovatin

ISBN 0-8092-9988-7

Douglas Green

For Elizabeth Grace

For her dreams and the smiles she gives me,

I can only confess a father's love.

Contents

Preface

Let's admit it right at the start. The main reason we all—and I include myself in this group—garden with perennials is to replicate those glorious, lush, ever-blooming gardens whose photographs we drool over in magazines and books. Our gardening dream is to be the envy of the neighborhood, with a vibrant garden gracing our home from spring through fall. All winter, we conjure visions of fully loaded flower stems and fragrant bouquets. In our mind's eye, we see wonderfully crowded beds full of healthy, dazzling flowers just waiting to welcome our less fortunate guests. If we close our eyes, we can picture each and every flower.

The reality is often different. Oh, we plant, feed, and prune with care, but somehow the garden can never compare with the flower beds of our dreams. We continually move plants about, seeking that ideal arrangement that will set them all off to perfection. We run ourselves ragged, trying this technique and that, this new and "scientifically guaranteed" fertilizer or that pair of ergonomic hand pruners. Yes, we haunt specialist nurseries and pore over catalogs, looking for just the right plant to make our gardens come alive. We take notes at garden club meetings and ask our garden writers and radio gurus for their secrets. Still, that elusive perennial garden that blooms all season is out of our reach.

The trouble is that we're looking for the answers in all the wrong places.

It's in the design. The reality of perennial gardening is that the way in which the bed is laid out determines how lush it will look.

It's in the plant selection. No matter how good a gardener you are, if all the plants in your garden bloom in May and June, your fall garden will be a wasteland.

It's in the plant arrangement. Great combinations are not accidental. There are guidelines and rules of thumb to create those seemingly simple, cottage-garden perennial borders.

It's in this book. In *Perennials All Season*, I've combined all the tricks of the trade into a simple system of garden design. The guidelines given here will allow any gardener to create a garden that blooms all season. Gardening is not rocket science, nor should it be artistic psychobabble. It is easily learned and almost as easily accomplished.

In the pages that follow, you will discover that you can and will get your garden to bloom all summer long in the colors you love. So, let us begin to turn that lush, fragrant vision you hold in your mind's eye into a reality that greets you every time you step outside.

Acknowledgments

*A*ndrea is the person responsible for my color education and for slowly changing this plantsman into a gardener.

Jeanne Fredericks, my agent, who thankfully never gives up on works-in-progress.

Anne Knudsen, my editor at Contemporary Books, who believed in the project and wanted it done.

Dan Heims, at Terra Nova Nurseries, for the fine photographs and the plants in my garden. Sharing is a great gardening tradition.

The folks at Blooms of Bressingham North America for lending me slides of their great perennial plants. I like the slides, but I really like their plants better.

All the writers and correspondents on alpine-l who have challenged me to think about gardening in new ways.

The fellow members of the Ottawa Rock Garden Society and Ontario Rock Garden Society who have shared seeds, plants, and ideas faithfully and wonderfully for many years. My gardens would not be the same without their help.

Dreaming of an Ever-Blooming Garden

I can't even begin to tell you how good I feel when I see that first spring crocus or smell the first sweet rose of the season. You see, flowers speak to my soul in ways that my written words can never quite convey. To keep myself happy and sane in an increasingly busy world, I made a garden that is constantly in glorious bloom and that speaks to me all season long. I was able to do this in my own garden because of the design and plant choices I made, and I have to confess I do revel in its glory. My dream of a garden that is ever in bloom has become a reality.

Unfortunately, some garden designers would have us believe that garden design is an arcane science, only open to those who know some magic formula. Well, magic formula or not, I have seen some pretty good gardens put together by gardeners who would not know a magician's spell from a design principle. There is no reason at all why our first attempts at design should fail to result in a garden that flowers all season. Oh, to be sure, there is no question that gardeners with a little artistry in their souls can create better first attempts than most of us. Gardens are, after all, artistic creations. Yet, this book gives *any* gardener—even those who have never yet put spade to dirt—the tools to create an ever-blooming garden that will be a haven of color and fragrance from the first spring flush through to the last gasps of fall.

PICTURE-PERFECT?

I love the photographs of gardens that spill from the pages of books and magazines. And like most gardeners, I use them to help me transform my own perennial beds. But the funny thing about photographs is that they rarely tell the whole story. The pictures of enviably glorious, lush flower beds are usually taken when the gardens are in their prime, at the very height of their bloom cycle. The photographs are taken on longed-for days when the light is perfect and are shot using high-intensity film that saturates the eye with color. No editor would dare put anything less in a book or magazine.

The hard reality is that it is impossible to create a garden that is at this exaggerated height of bloom for the entire growing season. No plant maintains its bloom from April through September. No matter how well planned the garden is, after a spring-blooming plant is spent, there will be a spot in the garden without color. In a later chapter, you will discover many longer-blooming plants that help solve this problem, but accept that there will be nonflowering areas of your garden at all times of the gardening season. Your objective as a gardener is to minimize these spots and create your own stunning color combinations that take the eye away from them. You and your visitors will not notice them if you create wide swaths of color around them.

MICK HALES

All-Season Bloom?

While the goal of this book is to show you how to create a perennial garden that will be in bloom from spring through fall, you may not find this to be practical. If your garden is at the summer cottage, there is no value in planting wonderful early-spring-blooming plants. Other than the mosquitoes, no one will be there to view them. Similarly, if cottage or camp life ends on Labor Day, fall-blooming chrysanthemums and the newer varieties of *Solidago* would be a total waste of garden space. Instead, a single-season garden with flowers that bloom for an extended period in high summer is the ideal choice.

Some gardeners find it easiest to concentrate all their spring-blooming plants in one garden and the summer bloomers in another. They ignore the fall because they are tired of gardening by then.

The point is that each garden is different and it is up to you to decide which bloom cycle is important for your own garden. Just because an ever-blooming perennial garden is the ideal of many gardeners does not mean it has to be your goal.

Turn the Dream into Reality— Three Secrets

1. More Is Better

It is impossible to have too many perennials in your garden. The pictures we all drool over rarely consist of single plants. When you look at them closely, you will see that that huge mass of blooms is not coming from a single plant but rather from several plants of the same kind planted together. The first general planting rule is that a minimum of three plants of any kind are always planted together to create a color mass. After a few seasons of growth, the flowering mass will grow together to create the special effect we see in magazines. It is not that you cannot grow plants as lush as those of the gardens in the pictures; it is that you do not plant enough of the plants together to create that effect.

As a frugal gardener, I do know that the best plants are often the most expensive and planting three of them can do serious damage to the budget. You have the option of planting one and allowing it to grow and spread. Or you can do as I do: pretend that you have a garden emergency and the costs will only happen "just this once." Creating that perfect flowering picture demands using the correct number of plants; any reduction in numbers will reduce the effect and the magic.

2. Bigger Is Better

There is no way to sugarcoat this main point: bigger is better. Perennial gardens look better when they are larger. Herbaceous perennials do not look good in small beds. Alpine plants look good in small gardens; but then again, alpines are small plants. The question is one of proportion, and the proportion that beginning designers should remember is 3:1. For every 3' (90 cm) of length of the garden bed, the width should be 1' (30 cm). This means that a short 10' (300 cm) bed has to be at least 3' (90 cm) wide (let us not quibble over an inch or two) to be in proportion. A backyard garden of 20' (600 cm) in length along the back of the property should then be at least 6' (180 cm) wide. Beds can be made wider than the formula would suggest but they are made narrower only at the designer's peril. The maximum width for longer borders in many of the classic designs seems to be between 14' (420 cm) and 20' (600 cm). If the flower bed stretches past 45' (1,350 cm) in length, it is not necessary to widen the bed past 14' (420 cm). You may, but it is not absolutely necessary.

Wide gardens, which offer a front as well as a back to the bed, give the garden designer the space needed to create bloom that lasts all season long. Without this needed space, it would be almost impossible to create a good display. Narrow garden spaces that cannot be enlarged are perfect homes for single-season gardens or single-plant gardens. A very narrow, shaded space along a property line in a city lot, for example, would be a perfect spot for a fern garden or a *Hosta* garden. One of the nicer narrow gardens I have seen was a *Hosta* garden with only stepping-stones between the plants in the dark, shady section between two homes.

If the garden has room for a back, it allows the gardener to create a backdrop against which to show off the flowers in the front of the border using tall perennials or hedges. Examine magazine or book photographs with an eye to the backs of the gardens. You will see that most of the wonderful shots show the flowers against a dark background of some kind. Following the 3:1 ratio of length to width creates the space for these backgrounds.

3. Annuals Aren't Better; They're Just Necessary

This gardening secret is sometimes considered heresy in the perennial garden world, but I advise you to use annuals sparingly to create consistent and ongoing color patches. Gertrude Jekyll, the doyenne of the British cottage-garden style, used annuals. If they were good enough for her, how can I suggest otherwise?

In my own gardens, I use hardy annuals to give a splash of color to tide the garden over during dull periods. Hardy annuals are annuals that either are sown in the garden in the spring, such

Rose container with annuals in background   DOUGLAS GREEN

2

Designing for All-Season Bloom

Most design books lead off with a range of information about the hows and whys of garden design and how to effectively use color, but I've put all that in other chapters. You want to know how to get blooms that go on and on all season long in your garden. So, here's how to do exactly that.

To plan for blooms that go on and on all season long, begin with a pencil and paper. This is by far the best way to do your initial designs, as it is much easier to correct a mistake with an eraser than it is with a shovel. This simple system works with a bed of any shape. For the purposes of illustration, I've started with a rectangle.

MICK HALES

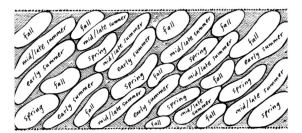

Add fall-blooming perennials.

Fall is also the time that individual ornamental plants such as fall mums can be moved into the garden to fill in any holes in the design. A mum is one of the few plants that can be dug and moved while in full bloom and, as long as the roots are not severely cut back, the plant will not wilt or show signs of the upset. This is why I often recommend growing fall mums in the vegetable garden under full sun and high-fertility conditions and then moving them in the fall to repair or balance out the fall flower garden. Leave the mum in the perennial garden for the winter and then move it again in the spring back to the vegetable garden. Now you see why I would put wheels on my mums if I could. Let me give you a quick tip about fall mum blooming: If you move them from one area of the garden to another, ensure that they do not lack for water during the bloom season. Any lack of water caused by the shortening of the roots during digging will shorten the bloom time.

*T*he many multiple-season bloomers described in Chapter 10 are really the backbone's backbone in this process, if I may stretch a concept a little way. If you use multiple-season bloomers as often as you can in the garden, you will find the increased bloom well worth the exercise of fitting them into the design. Most multiple-season bloomers begin blooming at the height of summer.

You now have a fully laid out diagram of bloom times in the garden. Let me emphasize that if you do not want fall-blooming plants in your design, then increase the numbers of plants from other blooming periods for that particular garden. Similarly, if you don't want spring bloomers, eliminate them and start the process with the early-summer bloomers. Even though I've run through a quick system here, the modification of that system to fit your individual needs is what makes the system work for you. Use it as a base, but do not be a slave to it. I know that even though I do something like this with new gardens, there's always "just this one plant" or "try this one" that does not fit into this system and gets put into the real garden. These are great guidelines, but as you get out in the garden, it is more important to enjoy what you are doing than it is to follow a plan made indoors in January. Also note that there is never a perfect perennial garden plan. But just having sketched out your plan in advance is going to make your perennial border much better than 99 percent of all perennial gardens you'll see.

Step Five: Drift Master Sheet

Copy the plan layout to a clean sheet of paper, but do not enter the blooming times onto this master sheet. I often make a notation in one or two letters in each plant area to remind me of the bloom time for that area, but I want all the rest of the space for plant names. I usually refer to this as the *drift master sheet*. Some gardeners will want to skip steps one through four and simply draw the drifts on paper and go directly to placing plants. This is fine if you've done the process before or have a simplified concept of bloom times. Otherwise, it is a good idea to follow the steps as described in this chapter.

Make at least a dozen copies of your drift master sheet. You'll likely need at least that many before you are finished. I usually keep one as a master and make as many copies as I need.

With your diagram in front of you, start leafing through the basic plants in Chapters 5 and 6 for spring bloomers. Write the name of a plant (in pencil!) into a space. Continue writing the names of spring-blooming plants into the spaces until all the spring spaces are filled up. The size of the space will determine how many plants you will require to fill it up. A space that is 3′ (90 cm) long will not be easily filled with a single plant; you will have to estimate how many plants you will need by using the "plant apart" data in the plant chapters.

A young perennial garden filled out with annuals   MICK HALES

Color in drifts   MICK HALES

Do the same thing with summer and fall bloomers, picking your favorite plants and putting them into appropriate spaces. This is the time-consuming part of the process; this is also where the fun and the dreaming start. "I wonder what it would look like if I put this plant in that spot?" You can easily erase one plant and put in another to improve your design; this is why erasers were installed on the ends of pencils. Once you've filled up and made a mess of the first page, pull out a new page and keep on going.

When you are finished, you will have a plan for a perennial garden that will bloom all season long. Or you will until you start thinking about it and decide to change "just this one plant" here and there and there again. Relax; it's all part of the fun of garden design. And what else do gardeners do all winter but dream of their garden? You're simply dreaming on paper instead of in your mind's eye.

Designing in Color Drifts

Once you've created drifts of blooming areas for time of bloom, an alternative design method is to create colored drifts of bloom.

First create your drift shapes, and then take colored pencils or crayons and lightly color in the drift shapes in colors you find attractive and that go together well. Once the colors are picked for each season, then you can go hunting through plant lists in books or magazines and seed catalogs searching for just the right colors to complete your garden.

For a beginner, integrating colors is not as easy as using the simpler bloom-times method of design described in this chapter. The perfect model is to combine the two methods to create a garden that blooms from early spring through fall in the colors of your choice. Ideally, this is what we are all searching for as we constantly try

*Y*ou'll notice that there are always spaces between the drifts in your plans. This is quite acceptable. What you will find when you get out into the garden is that the plants will expand into each other to eliminate excess planning space. Just don't leave too many spaces. What you may not have considered is that in the first year or two of a perennial garden, the plants are not their mature size. For the time it takes to grow perennial plants up to flowering size, plan on using annual flowers to fill the spaces.

to design the perfectly color matched, everblooming perennial garden. To help you, Chapter 3, Color in the Garden, on designing with color, will get you started down this artistic pathway. It is a path you'll never want to leave.

At this point, you have everything you need to make a great flower bed design. There's no need to fuss about color or other design aspects; you can go directly to the plant selection chapters and start choosing your plants. Your garden bed will be an ever-blooming one.

3

Color in the Garden

Once you have a plant plan, you must decide which color school of plant design you will join. The first color school of garden design says that with certain exclusions (white and magenta) every color in the perennial garden matches every other color and it is impossible to have a bad combination. It is possible to have *better* combinations but impossible to have really bad ones. This is the school of the gardener who wants to have a good time with perennial plants of all kinds and colors but isn't overly concerned about artistic merit. This is the fun school.

The second school, espoused by most professional garden designers, is that only certain colors and plants should go together in the garden. Certainly, if you are trying to create artistic color schemes or moods in the garden, then this is the school of color design you'll join, and instructions for beginning this process appear later in this chapter with the sections describing the color wheel and color-chord applications. This color school of gardening design is a lot of work but can be used to achieve masterpieces of design.

If you are a real beginner, join the first school. Like kindergarten, it's easier, it allows you to experiment, and it is far more fun. You can switch at any time, as gradually as you wish. My artist wife has been working on her plantsman husband for many years now.

Verbascum/poppies   DOUGLAS GREEN

Johannes Itten (1888–1967) was considered to be one of the greatest teachers of color theory in modern times. Although he was an exhibiting painter in Europe, he was much better known for his writing. His *The Art of Color* is still one of the most important works on the subject. In *Elements of Color* he describes how he discovered that none of his students could agree on what made a harmonious color combination. What was most harmonious to one student was not the most harmonious to another. In his experience, specific color harmonies were based on individual preferences and perceptions.

The importance of this to gardening cannot be overstated. While there are general rules (never put a red rose against a red-brick wall, for example), specific combinations of colors and plants are enjoyed by one gardener and may or may not be appreciated by others. My point is that your decisions about color and color combinations in your garden are made based on what pleases you. This book can be a guide to the general rules, but the ultimate decision is yours and should be.

And if you *really* want to plant a red rose against a red-brick wall, well, that too is your decision.

difficult to master all the time. There is a difference between a beginner's efforts and those of a competent color designer, and we should all be glad that this is so. It means we can all continually improve our gardens and our color sense.

We start by comparing color in the garden to music. If you ever took piano (I took guitar), then you know that there are two-note chords, three-note chords, and four-note chords in music. The notes were combined to create different sounds. It is exactly the same in color design for the garden; we use two-color chords, three-color chords, and four-color chords to create different looks for our gardens.

How the Color-Chord System Works

In my description of the chord system that follows, you will first find basic instructions on the use and effect of each chord. If you want to use the chord system, simply read the instructions contained in the introductory paragraphs. You'll be able to drastically improve your garden color choices. If you want further theoretical information, keep reading, through each of the sections titled For the Color-Curious. If your color curiosity goes even further, read the sections titled Foliage Color, Color Contrast, and Spatial Effects of Color.

Designing with Color

If at the outset you do decide to use color to help you design your garden, then the single best starting point is right here. Designing around color is not particularly difficult to accomplish, but it does take more work than simply evaluating perennial choices based on their bloom times. As an aside, I note that while it is not difficult to start designing with color, it is hugely

Two-Color Chords

Two-color chords are formed by colors on opposite sides of the color wheel and are found by putting a ruler across the center point of the color wheel, connecting opposite colors. For example, blue and orange, yellow and purple, and red and green are opposite each other on the wheel. Any two colors opposite each other on the color wheel are referred to as "complemen-

CHORDS OF COLOR

Get out some stiff cardboard and scissors. The cardboard from a cereal box works really well because it is about the right stiffness. Trace and then cut each of the four shapes on the color wheel. Then, depending on which type of color chord you'd like, lay one of the shapes over the color wheel and rotate until you find a color chord to your liking.

A straight line passing through the center of the color wheel forms a **two-color chord**.

An equilateral triangle (all angles and sides equal) or an isosceles triangle (two sides and two angles equal, one side and one angle unequal) placed on the color wheel forms a **three-color chord**.

A square or rectangle placed on the color wheel forms a **four-color chord**.

Eupatorium maculatum / Helenium hoopesii 'Kanaria.'
Complementary pairing.   Douglas Green

more likely we are to incorporate foliage into our garden designs. My advice to beginners is to focus on bloom color for most perennials. If a plant has been purchased because of its foliage color, however, the design should concentrate on that color.

To increase color contrast in the garden, determine the color of your chosen plant either from memory, from catalogs, or from the photographs in this book. Then look directly across the color wheel to find its complementary color. That color is the one you are searching for. Naturally, you will have to find it in a plant of similar bloom time and height so that the contrast is evident. There is little point in having a spring-blooming yellow plant and a fall-blooming violet one because they will never be seen in bloom together.

For the Color-Curious: Stability and Analogous Colors

Not only does the combination of complementary colors give us maximum excitement, it also gives us maximum stability. An interesting consequence of human perception is that the eye and human psychology automatically seek to find color complements. If we see red, our psyche demands that green be present and unconsciously will look for it. By giving the eye the complementary color, the psyche is satisfied and does not have to look further; it relaxes. This relaxation state is stable. When we see a yellow flower, we immediately want to see a violet one as well and the eye searches for the color violet. By providing a violet flower close by, the perception of the viewer is quickly satisfied. The garden view is stable.

Stable color combinations, whether in the garden or home, are reassuring. We may find them exciting if the colors are hot or relaxing if the colors are cool, but we will always be comfortable with the combination.

tary colors." When these pairs are used together in the garden—that is, when the flowers of complementary colors are planted side by side—they will generate the maximum possible color excitement.

This is as good a place as any to point out the obvious fact that foliage color is very important in garden color design. Advanced gardeners design for foliage as well as flower color, and as every plant in our perennial gardens has foliage, we could do the same. The simple fact is that most of us only design for foliage color when we are dealing with small flowering plants such as hosta or plants with highly colored or variegated leaves. The more practice we get at design, the

We used two colors opposite each other on the color wheel to make a maximum-impact color effect, but what happens when the colors are not opposite each other? The closer the colors are on the wheel, the less the impact of contrast will be, until they are right together on the wheel and the contrast is minimal. Colors that are beside each other are called "analogous." While there is still contrast because they are different colors, the impact on the viewer is not as great nor does it have the visual kick that gardeners often seek. Analogous colors do have their place in garden design, so see the section later in this chapter titled Color Contrast for further discussion of analogous colors.

Where some designers get into trouble is when a flower of a color such as yellow is put next to a pale green leaf. Both colors look sick, and the garden appearance suffers. Variegated foliage can cause a similar problem. The contrast in the leaf colors is high and attractive, but the white in the foliage can make obtaining a good contrast difficult if the flower is also a light color. The flower winds up looking sickly, as in the case of *Phlox paniculata* 'Norah Leigh.' (See photograph in Chapter 10.)

Astilbe arendsii on a concrete patio. Here, the foreground patio stones and furniture help create a wonderful two-color chord.   Douglas Green

*Y*ou'll often hear the word *contrast* tossed about in discussions of color in the garden. "Oh," a visitor will say, "that plant contrasts so well with that other combination." Or "Those plants go well together." What they are really saying is that in their opinion the *comparison between* the plants is good. Contrast is about comparison, and there are many ways to compare plant colors. It probably sounds trite to say that you can't have contrast without comparison, but this is true. Why it is important in the garden is because there is always contrast happening. It may be happening with the dull brown, unpainted-board fence behind the garden that reduces the intensity of all flower colors or with the dark green cedar hedge that makes every flower sparkle, but it is happening.

Your job as a color designer is to figure out what the contrasts are in your own garden. Is it the board fence? Is it the greenery of the hedge or other leaves in the garden? Is it other nearby flowers in bloom at the same time? Is it the house color or a brick wall? Does the neighbor's swimming pool feature prominently in your garden view? What dynamics and contrasts exist in your garden to influence your design? For further information on this subject, see the section later in this chapter titled Color Contrast.

Red *Monarda*/pink poppies.
Poor contrast. Douglas Green

Blue *Veronica*/*Phlomis russeliana*.
Good contrast. Douglas Green

Three-Color Chords

It is quite rare that a perennial garden comes only in two colors. Even the celebrated "white" garden of Vita Sackville-West had more than simply white and green in it. To help sort out the color combinations in three-color combinations, use the triangles from cardboard as described earlier in this chapter. To further the analogy with music, a three-color chord determined with an equilateral triangle is a major chord while one determined with an isosceles triangle is a minor chord. Both sound fine (and look good, too) when used appropriately. What happens most often with beginning piano players and garden designers is that two notes are struck well but the third note (or color) is a disaster, effectively ruining the chord and its effect.

If, for example, a three-color combination of yellow, red, and blue is one of the most powerful combinations possible, it will ring true in the music of the garden. But if the choice is red, yellow, and violet, the entire effect will be lost, as the bottom of the triangle has not stretched out far enough to make a good chord. The color chord has been misplayed, and while it may be interesting, it will never achieve the impact of a well-planted color chord.

The triangles can be rotated on the color wheel to pick and match any color with its associated chord colors. You can do this now as part of your design efforts, you can do it in your garden, or you can do it even while shopping at the garden center to check out whether a new plant matches your existing garden.

Using a minor chord (our isosceles triangle) in the garden creates powerful combinations but with more subtle effects. Again, it is important that the chosen colors hit the points of the triangles as closely as possible so the effect of the chord in the garden will ring true to garden viewers.

For maximum impact in the garden, use major chords produced by the equilateral triangle, and

Ligularia przewalskii/*Achillea* 'Heidi'/*Veronica* 'Blue Charm.' A three-color chord planting.
Douglas Green

for more relaxed, subtle combinations, use the minor chord of an isosceles triangle.

For the Color-Curious: Primary Colors

The primary colors—red, yellow, and blue—are the most intense and offer the highest contrast in the garden. A three-color chord of these colors is going to create the most visual excitement possible. Visitors will not understand exactly what is happening, but they will be visually stimulated and your good reputation as a designer will be ensured. For example, in the fall garden, with its emphasis on yellow flowers, the addition of blue and red asters, blue gentians, and blue *Perovskia* will all contribute to making an exciting primary color contrast.

As you add secondary colors—orange, green, and violet—you decrease the color contrast and the visual excitement.

Four-Color Chords

Four-color chords are simply an extension of three-color chords. Use the square and rectangle from cardboard as described earlier. The square provides the major four-color chords, while the rectangle provides the minor four-color chords. Both can be rotated around the circle to provide interesting color combinations.

Four-color chord   MICK HALES

Using Color Chords

Color chording is the single easiest way to answer the question, "What goes well with this plant?" By using the color wheel and your cutout chord shapes or ruler, you'll be able to instantly pick a flower color that goes with your existing garden scheme. Put one corner of your triangle, square, or ruler on the color that is closest to the flower you want to match, and the colors indicated by the other corners or end are your choices.

I can hear a question forming on your lips right now. "Why do I need a three-color chord when four (or more) colors are in my garden?" It depends on your own garden design and color sense. Three-color gardens are lively and are high-impact gardens. When done properly four-color gardens are equally attractive, but they are a bit more complex to create. You may also use the ruler, the triangle, and the square in the same garden—just at different times. For example, a triangle might be used to create pleasing spring combinations and a square for mid-summer blooms, and then you could switch back to the triangle for fall color choices. This allows different color schemes and themes for each of the major flowering seasons.

Physostegia 'Summer Snow' / *Achillea* 'Credo.' If you place a triangle on the color wheel so that two of its corners touch red and green, the third corner of the triangle will land on blue. In this planting, white replaces blue to create a three-color chord.   DOUGLAS GREEN

For the Color-Curious: White

The color white is always a problem in the garden. It seems gardeners can never figure out how to incorporate it without destroying the color scheme. The same situation exists for the color black, but it is less of a problem because of the dearth of black flowers. You'll have to do some mental gymnastics, but this is how you design for these two colors:

1. Place a square or rectangle on top of the color wheel so that the corners are touching specific colors. Any four corners make a chord. (You can do the same with a triangle: any three corners make a chord.)

2. In practice, if not in theory, you can now substitute the color white for any single color. White will make a color chord with the other colors indicated on the square or rectangle. (You can do the same for black, but as we don't have any truly black flowers, it is not really possible to design for true black.)

3. Before you go planting white flowers in your garden, however, it is important for you to read the section titled Contrast of Extension later in this chapter. The amount of white in the color balance is as important as the other colors that go with it.

Dianthus barbatus, pink and red. Cold/warm contrast.   DOUGLAS GREEN

painted in "hot" reds and yellows can be consistently cooler without complaints from those in the room than rooms painted in "cool" blues and greens. For some reason, we see and feel the heat of the color and our body reacts to it in a physical manner. Bright reds and yellows will therefore increase the heat in the garden, while cooler blues and soft greens will cool it down.

This is a relative concept, and it should be noted that while there are extremes of heat and cold in color, the position of the colors influences how they are seen. Let me illustrate. The right side of the color wheel is the hot side. A color such as yellow is quite hot, and the colors cool down as they progress down the wheel toward blue. Yellow is much hotter than orange. If these two colors are seen together, then yellow is hot and orange is cool, relatively speaking. However, if we compare orange and red, we see

that orange is hotter and red is the cooler color. Orange becomes hotter when it is in the company of a cooler color and cooler when in the company of a hotter color. The contrast then is all-important. You can make a flower that is a relatively cool color such as violet or purple hot by putting it next to a flower that is a clear blue.

In practice, this means that in designing a cool garden of blues and violets, the addition of a soft pink will add a touch of heat, of excitement, to emphasize and lend some energy to the garden. You do not have to add yellow to increase the energy or heat level. It is a question of relative energy. If you want a bit of energy in a cool garden, then you can determine that energy by increasing or decreasing the number of plants or the relative heat value of the plants involved. For example, adding one or two soft pink plants or adding one blazing yellow plant will create different kinds of contrasts and effects in the same garden setting. The previous example was adding a touch of pink to a cool garden; the same holds true for a hotter garden. Remember, it is all relative. If my garden is designed around reds, violets, and oranges, a touch of yellow will still contribute relative energy to the garden and create a warm-cool contrast. The yellow is hot, while the oranges will be cool. Similarly, I could add a touch of blue *Nepeta* to a stunningly hot bed of orange and red *Hemerocallis* to cool it off and add contrast.

Complementary Contrast

I touched on complementary colors earlier in this chapter, under the section titled Two-Color Chords, but it is useful to consider some other qualities of contrasting pairs of complementary colors when applied to the garden. Remember that complementary colors are opposite each other on the color wheel.

Flowers that are yellow and violet are also a perfect example of a light-dark contrast. Yellow *Oenethera* and violet *Nepeta* are not only complementary, but they are light and dark.

Reddish orange and blue green are complementary but are also the most extreme examples of hot and cold colors in the garden.

Contrast of Saturation

Pure colors, as we see on the color wheel, are rare in the garden. Unfortunately, flower colors rarely conform to the designer's desires for clarity and consistency. The vagaries of the weather and growing conditions change flower color from day to day and season to season and prevent

Echinops/Helenium. Complementary contrast.   Douglas Green

us from designing in pure or consistent flower colors. Keep the following points in mind when examining those wonderful flower pictures:

- Any flower that is paler than another (as if white were added) is cooler. Pale flowers are cooler than more intensely colored flowers. Any flower that has more violet or "black" in its mix increases in warmth. Darker colors are warmer.
- Green is very important in this, as the darker green the leaf, the more intense the contrast with the surrounding flowers will be. A perfect example of this is the new breeding of Christmas poinsettia plants. The newer varieties have much darker leaves, which make the red bracts stand out so much more.
- Say you have a choice between a light green leaf on a plant and a darker green leaf. The plant with the darker green leaf will provide more flower color, making the bloom explode with light and color. The lighter green leaf is useful if the leaves are the primary color source. The best example of this is found in the *Hosta* family. We pick darker and lighter leaves to work together in the garden regardless of the flower color. We grow pale or less-saturated green-colored leaves next to darker leaves to increase the contrast.

Contrast of Extension

While the concept of contrast of extension sounds complicated, it is pretty simple to understand the essentials. "Contrast of extension" is the contrast between two color areas of different sizes. The primary question that contrast of extension is answering is "What is the proportion of this color that I need to balance the proportion of that color?" This is one of the most important questions of garden color design. An overpowering abundance of yellow in the fall

garden is one such problem. We've got far too many hot yellow and orange *Coreopsis*, *Heliopsis*, *Helenium*, and *Solidago* plants to work with when compared to plants of softer colors.

We can balance designs in a rough way by using the light values (originally designed by Goethe) as follows:

Yellow = 9	Violet = 3
Orange = 8	Blue = 4
Red = 6	Green = 6

As an example, the combination of complementary colors of violet and yellow give us a ratio of 3:9 (or 1:3). Because yellow is so much brighter than violet, we have to use one part of yellow to equal three parts of violet. (You have to reverse the ratio to get the correct amounts.) In the garden, we might say that we need 3' (90 cm) square of violet blooms to balance the color provided by 1' (30 cm) square of yellow blooms. Yellow is much brighter and carries more power in the contrast of extension.

The combination of orange, with a value of 8, and blue, with a value of 4, is a simple ratio to calculate. At 8:4 (orange:blue) we balance an area of orange with an area of blue that is twice as large. The ratio of the combination of yellow (9) and red (6) is 9:6, or 3:2, so that three parts of the darker red balance two parts of the brighter yellow. We always require less of brighter colors to balance darker colors.

The reality in the garden is that this is never a perfect science. A *Coreopsis* plant might be several years older than a *Eupatorium* or *Aster* and bear more flowers. Growing a well-designed flower garden is as much an art as it is a science. We don't think in terms of individual plants; we think in terms of square footage (or centimeters) of blooms or areas of contrast of blooms. We have to think in terms of wide swaths of color as painters do rather than the individual flowers of gardening imaginations.

I have to point out that the ratios designed have validity only if the flower color contrasts of hue are the same. In other words, a bright blue fall aster has to be compared to a bright yellow *Helenium* and not a much softer yellow *Solidago*. When a color is paler, it will require a corresponding increase in ratio or area of bloom to balance a more intense color. Thus contrast of extension is not an exact science but rather more of a guideline for the gardener. We don't use our tape measures to evaluate the flower sizes and relative contrasts of extension, but we do use our eyes and our judgment. Over the years, with practice, our judgment becomes able to determine a good color proportion.

As a last note, white is not mentioned on the light values chart, but you can very quickly see that it will have a much higher number than even yellow. This means that a little white goes a very long way in the garden when compared to the rest of the colors.

Sedum kamts/Iberis semp. Contrast of extension.
Douglas Green

Spatial Effects of Color

So far I have pointed out several times that the spatial effects of color are relative. That is, there is no hard and fast rule that applies to all colors; the spatial effect of a color depends on its size, shape, and position in the garden to determine the effect it has on the eye. Let me add another bit of information to the mix. If on your color wheel you start at yellow and follow the wheel around to violet, you'll get a sense of how colors recede or advance when we look at them in the garden. If all the colors were lined up in a straight row across the garden, yellow would advance and seem closer than all other colors. Violet would appear to be the farthest away from us. All other colors recede or advance based on their position on the color wheel. So, if yellow and red were side by side, the yellow would appear to be closer. If red and blue were side by side, the red would appear to be closer.

The intensity of the background influences how far forward the colors will come or how forcefully they will appear to do so. Dark green or black backgrounds force yellow flowers to the foreground, while darker blues disappear into the distance of the background. If you have dark siding on your house, this rule holds true. If, on the other hand, you have a white background, you reverse the effect, allowing violet and the darker colors to punch out closer to you.

This is interesting if you wish to create depth in your garden. If you have a darker background such as a hedge, you can plant dark-colored flowers to the rear to make them appear to recede even further. Planting light-colored flowers at the front makes them appear to be even closer, and between the two plantings you visually increase the depth of your garden. Your garden will look deeper and bigger than it really is.

Color in the garden is one of those amazing things that you'll work on for the rest of your life. As you change, you will likely change the way you garden. That means your garden is never static, never perfect, and never quite exactly how you want it to be. Isn't that wonderful? You always have next year to get it right.

4

The Hard Part:
Choosing Which
Plants to Grow

The toughest task in writing a gardening book like this one is deciding which plants to include. There are so many truly outstanding perennials that it is easy to find good plants; the problem is fitting them all in. I finally made my selections based on what I call the "backbone effect"; I chose the plants that will give your garden structure. More than just pretty faces, these plants add background, movement, and line to the garden design. All the plants selected look good and anchor the garden's entire flowering season.

A cursory look at a garden center's perennial shelves will quickly show you that there are many more plants available than have been described here. I suggest you start with these backbone plants and move on to the other plants as your garden and wallet allow. Quite frankly, there's more fizz in some of the newer plants than there is garden performance. The ones I list in Chapters 5 through 10 have worked for me and for thousands of beginning gardeners. That is why I have chosen them for you to use.

MICK HALES

What Makes a Plant Outstanding or Choice?

With tongue firmly in cheek, I define an outstanding plant as one that your next-door neighbor doesn't have. A choice plant is one that nobody on your block has. Once a plant becomes commonly available, it is neither outstanding nor choice.

Rearranging my face, I might say that outstanding plants are fairly easy to describe. These are plants that perform well in spite of poor conditions. Or they have characteristics that make them attractive to gardeners. They might flower longer than others in the same plant family, or they might be more disease-resistant. Any characteristic that improves their garden performance over other plants in their family makes them outstanding garden performers. Their rarity is not an issue. A choice plant is both a rare plant and an outstanding plant.

Finding Good Plants

Obtaining good plants for our gardens was once a real challenge. Luckily, it is becoming easier and easier. Even the major perennial nurseries are responding to consumer interests by searching out and bringing to the mass market plants that perform well under a variety of conditions. We see many new outstanding introductions every year that bloom for a longer time, are more upright, or have colors that are more intense than older varieties.

Finding choice plants is not an afternoon's work. Oh, to be sure, every now and then, you'll make a find at a garden center, but for the most part, the smaller, out-of-the-way nurseries that collect and propagate their own perennials will be the source of your finest plants. It is the dedicated gardener's expeditions down backcountry roads to find these small family nurseries that result in the most interesting plant selections.

You see, many of the truly choice plants are a little tricky to propagate and do not fit into the mass-market production system. It takes a dedicated plantsperson to nurture a tiny seedling through three to five years of growth before presenting it to you for your garden. And often, it takes a deep wallet to afford such a wonderful plant.

You find nurseries like this by searching through Yellow Pages directories and by listening to experienced gardeners in your area. Read the yearly reviews in gardening magazines that list all the specialized mail-order nurseries and scour the back-page ads for catalogs that list the plants you are searching for. By the way, this is an ongoing adventure. You never run out of new nurseries to find, as plantspeople regularly give

Campanula persicifolia with *Heliopsis* in rear
DOUGLAS GREEN

COLLECTORS' PLANTS

*Q*uite apart from plants introduced by nurseries, there are many that never see the sales benches. These are "collectors' plants." To find them, you must find the collectors. (See Resources.) Generally, there are two organizations you can join that help you obtain good perennial plants not normally found in garden centers. The first is the North American Rock Garden Society (NARGS). Join this group not because you want to grow rock garden plants but because those who do grow interesting alpine plants also grow interesting perennials. It is the seeds of these interesting plants that get shared and traded on the seed exchanges run by this organization that will appeal to the discerning plant collector. Attend regional meetings because this is where you will meet talented gardeners to learn from and share plants with. And you, in your turn, can help other beginners after a few years. The second organization is the Hardy Plant Society (HPS)—an organization devoted to perennial plants. The HPS is based in England but opens up the European window of plant collecting, and sooner or later, plant collectors wind up dreaming of European plants. Contact information for both of these organizations is listed in Resources.

Ligularia palmatoloba/ Hakonechloa macra
DOUGLAS GREEN

up their day jobs to open nurseries and dedicate themselves to sharing their plant loves.

The Internet is also a source of interesting plants. You can enter the name of the plant you want in a search engine, or you can enter any rare plant name. You see, once you find a nursery that grows one rare plant, the odds are that it will be growing more than one. You've found a new source! See Resources for some helpful search techniques.

Naming Perennials

Before I launch into a description of perennial plants in the chapters that follow, it is important for you to know how plants are named, so that you can find your way around quickly. I've used horticultural Latin to organize all plant lists. It is a common currency among gardeners and at garden centers; by using Latin names, we know we are all speaking of the same plant and we can describe it in precise ways. The Royal Horticultural Society's *Dictionary of Gardening* and *Plant Finder* are the main references I used in compiling the lists in Chapters 5 through 10.

However, just to make life more interesting, in my lists I also present many of the common names for each plant, along with a bit of historical background about how the plant got its name. It is these common names and backgrounds that breathe real life into our plants and gardens. As Dr. R. Prior wrote in his 1863 book, *On the Popular Names of British Plants*, "There are distinguished botanists at the present day who look upon popular names as leading to confusion, and a nuisance, and who would gladly abandon them, and ignore their existence. But this is surely a mistake, for there will always be ladies and others, who, with the greatest zeal for the pursuit of Natural History, have not had the opportunity of learning Greek and Latin, or have forgotten it, and who will prefer to call a plant by a name that they can pronounce and recollect." In 1863, Prior may have been able to get away with assuming that ladies would not know their Greek and Latin. Today, very few of us—ladies or others—have had the pleasure of studying these classical languages. Thus, as Prior so eloquently puts it, getting rid of common names would be a mistake.

Which Plants Grow in My Zone?

Every gardener I know worries about plant hardiness. "Is this plant hardy?" is a question I get all the time when I talk about perennials. There are so many variables to hardiness that saying a plant is hardy or not is almost meaningless. Let me begin by saying that I have grown all the plants listed in Chapters 5 through 10 in my USDA zone 4 garden (unless I note otherwise). Does that mean they will grow for you? Maybe.

Let us examine USDA zones and plant hardiness briefly before going on. While hardiness zones can be a complex issue, let us try to keep it to practical realities. The most useful guidelines given to gardeners are the zone maps that grace many gardening books. A beginner would assume that if a plant has a zone 4 rating, then it should thrive in a zone 4 garden. For the most part, this is true. However, the conditions of that garden are much more important to the plant than the zone rating. One simple example is lavender. I can grow lavender in my garden because I have sandy soil; it grows, self-sows, and keeps us in fragrant cuttings for much of the summer. A few miles away, a friend cannot grow this plant (even though he is in the same zone) because he has a clay-based soil. The lavender's feet are too wet during the winter, and it dies. So, lavender grows in my zone 4 garden but not his. Soil, along with a multitude of other factors, determines the ability of plants to grow and thrive. To help you make selections that suit your garden, I list the basic soil type that best suits each plant as well as its hardiness zone in the plant descriptions in Chapters 5 through 10, as this is the single most important factor in keeping perennials alive.

So, we can see that zone ratings are guidelines, but there are other factors involved in growing a plant. The practical questions then become, "Given the right soil and habitat conditions, can I grow plants out of their zone?" and "What are these habitat conditions, and can I manipulate them in my garden?"

Answering the first is fairly simple. Because zone ratings for each plant come from a multitude of gardeners across North America, the rat-

1. R. C. A. Prior, M.D., *On the Popular Names of British Plants* (London: Williams and Norgate, 1863), page ix.

NURTURING TENDER PLANTS

The most commonly used method of keeping tender plants alive is to apply a thick mulch over the top of the plant in the fall to keep the frost as far away as possible. This is an excellent method, and I would recommend at least several inches of mulch—be it straw, leaves, bark, or compost. If the plant is herbaceous (that is, it dies to the ground), the deeper the mulch, the better.

If the plant is not herbaceous and some parts of it stay above the ground for the winter, such as lavender and *Dianthus*, then a thick mulch may lead to keeping too much water around the stem and crown (located where the plant and soil meet). This in turn leads to winter rotting. These tender nonherbaceous plants are a little trickier to insulate. Dry peat moss is the single best winter mulch for these plants. A thick layer of dry peat moss, applied after the plant is fully dormant and just before snow falls, will not normally wet all the way to the ground and will still be dry at the crown the following spring. *It is important to apply the peat late in the fall and remove it early in the spring before it has a chance to soak up water and rot the crown.*

Peat is not a good all-purpose garden mulch because of its resistance to absorbing water, but it makes an excellent insulating winter mulch for the same reason. Use it as winter mulch over specific plants and then spread it evenly over the garden as a soil amendment. *Do not use peat moss as mulch over the summer.*

Some gardeners have very good luck laying evergreen or well-branched woody stems over their aboveground-wintering perennials. The theory here is that the branches hold the snow cover and this insulates the plant from the worst of winter's blasts. This works. The other option is simply to move the entire plant south to a warmer climate—along with the gardener, of course.

For the record, I know a gardener who, using extremely deep layers of mulch and a south-facing planting next to a brick wall, overwintered a banana tree outdoors in the zone 4 city of Ottawa, Canada. While the top obviously died, the roots stayed alive to produce a huge banana plant the following summer. This is a pretty amazing accomplishment and shows how far a gardener will go to protect a favorite plant.

Achillea 'Cerise Queen'/*Hemerocallis* 'Bay State.' Herbaceous plants. Douglas Green

ings are general; they do not take into account any cultural differences. To make matters worse, there is no central authority that says, "This plant is a zone 4 and that plant a zone 6." Each nursery and each author ranks plants independently—and often there is significant disagreement among them.

In my zone 4 garden, I regularly grow plants with a zone 5 rating when I give them the soil conditions they demand. I can, with some gardening manipulation, grow plants with a zone 6 rating. I once overwintered a plant with a zone 7 rating, *Arundo donax*, the giant reed. I had been looking for it for some time and discovered that the Royal Botanic Gardens had a plant. The director kindly had a chunk divided for me, and I planted it in my front garden. The following spring I sent him a celebratory postcard saying mine had overwintered. From his zone 6 garden, he telephoned back to say his had died and would I return him a division the following fall. I had heavily mulched mine and he had not.

Plant Habitats

And that brings us directly to the conditions, or habitat, we create in our gardens. First, understand that there are seven major plant habitats. Once you understand where your plant comes from and how it grows, then you can manipulate conditions to allow it to grow successfully for you. The seven plant habitats are as follows:

1. Woodland
2. Woodland edge
3. Prairie
4. Meadow
5. Alpine
6. Waterside
7. Water

There are just three variables you have to manipulate: soil, including fertility; sunlight; and water availability. Remember that your success as a gardener lies in giving the plants the conditions that they have in their natural setting.

Woodland

Native woodland areas have consistent shade throughout the season with the exception of early spring before the leaves have unfolded. The soils are heavy with humus, and there is a good mulch of decaying organic litter. Fertility is good because of this decaying organic matter. There is a high degree of biological microorganism activity in the soils to fight diseases and pests. Water availability is variable because of the demands of the larger trees. Winter soil temperatures are stable because of all the protection offered by the trees and leaf litter. Once the soil freezes, it will not thaw until spring has arrived. There will be no sudden thawing and refreezing to damage plants.

Woodland Edge

Woodland edges are part-shade spots. They typically produce plants that thrive in semishade. They tend to have soils high in organic matter because of the leaf litter from the nearby trees. Similar to the woodland area, fertility at the woodland edge is good because of this decaying organic base. The major difference is more available sunlight—soils, and water availability will stay the same because of the proximity of the trees.

Prairie

Prairie areas have full sunlight, with deep, rich, sandy soils. They are characterized by excellent drainage and variable water availability.

Meadow

Meadow areas tend to have rockier soils in areas of transition between prairies and woodland areas. Or they are transition areas in the middle

Woodland habitat   MICK HALES

Woodland edge habitat   ©JUDYWHITE/GARDENPHOTOS.COM

Prairie habitat   MICK HALES

of woodland areas. Meadows may also be areas where trees have—for one reason or another—not been able to successfully establish themselves or have been removed by the hand of man or nature. The fertility is typically not as good as that of a prairie, and the water availability is variable depending on the location.

Alpine

Alpine areas are areas of full sunlight, with excellent drainage, springwater from snowmelt, and often summer drying because of a lack of rain. The soils are mineral-rich but not high in the macronutrients nitrogen, phosphorus, and potash. What's noteworthy about an alpine area are the excellent drainage and the lack of standing water. Using an organic mulch, such as bark chips, that holds water around the plant crown will kill an alpine plant.

Waterside

Waterside areas vary in almost every aspect, sharing only the feature of constant moisture. The soils vary from clay through sand, and the light varies from full sunlight to full shade. Without the moisture, a plant will not thrive. The requirements for sunlight of each waterside plant will have to be dealt with individually. Soil fertility is usually medium to low; the mineral content of the soils is usually adequate, but the macronutrients will have been washed away in the water. My own gardening experiments have shown that the richer the soil or the more fertilizer given to this class of plants, the more aggressive they will be in spreading.

Water Plants

Water plants thrive in water. Normally, they also require full sunlight or a very light shade. Their nutrient needs tend to be much higher than waterside plants, requiring a gardener to feed

Meadow habitat   MICK HALES

water plants such as water lilies much more heavily than their waterside cousins.

The best strategy then is to grow a water plant in the soil and light conditions of its native habitat. You'll find you can grow some but not others, and that really is the message of zones and gardens. Try to grow what you like, but do not be overly intimidated by a plant's zone listing. Also, just because you've killed a plant does not mean it won't thrive in your garden. It simply

Alpine habitat   MICK HALES

Waterside habitat   MICK HALES

won't live in the first place you put it. Maybe there's another place that will do better—you simply have to keep experimenting.

When Do Plants Bloom?

I confess that arranging the plant listings in Chapters 5 through 9 by early- and late-spring, early- and late-summer, and fall bloom times creates some potential disagreement for me and readers. It is quite easy to say that *Brunnera* is a spring bloomer, but is *Geranium macrorrhizum* a late-spring bloomer or is it an early-summer bloomer? I suppose it depends on your definition of spring and summer.

To make life easy for us all, I have assigned early-spring-blooming plants and late-spring-blooming plants their own chapters. In this way,

Water habitat   MICK HALES

you won't be surprised when there is overlap between the late-spring and early-summer bloomers. This overlap is something to take into account when you are designing a garden and trying to tie the spring flush of blooms into the summer flush. Overlap plants fill a very useful place in the garden, as they keep the garden in

bloom and create interest during the inevitable lulls. If you designed a garden with nothing but early-spring bloomers and late-summer bloomers (easy to do), then there would be a gap in the garden blooming that would be quite conspicuous. Make selections from each of these seasons, and you will succeed in filling the gap.

WHY DIDN'T YOU LIST MY FAVORITE PERENNIAL?

*L*iterally hundreds of new plants are being introduced to a plant-hungry gardening populace every year. The reality is that any single book doesn't have room to list all the wonderful plants we'd all like to grow. What I have done is listed what I consider the best perennials for general gardening purposes, the backbone plants for the garden. I don't expect you to agree with me. Gardeners enjoy debating the merits of plants about as much as they enjoy growing them.

The last time I counted such things, I had close to two thousand varieties in my own gardens, so there are many more plants I've fallen in love with than the ones listed here as backbone plants for the garden. I'm sure you'll find a few of your own favorites here, but, yes, I've omitted a few as well. It is a necessary concession, intended to make your gardening life easier.

Cornus x rutgersensis
'Constellation'
(cv. Rutcan)
Cornaceae

Rhododendron
x Mary Fleming
Ericaceae

5

Early-Spring Bloomers

Tennyson certainly had it correct when he wrote "spring and a young man's fancy lightly turning to thoughts of love." I suspect that gardeners, whatever their age or sex, will forever lightly turn to thoughts of love when they think of spring-blooming plants. In my garden, these beauties tell me that winter is finally over and that my gardener's soul should stir once more. It is love I'm thinking of when the buds start to break and the flowers emerge in all their glory—gardening love. I am no poet, but spring flowers would be at the top of my writing list if I were.

MICK HALES

BERGENIA

Common names: heart leaf, heart-leafed bergenia, Siberian tea

The *Bergenia* plant family was named after Karl August von Bergen (1704–1760), a professor from Frankfurt an der Oder. He wrote the descriptive *Flora Francofurtana*, which was published in 1750. Native to eastern Asia up into Siberia, the plant was given the common name *Siberian tea*. I have to assume some part of the plant was used for tea, but I have been unable to find a reference that recommends this use.

Bloom time: Early spring
Height: 12″ to 18″ (30 cm to 45 cm)
Sun needed: Full sun to light shade
Bloom color: White, shades of red/violet
Planting space: 12″ to 18″ (30 cm to 45 cm) apart

Soil preferred: Light soil—no standing water, although it is a plant native to damp meadows
Propagation method: Division or seed

Recommended Varieties

Bergenia cordifolia

Bergenia cordifolia is the most commonly available species, from both seed companies and nurseries. While the plant is easily started from seed, it is slow to grow and will often take three years to bloom. For this reason, impatient gardeners often purchase larger, nursery-grown plants.

'Red Bloom' (also sold as 'Rotblum') has rose-red flowers.

Bergenia crassifolia

Bergenia crassifolia is a hardy species whose leaves may be less damaged by winter than others. It is not as easy to find, but if you do see it, purchase a plant or two.

'Red Star' is a good red color.

Bergenia x hybrida

'Bressingham Ruby' is a compact-growing variety with deep pink flowers and dark red fall foliage.

'Bressingham White,' the white counterpart to 'Bressingham Ruby,' is not "dirty" white like other whites but is a clear white bloom.

'Morning Blush' is also sold as 'Silverlight' and 'Silverlicht.' Early-spring flowers are white fading to reddish. This one is more drought- and sun-tolerant than the species.

'Baby Doll' is compact with flowers in multiple shades of pink on the same stem. It changes color as it ages to produce this effect.

Growing *Bergenia*

Bergenia is an easy plant to grow; simply put it in the ground and it seems to live. Do note that the plant does not like clay or standing water, even though it is native to damp meadows. The soil is best if it is evenly moist, and permanent mulch is an excellent method of creating that environment. Getting *Bergenia* to flower is a bit trickier if you live in zone 4 or colder. Even though it is native to colder zones, it has never done that well in my garden. Because it wants to bloom very,

very early in the spring, I often find that the buds are frozen by a late freeze and the resulting flowers are deformed and ugly. Perhaps when it thaws up in the far north, it does not have to contend with a secondary freeze. *Bergenia* is also sold as an evergreen perennial, which it is if you grow it in a zone warmer than zone 4. While the leaves do stay on the plant over the winter, by spring they are very brown-edged and ratty looking—not something I was ever pleased to have in the garden. The winter weather is not kind to it. These problems will not be an issue if you live in zone 5 or warmer. In warmer and hotter gardens, *Bergenia* also will thrive in dappled shade along with *Hosta*. Do mulch to preserve soil moisture in hot climates.

Bergenia is very slow to come from seed, and the seedling seems to take forever to develop into a plant big enough to be transplanted into a pot. It is much easier to purchase a two- or three-year root from a garden center. Making divisions in the early spring or fall is the easiest way to obtain new plants.

In our increasingly legalistic world, you'll notice that many plants in seed catalogs are suddenly being labeled as poisonous. The reality in the plant world is that many of our common plants have poisonous qualities if sufficient quantities are consumed. Indeed, if you search the literature, you may very well find that some of the plants now sold with caution flags have been used for decades as either a food source or a medicinal cure. For example, *Digitalis*, or foxglove (see Chapter 7), is the original source of a potent heart medicine. However, if you chow down on it from your garden, you'll be an unhappy camper very quickly. Do we ban it from cultivation because it has deadly as well as positive properties? You are responsible for your own safety. Just as you wouldn't swallow garden chemicals, I trust you won't go around eating your garden plants.

Bergenia 'Bressingham White'
BLOOMS OF BRESSINGHAM NORTH AMERICA, BARBERTON OH

Bergenia 'Bressingham Ruby'
BLOOMS OF BRESSINGHAM NORTH AMERICA, BARBERTON OH

EPIMEDIUM

Common names: barrenwort, bishop's hat

*E*pimedium was apparently named *barrenwort*, meaning "plant not able to conceive" because when eaten it was thought to prevent conception. *Bishop's hat* is an obvious reference to the shape of the flower.

Bloom time: Early spring
Height: 8" to 12" (30 cm to 45 cm)
Sun needed: Shade to part shade
Bloom color: Pink/yellow
Planting space: 12" to 18" (30 cm to 45 cm) apart

Soil preferred: Well-drained woodland or woodland edge
Propagation method: Division

Recommended Varieties

Epimedium alpinum 'Rubrum'

Epimedium alpinum 'Rubrum' is a dwarf with reddish pink blossoms.

Epimedium grandiflorum

Grandiflorum is horticultural Latin for "large flowered," and *Epimedium grandiflorum* 'Album' carries its large white blossoms above the foliage on long, graceful stems.

A Korean plant, variety *Epimedium grandiflorum* 'Lilafee' has purple flowers. Like all the *grandiflorum* species, it carries its flower well above the foliage.

The deep pink blooms of *Epimedium grandiflorum* 'Rose Queen,' carried above the foliage, make this a candidate for the best garden performer. It is more a clump grower as opposed to having a spreading habit.

Epimedium x versicolor 'Sulphureum'

Yellow-flowering *Epimedium x versicolor* 'Sulphureum,' easily found in garden centers, is quite a good bloomer. Fall leaf color is reddish and attractive. I cut mine to the ground in the fall, and they regrow nicely in the spring.

Epimedium x rubrum

With red blossoms in early spring, the leaves of *Epimedium x rubrum* are red-veined and attractive in their own right until the coloring fades later in the summer.

Epimedium x youngianum 'Roseum'

Epimedium x youngianum 'Roseum' is a dwarf *Epimedium* that forms clumps of semievergreen foliage. It has soft pink flowers, is easy to grow, and is excellent for small city gardens.

Growing Epimedium

Epimedium is a wonderful ground cover. While it is technically an evergreen, the foliage does get pretty ratty by spring in our zone 4 garden and dies to the ground in snowless winters. In warmer areas, it would be an excellent alternative as an evergreen ground cover. This plant

Epimedium x versicolor 'Sulphureum'
Douglas Green

does reasonably well in dry shade (once established), so it is a candidate for that problem garden space. *Epimedium* does bloom, but unless you clip the foliage back to the ground in the very early spring, you may miss the flowers. These attractive flowers are held just underneath the top foliage of the plant. If grown in decent soils with average moisture, *Epimedium* is a medium-fast-spreading plant. Note that the *grandiflorum* varieties all carry their flowers above the foliage and are likely the showiest in the family. If given average garden woodland soils, this plant will thrive handsomely.

Epimedium x rubrum   Douglas Green

Potions and Poisons

Epimedium is a plant that if eaten has been claimed to have some abortifacient properties, even though no modern data I can find suggests this. Properties suggested by old names often have a basis in truth even if they were the products of the imagination of some classical Greek author looking to sell his own botanical services.

HELLEBORUS

Common names: Christmas rose, Lenten rose, hellebore, melampode

The name *Christmas rose* is easily understood, owing to this plant's ability to be one of the earliest-flowering perennial plants. In the mildest of climates, it can indeed be in flower by Christmas. It is said that the Greeks gave us *hellebore* from *elein*, "to injure," and *bora*, "food," clearly indicating the poisonous nature of this plant. Pliny wrote that Melampus, a physician living some time around 1400 B.C., used the plant as a purgative, giving it the common name *melampode* in the process.

Bloom time: Very early spring
Height: 18″ to 24″ (30 cm to 45 cm)
Sun needed: Shade to part shade
Bloom color: Full range—from green to bicolors, reds, blues, and whites
Planting space: 18″ to 24″ (30 cm to 45 cm) apart

Soil preferred: Well-drained but humus-rich
Propagation method: Seed is best. You may divide established plants if you are very careful—some plants resent being divided and die.

Recommended Varieties

Helleborus argutifolius

Helleborus argutifolius is a pale-green-flowering species grown mostly by collectors. There are two varieties, 'Pacific Frost' and 'Pacific Mist,' available in Europe, but I have not seen them in North American sources yet. The species is not something you will write home about. I've grown it but discarded it as not particularly attractive.

Helleborus foetidus

Known as the stinking hellebore (now there's a name that is guaranteed to sell a plant), *Helleborus foetidus* is another green-flowering species, although it does have some red streaking at its base. It's another collectors' plant that is not worth garden space unless you are a plant collector, and then you'll have to have it.

Helleborus niger

Also known as the Christmas rose, *Helleborus niger* is one of the classics (along with the *Helleborus orientalis* varieties, following) that the breeders have used extensively. There are at least four major color hybrid families available to consumers: Blackthorn Group, Harvington Hybrids, Sunrise Group, and Sunset Group. There is a wide assortment of plant sizes (including dwarfs) as well as flower colors. It is hard to go wrong with this family.

Helleborus orientalis

Helleborus orientalis is the Lenten rose and the most hybridized member of the family. There are simply more *orientalis* hybrids on the market than any other species, and they come in a dazzling array of colors ranging from blues through yellows and pinks along with picotee bicolored blooms. This plant crosses easily with almost

Helleborus MICK HALES

every other member of the family, and it will do so in your garden as well. Seedlings show great variation in color. I've seldom met a *Helleborus orientalis* I didn't like.

Helleborus x sternii

Helleborus x sternii is another of the hybrids you'll often see in seed catalogs. It is reputed to be tender, but I have several in my garden. Try to purchase them in bloom or with color guaranteed by the grower; they often have drab flowers. This is another of the hybrids that flowers green or flowers green with flushes of rose in the petals. As you might be able to tell, as a gardener I am not all that enthusiastic about green flowers in my garden.

Growing *Helleborus*

Some person wrote that *Helleborus* grows well in dry shade, and this mantra has been picked up by many gardeners who have never grown this plant. The bottom line is that it might survive in dry shade once it is established there, but it will never thrive in dry shade nor flower as profusely as when grown in conditions it prefers. And what it prefers is shade or part shade as well as evenly moist soil. Grow this plant in a woodland or woodland edge habitat and ensure it has constant moisture (a mulch helps here), and you'll get all the blossoms you could want. If you insist on growing it in dry shade, ensure that the organic matter of your soil is quite high (organic matter holds moisture), and the plant will do better. Do not bother to torture the plant by growing it in dry, sandy soils under evergreens or out in the full, hot sunshine. Its demise will be painful for you both.

Helleborus also has a reputation as being hard to propagate from seeds. Nothing could be further from the truth as long as the seed is fresh. If the seed is dried out and dormant—well, yes, seed propagation can be difficult. What you'll find if you grow this plant in a woodland edge habitat is that it will self-sow to provide you with all kinds of young plants to share with friends and spread around your garden. Look around the base of plants in the early summer and gently transplant the new seedlings. While new seedlings move easily, the established plants sulk quite badly for several years (or worse, they simply die) when moved before they will flower again. Similarly, you *can* theoretically divide this plant, but you take the chance of losing it when you do. It is much easier to pick small seedlings than divide or move the mature specimen. I note that *Helleborus foetidus* simply will not divide but rather will die if you attempt to divide it.

This plant is usually a heavy feeder, so a yearly (fall) application of compost is necessary if you want to maintain its heavy blossoming.

In warmer climates than mine, the evergreen foliage is quite striking over the entire year. It is glossy green and makes an excellent accent in an otherwise drab season. In our zone 4 garden, the evergreen species look very tattered after Old Man Winter gets finished with them.

Potions and Poisons

Helleborus is a *poisonous* plant. This family of plants has high alkaloid levels in the roots, and these are not to be eaten. It has been used in the past for medicinal purposes both on humans and animals, and the powdered root has even been scattered or spread over animals to ward off evil spirits. One old herbal recommended that if an animal had a cough, a bit of hellebore root be passed through a hole cut in the ear of the animal to remedy the cough. While its poisonous—as well as a few positive—effects have been noted in most of the old herbals as well as the more modern ones, it is not recommended for general use.

The easiest way to germinate perennial flower seeds like those of the hellebore is to employ Mother Nature as your helper. Cut the bottom off an old nursery container. The smaller 1 gal. (3.8 l) or 6" (15 cm) sizes are best. Sink this pot into the ground so only 1" (25 mm) of the rim is above the soil. Pour 1 gal. (3.8 l) of boiling water slowly over the soil inside the pot to sterilize it. (Alternatively, you can bury the bottomless pot and fill it with sterilized soil.) Sow the fresh perennial seed inside the pot. Cover it with only enough soil so you lose sight of the seed—and write a name label for the seed. Bury that label at the front of the pot so it is not visible. By doing this, it will not fade or break off; and if you always put the label in the same spot in your pots, you'll know where to look to find out what is growing in the pots. Keep the soil moist for the remainder of the season by using a fine rose on your watering can. (A *rose* is the holed end of the spout where the water force is broken up into tiny streams. Good watering cans have changeable roses.) Forget the pot and seeds for the winter—even if they start to germinate in the fall; allow the plant to remain in the pot until spring. The following spring when the newly germinated seedling has four true leaves (the same as a mature plant), you can transplant it safely to another part of your garden. Regularly water the newly transplanted seedling so it is not overly stressed by the move. Enjoy the flowers.

HEPATICA

Common name: liverwort

*H*epatica comes from the Greek *hepar*, which means "the liver." The color and shape of each leaf resemble the human liver. The old herbal Doctrine of Signatures suggests that if a plant looks like a bodily organ, it will have an effect on that organ. *Hepatica* was used as a treatment for liver problems so it was named *liverwort*, or "liver plant."

Bloom time: Early spring
Height: 3″ to 5″ (7 cm to 13 cm)
Sun needed: Shade to part shade
Bloom color: Whites through blues
Planting space: 8″ (20 cm) apart

Soil preferred: Organic soil—well-drained, such as a typical forest floor with good organic matter from leaves
Propagation method: Seed or division

Recommended Varieties

While there are ten species, the one of note is *Hepatica nobilis*. Search out varieties such as the following:

Hepatica nobilis
'Ada Scott,' is double-flowering in dark blue and an excellent grower.

'Barlowii' has rounded flowers and sky-blue coloring.

'Little Abington' is also double-flowering in dark blue. It's hard to find and expensive, but you'll fall in love with those double flowers.

'Rosea' is a pink-flowering single bloom.

'Rubra Plena' is a double-flowering red bloom. It's excellent but difficult to find.

Growing *Hepatica*

Hepatica is a spring-blooming plant for the shade and is considered by many to be one of the best spring bloomers. The North American varieties come in a range of colors, but for really interesting garden varieties, it is necessary to spend some money for Japanese hybrids. (See Resources.)

Hepatica is one of the earliest bloomers in my shade garden and performs well in a soil that is high in organic matter and moist but well drained.

Potions and Poisons

It is said that a mild infusion (tea) of this herb acts as a remedy for disorders of the liver and indigestion. It is also said to help coughs, bleeding of the lungs, and diseases of the chest. Frequent doses were given at the initial stages of consumption.

Hepatica nobilis   DOUGLAS GREEN

PRIMULA

Common names: primrose, cowslip

*P*rimula is a contraction of the Latin *primus*, "first," an obvious reference to the flowering of the plant first thing in the spring. In medieval times, *Primula veris* was known as the "firstling of spring."

Where did *cowslip* come from? It's a long story. Botanically, the *Primula* and *Verbascum* families were once thought to be related, and both were called *Verbascum*. One member of the *Verbascum* family (called bullocks' lungwort) was used to treat pneumonia in cattle. Its thick, woolly leaves resembled a cow's dewlap (a prominent flap of skin running down its chest), and as I have noted, according to the Doctrine of Signatures, if a plant resembles an anatomical part, it was used to treat illnesses of that part. The Anglo-Saxon word for *dewlap* was *lappa*, "lap or border." It is a short, slurring leap from there to *cow's lappa* or *cowslap* or *cowslip*. When *Primula*, no longer a *Verbascum*, was given its own family classification, it took the cowslip name with it. I told you it was a long story.

The older herbals use a variety of names for this very popular plant. *Keyflower* is one—the flowers drooping down were said to resemble a bunch of keys on a ring. *Herb Peter* is another—the drooping flowers (keys) were said to be St. Peter's keys guarding the entrance to heaven.

Bloom time: Early spring
Height: 8″ to 24″ (20 cm to 60 cm)
Sun needed: Shade to part shade
Bloom color: Yellows, reds, blues, bicolors
Planting space: 8″ to 12″ (20 cm to 30 cm) apart

Soil preferred: Open, well-drained soil high in organic matter, with no standing water
Propagation method: Seed, root cuttings, and division of fancy hybrid varieties.

Recommended Varieties

Primula is a huge family of plants—with over four hundred different species in the family—and while a few are the province of collectors and specialists, most make good garden plants. The numbers speak to the ease of breeding this plant and its delightful tendency to produce huge amounts of seed. Following I list some of the more easily available species. There are simply too many to mention them all.

Primula allionii

Primula allionii and varieties will grow in the shade garden but do not want to be exposed to hot sun at all. There are a significant number of varieties on the market and all share a dislike of acidic soils. *Primula allionii* is not a plant to be grown under evergreens or with rhododendrons and azaleas. We have no problems with dry dormancy here in zone 4, as the ground freezes solid, but if you are growing this plant in a

Primula veris   © GRAHAM RICE/GARDENPHOTOS.COM

slightly warmer area, keep it dry during dormancy. Soggy, damp winter conditions will doom it.

Primula auricula

Primula auricula is the show class of *Primula* that we most often see as a double, "gold," or in mixed colors in catalogs. While it is fancy, it is just as easy to grow as any other species. It does not breed true so the seed you collect will likely give you something quite interesting but not identical to the parent plant. Division is the best method of propagation for maintaining the hybrid flower form. The wild plant is hard to find because it has been overcollected in its native areas. *Primula auricula* will tolerate a bit more sunshine than many other *Primula*, but avoid planting it in hot, noonday sun. This species will grow nicely in a semishaded rock garden where adequate moisture is present. Drainage has to be perfect—it cannot sit in wet, boglike soils, or it

will die. This species is often grown as a potted plant because of the beauty of its flowers.

Primula denticulata

There are not too many hybrids of species *Primula denticulata* on the market here in North America, and this is more the pity. Over the years, this has been one of my hardiest and most favorite *Primula*. It is a Himalayan plant and demands shade and rich, organic soils. The blooms are drumsticklike (which is why the common name for this plant is *drumstick primula*) and bloom very early in the spring.

Primula juliae

Primula juliae is one of the species used in creating a series of hybrids called the Juliana series, and these Juliana hybrids are quite hardy in zone 4 and easily grown in the shade garden. One of the earliest and still the best known of this series is 'Wanda,' a violet plant that is quite tolerant of any soil type and accepts a bit more sun than the species. There are two clues that you are getting a member of this family at a garden center. The first is if the plant's tag says *Juliana* anywhere in the description. The second is if the tag says *hybrid*; many of the more modern hybrids come from this group. This is assuming of course that the tag does not mention one of the other species or variety names of the *Primula* family—especially the Polyanthus types listed below under *Primula vulgaris*.

Primula veris

Primula veris is the traditional yellow cowslip and one of the more easily shade-grown yellow-blooming *Primula*.

Primula vulgaris

How anyone could name this plant *vulgaris* is beyond me. It comes in a wide range of colors, and the breeders have worked their magic on it. To succeed with this one, simply keep it out of the sun. The breeders have used *Primula vulgaris* and *Primula juliae* to produce a variety of hybrids. One result, called Polyanthus, is commonly sold in garden centers and seed catalogs. With the Polyanthus varieties (Pacific Giants, Regal, and Posy series are some of the readily available plants), I've found that the yellows are quite hardy, but the blues and reds tend to be much shorter lived. They tend to grow and flower themselves to death, and while quite lovely for the first year, they rarely make the second year. I'm sure other gardeners have a better track record with them, particularly if they have a slightly warmer garden.

Growing *Primula*

Primula is a very large family of plants found in many different growing conditions. For the most part, however, *Primula* plants found in garden centers are plants of the woodland or woodland edge. Some species are bog plants or mountain meadow plants, but these are mostly collector plants and not easily located. The one rule of thumb is that North American species will survive and grow well enough in sunlight, while Asian species demand shade if they are to be successful.

In general, the family wants a soil that is well drained yet high in moisture. Standing water will rot the crowns of the plant, particularly during the wintertime. While this soil water would be frozen in our zone 4 garden, if allowed to collect around the crown of the plant, any thawing and subsequent freezing during the winter would kill. Avoid deep mulches for this reason. High summer humidity is excellent, so shady areas with reduced air movement are good spots. *Primula* does not like hot summers but prefers a cooler area; grow it in the coolest part of the garden. For the most part, it prefers a more alkaline soil, so adding lime rather than peat moss is a good starting point. Compost is welcomed both for its nutritional value as well as for its soil-amending properties.

Potions and Poisons

Primula has been used medicinally for centuries, even, if you believe the recipes, in the making of a particularly potent liquor called cowslip wine. The young leaves were eaten in salads, the flowers made into conserve. *Primula* was generally used as a sedative and antispasmodic, and the flowers were thought to strengthen the brain. In fact, if you read long enough, there are few ailments that this plant was not used for at one time or another—from wrinkle removal to headache relief to sedation for nervous afflictions. There are no dangers associated with *Primula*, so do not worry about growing it in abundance (and you'll need an abundance to make cowslip wine).

PULMONARIA

Common names: lungwort, Jerusalem cowslip

*P*ulmonaria comes from the Latin *pulmo*, or "lung." The spotted leaves were said to resemble lungs, so according to the Doctrine of Signatures, it was named after the lung. *Lungwort* is obviously "lung" combined with the Saxon *wort*, or "plant." Note that the word *lung* is almost the same in all Germanic languages and is related to the Greek *luft*, or "air." The origin of *Jerusalem cowslip* remains a mystery to me.

Bloom time: Early spring
Height: 8″ to 12″ (20 cm to 30 cm)
Sun needed: Sun to shade; does best in part shade out of the hot midday sun
Bloom color: White, red shades, blue-pinks

Planting space: 24″ (60 cm) apart
Soil preferred: Good soil with organic matter and no standing water
Propagation method: Division

Recommended Varieties

I confess that *Pulmonaria* is one of my favorite spring-blooming plants and that it is scattered throughout my garden. I try to grow it everywhere I have a few spare feet of garden because the flowers are early and the leaves are attractive for the entire summer. I've never had a disease or pest problem on *Pulmonaria*, and other than keeping it in bounds with a shovel every few years, it is a carefree and trouble-free plant. The breeders must agree with me because there are more and more of them appearing on the market every year.

Pulmonaria angustifolia

Pulmonaria angustifolia will do best on slightly acidic soils, so adding peat moss is a good idea. It will also tolerate more sunlight than some other species, and it is a candidate for naturalizing in meadows as long as there is no spring mowing until after flowering is finished. The leaves are narrower on this species than others, and in many of the varieties, they are unspotted or lack the heavy spotting so common in other species. Common varieties include the following:

'Rubra' has reddish-pink flowers.

'Azurea' has flowers of bright blue with a red tint in the bud.

'Lambrook Silver' is one of the more highly variegated of this species, with good blue flowers.

Pulmonaria x hybrida

An increasing number of hybrids are coming onto the market that are excellent garden-performing plants. Truth be told, unless I need a specific species such as *Pulmonaria longifolia* to grow on clay, I really don't care about the species of the plants I grow. I grow far too many of this plant family in my own garden because I like its spring flowers and ongoing foliar attractiveness, including hybrids such as the following:

'Beth Chatto,' with its heavily spotted leaves and dark blue flowers, fits my garden plans quite nicely.

'Victorian Brooch' has long leaves and silver-spotted foliage and gorgeous magenta-coral blooms with a ruby red calyx. This is one of the longest bloomers in this family.

'Lewis Palmer' has long, thin leaves with good-sized silver blotches and a very heavy blooming display of blue-violet flowers.

Pulmonaria longifolia

If you are cursed with a heavy clay soil, species *Pulmonaria longifolia* is one you should search out. It does better on clay than any other species.

'Bertram Anderson' is the most commonly available variety. The leaves are well spotted with silver, and the flowers are a mid-blue color.

Pulmonaria rubra

While species *Pulmonaria rubra* is said to be semi-evergreen in warmer climates by reference textbooks, it isn't so in my garden.

'Sissinghurst White' is a white-blooming plant with good coloring on the leaves.

'Trevi Fountain' has heavily silver-spotted leaves and large cobalt blue flowers, making this an interesting addition to any garden.

Pulmonaria saccharata

'Leopard' is a narrow-leaf variety but well spotted with silver markings. The flowers are early-spring bloomers in reddish tones.

Pulmonaria angustifolia   DOUGLAS GREEN

Growing *Pulmonaria*

All fourteen different species of this plant share the love of deep, rich soils that are high in organic matter. *Pulmonaria* thrives in the shade or part shade of the garden. There are some individual differences in cultivation, which are listed under the specific variety notes. My own experience is that these differences are preferences rather than absolute requirements and that providing a good soil high in organic matter is the single most important requirement for success.

Pulmonaria majeste   DOUGLAS GREEN

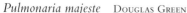

Early-Spring Bloomers   71

Pulmonaria saccharata 'Leopard'
BLOOMS OF BRESSINGHAM NORTH AMERICA, BARBERTON OH

Pulmonaria angustifolia   DOUGLAS GREEN

Consistently damp soil is also important for *Pulmonaria*'s success. This is *not* a plant for dry shade.

Most gardeners delight in the two-toned colors of the blossoms, and obtaining a variety of these plants will bring bright spring color to the garden as well as the season-long interest provided by the leaves.

Potions and Poisons

An infusion (liquid dose) of the leaves of lungwort was said to clear up mucous problems, reduce coughs, and clear up infections. As the original use was based on the shape of the leaves rather than the effectiveness of its treatment, this is no longer recommended.

Pulmonaria rubra 'Trevi Fountain'
TERRA NOVA NURSERIES

Pulmonaria 'Victorian Brooch'
TERRA NOVA NURSERIES

TRILLIUM

Common names: wake-robin, birthroot

The name *Trillium* comes from the Latin *tri* meaning "three." Leaves or other parts of the plant are in threes. The common name *birthroot* comes from its long use as an herb given to women during childbirth.

Bloom time: Early spring

Height: 12" to 18" (30 cm to 45 cm)

Sun needed: Part sun

Bloom color: White, pink, red, and yellow

Planting space: 8" to 12" (20 cm to 30 cm) apart

Soil preferred: Rich woodland soil

Propagation method: Division or seed

Recommended Varieties

Almost any *Trillium* you can purchase is a good one to grow. Because a salable *Trillium* can take upwards of four years in a nursery to grow, nursery-grown plants tend to be expensive. Cheaper plants are almost always those that have been dug from the wild. There are thirty-eight different species of *Trillium* found in North America, while only five are found in Asia. Not all are hardy in colder zones; nor are they commonly available except through specialist nurseries. (Some of these sources are listed in Resources.) The most commonly available *Trillium* species in the nursery trade are listed below.

Trillium catesbaei

Trillium catesbaei is a *Trillium* of Alabama, Georgia, the Carolinas, and parts of Virginia, and unfortunately for us more northern gardeners it is not hardy much north of these areas. With a delightful pink color with darker veins, this spring flower is a charmer. I've tried this one and unfortunately killed it in my zone 4 garden.

Trillium cernuum

Trillium cernuum is one of the most northern of *Trillium* species, being found all the way up to Hudson's Bay in Canada and down to the Northeast as far as Virginia. It prefers moist soils and part-shade spots. It is small-flowered and white but welcomed at the edge of shady ponds.

Trillium grandiflorum

Trillium grandiflorum is the *Trillium* you think of when you hear the name. It too is a northern species—found across eastern Canada and down as far as the Appalachian Mountains into northern Georgia. It prefers well-drained soils under maple trees on neutral soils. There are some cultivated varieties of this species:

Trillium grandiflorum 'Roseum' is a pink variation with large leaves.

Trillium grandiflorum polymerum 'Victorin' is a double-flowering white *Trillium* that is quite costly if you can find it in specialty catalogs. The double varieties are sterile and must be divided for propagation.

Trillium nivale

Trillium nivale, or *snow trillium*, is a small-flowering white *Trillium*. In its native area of West Virginia across to Ohio and Illinois and north as far as southern Minnesota, it is one of the earliest *Trillium* species to bloom. I've had this *Trillium* in my

Trillium grandiflorum DOUGLAS GREEN

Trillium grandiflorum DOUGLAS GREEN

garden for several years, and it has proved to be quite hardy. It is an excellent plant for the shady rock garden, thriving in cracks in rocks where there is little plant competition and the soil is well drained.

Trillium luteum

Trillium luteum is one of the sessile *Trillium* species, with spotted leaves and distinctive upward-facing sessile flowers (*sessile* means that the flower is attached to the plant without a stalk). In its native area of North Carolina and northern Georgia upward to southern Kentucky, this is a plant of deciduous forests. I've grown it easily in my zone 4 garden, and its yellow flowers are quite distinctive. Once you learn to recognize it, you'll not mistake it for anything else.

Trillium recurvatum

Trillium recurvatum is the *prairie trillium*, and its sessile blooms are found in Michigan, Iowa, and Missouri and down to eastern Texas and north of a line from there to northern Alabama. This red-bloomed species is found mostly on rich, moist soils. Easily grown, it is quite hardy in zone 4.

Growing *Trillium*

This is a plant of the deciduous forest. It thrives in humus-rich soils in shade to part shade. It will survive in full sun but quite unhappily unless the soil is quite rich and moisture is constant. Once established, *Trillium* is very long-lived and will flower regularly to welcome spring to the garden. Virtually trouble- and pest-free, it is an easy plant to grow. It does indeed make a good cut flower if you can bear to take the scissors to it.

Potions and Poisons

The common name *wake-robin* refers to two plants. The first is the *Trillium*, and the second is several members of the *Arum* family. Do not confuse these two plants, as they have vastly different effects. The *Trillium* has been used for many years as an antiseptic and for hemorrhaging control; this gives us the other common name *birthroot*—it was often given to women in labor to control bleeding. It is no longer used.

6

Late-Spring Bloomers

While the early-spring bloomers tell me that spring is thinking of coming, these late-spring bloomers tell me that spring has well and truly arrived. Winter is now officially banished in my garden, and I get my hands and mind fully into gardening delights. When the spring *Anemone* and *Aquilegia* blooms announce their presence, I once again fall in love with my garden. Spring is an enchanting time, and I confess I'm a willing participant in the affair.

ANEMONE

Common names: anemone, windflower, pheasant's eye

The name *Anemone* is rooted in Greek. *An* means "to blow," and a derivative of this is *anila*, which means "the wind." Hence the common name *windflower*. Legend has it that the tears Venus wept over the body of Adonis—gored to death by a wild boar—were carried away and became anemone flowers. This has led to the mistaken belief that *Anemone* flowers open only when it is windy. Some accounts say that the drops of blood spilled by Adonis grew into windflowers. This translation of the poem *Adonais*, a pastoral poem by Bion, circa 100 B.C., seems to lend credence to the tears derivation.

> But, oh the Cytherean! slain and dead,
> The fair Adonis slain!
> Her tears, as plenteous as the blood he shed,
> She pours amain;
> And flowers are born from every drop that flows,
> From tears the Anemony, from blood the Rose.

It has been suggested that Venus tried unsuccessfully to seduce Adonis and this, too, resulted in tears on his death. Whatever the cause of the tears, they produced flowers.

Just for the record, Adonis was regarded as the god of the plants, and it is said that he alone of all gods would disappear into the ground in the autumn and winter to reappear in the spring and summer. This is a fitting behavior for the god of plants, and *Anemone* is likewise a fitting plant to be named after him.

Bloom time: Late spring
Height: 8″ to 30″ (20 cm to 75 cm)
Sun needed: Light shade for most
Bloom color: White, pinks, blues, rose
Planting space: 12″ to 18″ (30 cm to 45 cm) apart

Soil preferred: Well-drained and high in humus
Propagation method: Seed or division

Recommended Varieties

To make things simple, there are three classes of *Anemone* we grow in our gardens.

- Tuberous-rooted: Summer-blooming and tender. These are normally sold as annual bulbs and can be found in any good bulb catalog. As annuals they are not described in this book.

- Fibrous-rooted: Fall-blooming and reasonably hardy into zone 3.
- Rhizomes and tubers: Spring-blooming and hardy.

---

1. R. C. A. Prior, M.D., *On the Popular Names of British Plants* (London: Williams and Norgate, 1863), page 7.

Anemone canadensis   Douglas Green

Anemone blanda (Grecian windflower)

The common name for species *Anemone blanda* is *Grecian windflower*. This small plant, 6″ to 8″ (15 cm to 20 cm) tall, is one of the earlier-flowering *Anemone* species. It is a tuberous species but is the hardiest of that group, surviving into zone 4 in mild winters or protected gardens. Part shade and humus-enriched soil will help this plant thrive. If you purchase dried-out tubers, they may take several years to establish themselves; if you have a choice, avoid the leathery-looking tubers, and instead pick a plump specimen. Planting can be confusing (which is the top and which the bottom?), so the generations-old advice is to plant the tubers vertically on their edges. The tubers will figure out top and bottom and will orient themselves. The following varieties are sometimes difficult to find but worth the search:

‘Blue Star’ and ‘Pink Star’ are exactly what they sound like and have good colors.

‘White Splendour’ is (surprise) a good white-blooming variety.

Anemone canadensis

Anemone canadensis is often sold in mail-order catalogs and is one of the more frequently listed *Anemone* species in European nurseries. See the following page for a warning about this charming but highly invasive plant. It grows best in light shade, although it survives in full sun. Our most invasive patch was in shallow, sandy soil in full sun. I do note that it is quite attractive and blooms for a long time.

Anemone x lesseri

Anemone x lesseri is another *Anemone* that blooms in late spring or early summer. Growing to 18″ (45 cm) tall, it does best in light shade with humus-enriched soils. This is one of the more heat tolerant of *Anemone* species and will grow in full sun in all but the hottest of areas. There is a hard-to-find red variety.

The short species *Anemone multifida*, 8″ (15 cm) tall is one of the more cold-tolerant in the garden. It is not readily available in the nursery trade but is a delightful little plant. It has creamy white flowers on a stem 12″ (30 cm) long. It's easy to grow if given a bit of compost and light shade.

Anemone nemerosa

Short *Anemone nemerosa*, 8″ (15 cm) tall, is the European wood anemone and is one of the more popular spring-blooming *Anemone* species in cultivation. Identifying this spreading plant can be difficult, as it is so variable in flower form, size, and color. This is the *Anemone* for deeper shade, although it does well enough in light shade as well, and it performs much better on an acidic soil than others in the family. (Hint: Grow it with rhododendrons.) Add copious amounts of leaf mold or compost to keep this plant thriving.

Anemone sylvestris

Fragrant, white flowers make *Anemone sylvestris* a desired garden member, although it can be a bit of a spreader if it decides it likes the garden. Give it light shade, humus-rich soils, and even moisture. If the soil is well-cultivated or sandy, it will increase in invasiveness.

The white, fragrant blossoms of 'Grandiflora' make it a winner.

Growing *Anemone*

Once planted in the appropriate sun location at the front of the perennial garden, the *Anemone* can be forgotten. It is quite hardy and produces its blooms regularly late spring and after late spring. The blooms are not long-lasting when compared to their fall-blooming cousins, but they are welcome nevertheless. There is a full range of sun- to shade-lovers in this family. Plants such as *Anenome sylvestris* and the thug *Anenome canadensis* (see the following paragraph) prefer a semishaded spot, while *Anenome x lesseri* varieties prefer a bit more sun. If you give *Anemone* a well-drained soil but one that is high in humus, you will have very little trouble growing it. It does make an excellent alpine or rock garden plant.

Sometimes, you'll find *Anemone canadensis* for sale in garden centers as a wildflower. Do not let this plant into your garden unless you want it to grow wild everywhere. This is a true garden thug. It is delightfully pretty in the late spring and early summer, with its white blossoms, but it is a rampant spreader and cannot be controlled without excessive zeal. I had an entire bed ruined by this plant—it occurs naturally in our area—and will no longer allow it anywhere near the garden. Each emerging shoot is quickly dug up and removed from the garden; I make an extra effort to get all the roots, as any that are left will produce new plants. One of the main keys to identifying *Anenome canadensis* is that the flower buds are held very close to the leaves, almost cupped by them before they open and develop a very short stem. Other *Anenome* species have a much longer stem, and the flower develops clearly on the end of a stem—not cupped down with the leaf.

Do note that some *Anenome* species, *Anenome blanda* and *Anenome nemorosa* in particular, like hot, dry conditions after they are finished blooming and will likely go dormant in midsummer when given these conditions. Their disappearance at this time is no slight to the gardener; they will simply disappear when they have stored enough energy and will reappear once again to bloom the following spring.

Potions and Poisons

Anemone has a long medicinal history associated with it. The root is an irritant and somewhat poisonous, although older herbals recommend it be chewed as a purgative. In other words, chew the root and you'll throw up. The leaves are acrid, and it's possible to make vinegar from them; old herbals also report cattle being poisoned by eating them. Their taste is likely to deter any child from eating them, so this is not likely to be a problem. Having said that of course, it is wise to keep small children away from roots if you are transplanting or working with this plant.

AQUILEGIA

Common names: columbine, culverwort

*A*quilegia is a delightful plant, and its name is equally wonderful in that it is derived from the Latin *aquila* meaning "eagle." This is a reference to the individual petals. The common name *columbine* refers to the shape of the flower, which is said to resemble doves drinking around in a circle. The Latin word for *dove* is *columba*. *Culverwort* comes from the Saxon words *culfre* "pigeon" and *wort* "plant." Use your imagination and you'll be able to see a flock of pigeons sitting around in a circle drinking together.

Bloom time: Late spring or early summer
Height: 3″ to 30″ (7.5 cm to 75 cm), tending to grow taller in hotter climates
Sun needed: Preferably full sun in cooler climates; part shade in hotter climates
Bloom color: Blues, pinks, whites, and yellows as well as shades and combinations of these

Planting space: Depends on variety; average 12″ (30 cm) apart for garden center varieties
Soil preferred: A loose, well-drained soil without clay
Propagation method: Seed

Recommended Varieties

Aquilegia alpina

Aquilegia alpina is a delightful plant if you can find it. It has deep sky-blue flowers on 12″ (30 cm) plants. It is wonderful for the front of the border or rock garden. There is some mixed breeding going on with *Aquilegia alpina*, and taller varieties are appearing in garden centers. This is my second-favorite columbine.

Aquilegia bertolonii

Aquilegia bertolonii is my favorite columbine. This plant, 6″ to 8″ (15 cm to 20 cm) tall, is wonderful for the rock garden, and its blue-and-cream flowers are a spring tonic. You'll likely find this one in seed form rather than as a plant in garden centers. Try it in the rock garden either in full sun or light shade. It self-sows abundantly in part-shade locations in my garden rather than in

full sun. I did have it at the front of the main perennial border, but it doesn't self-sow in heavy mulches and I lost it there.

Aquilegia caerulea

Also known as the *Rocky Mountain columbine*, *Aquilegia caerulea* grows 18″ to 24″ (45 cm to 60 cm) in my garden and has blue-and-white flowers. An attractive plant, I'm told it is one of the parents of many of the hybrids on the market.

Aquilegia canadensis

Aquilegia canadensis is a smaller plant. It thrives naturally at the front of my farm and stands about 18″ (45 cm) tall in full-sun and part-shade spots. The flowers (red and yellow) are smaller than the garden center hybrids but are equally charming. It is easy to naturalize and grow (I didn't do anything—it just arrived one year to colonize the area). The textbooks say it prefers

Aquilegia alpina   Douglas Green

Aquilegia alpina   Douglas Green

moist, shady areas, but mine is growing on poor, rocky, thin soils in full sunlight.

Aquilegia flabellata

Aquilegia flabellata is also one of the parents of modern columbine breeding. One of the nicest species is the pure white 'Nana.' It is only 12″ (30 cm) tall with glistening white flowers to 18″ (45 cm). The foliage forms a wonderful rounded mass and is quite heavy and glaucous compared to other *Aquilegia* species. If you find this plant at a specialist garden center, purchase it. There are taller varieties, such as '*pumila*,' which have slightly less glaucous blue-green leaves with blue-and-white flowers and are equally desirable in the garden.

Aquilegia chrysantha

Growing to 3′ (90 cm) in my garden, wonderful yellow *Aquilegia chrysantha* is a delight when it blooms. I never staked this tall plant, although I know others have. The flowers are large and the spurs long, so it stands out in the garden. This is the plant that brought the yellow gene to the

columbine breeding program. Unfortunately, it has also been one of the shortest lived columbines in my garden, seldom living longer than two to three years.

Aquilegia x hybrida

Some wonderful hybrids (*Aquilegia x hybrida*) are being bred and introduced to the market. Note that most of these are not too stable in terms of colors. They do not breed true, and sometimes the original breeding is not stable either, so a plant may not be exactly as advertised because of the variability in the genetic mix.

'Biedermeier' is offered by many seed companies. The blue-and-white variety is acceptable; other colors are muddy and, in my experience, not worth growing.

One of the problems faced by gardeners who mulch their gardens for weed control is that plants like *Aquilegia* that self-sow have a major problem doing so through the mulch. In our gardens, we have established areas where the self-sowing plants are not mulched with bark chips or straw so they can propagate themselves to their heart's delight. Otherwise, they would disappear in a few years as the mother plants die and the offspring are smothered by the mulch. On the other hand, I do note that if you want to maintain a particular hybrid line, a protective mulch is a good way to do so. The mulch will stop the offspring from germinating, and when the original plant dies, it can be replaced with another hybrid.

'Dragonfly' is a color mix and grows to 24″ (60 cm) tall. It has a good color range and is worth growing.

McKenna hybrids are hybrids 18″ to 24″ (45 cm to 60 cm) tall quite commonly found in commercial nurseries. They've had good color ranges in my garden.

Music series is one of the better hybrids at 18″ (45 cm). It has a good color mix, and the colors tend to be more intense than other hybrids in my garden.

Aquilegia vulgaris

Aquilegia vulgaris is known in Europe as *granny's bonnet* and grows 18″ to 24″ (45 to 60 cm) tall. A difficulty is that this plant has been bred for so long with so many other species that finding the original plant is becoming difficult. This is the source of the Vervaeneana group, which has variegated or gold flecks in the leaves and can either be quite attractive or look quite sickly. Many doubles have also been bred from *Aquilegia vulgaris* genetics. The old standby 'Nora Barlow,' a pink-and-green colored variety, is quite stable and has bred true year after seeding year in my garden.

Growing *Aquilegia*

Aquilegia is a short-lived perennial in my garden, although with the copious amount of seeds it produces, there is never any danger of running out of it. It self-sows like crazy, particularly in the sandier soils of the rock garden where there is a pea gravel mulch to protect the seeds from mice. The gravel mulch and well-drained soil give *Aquilegia* a perfect seed bed, and I have to weed it out every year or it will take over the rock garden.

Aquilegia is also promiscuous. It interbreeds very quickly and easily, so it is quite difficult to maintain a pure line of species plants. This is usually thought to be a problem for plant collectors; however, this is also a problem of the newer hybrids found in garden centers. After a few years, the hybrids will self-sow and produce offspring quite different in appearance from the

Aquilegia 'Alba'   DOUGLAS GREEN

Aquilegia bertolonii   DOUGLAS GREEN

parents. The gardener has a choice at that time: select the blooming plants he or she likes and allow these to go to seed or pull the offending plants and repurchase the hybrid. I note that some of the colors of the hybrid offspring will be quite terrible, and gardeners should feel no compunction to grow each and every one. A few years of selecting the most desirable colors will give a relatively stable population. Some of the older doubles in our garden are quite stable in color and seldom produce any offspring that are not true to the parent color and form.

Potions and Poisons

The roots and seeds of columbine were used in the past to treat sore throats and liver problems. It is an astringent (contracts soft tissue internally or externally) and is reputed to be dangerous to children. Some seed catalogs now put a warning label on *Aquilegia* seed for this reason.

The major insect problem for *Aquilegia* is the leaf miner. Simply squeeze the ends of the tunnels to eliminate the problem. Some species such as *Aquilegia canadensis* and *Aquilegia bertolonii* are not as susceptible to leaf miners.

ARISAEMA

Common names: jack-in-the-pulpit, Indian turnip, dragon arum

*A*risaema is a widely seen wildflower in North American woodlands, and its Asian cousins are now being imported in order to grace our gardens. The name is derived from the Greek *aris* or *arum,* "plant," and *haima,* "blood." This combination refers to a relationship; that is, *Arisaema* is blood-related to *Arum,* or it could refer to the dark flecks on the blooms. It could also derive from the blood-red blotches on the leaves of some species.

Bloom time: Normally late spring or early summer
Height: 12" to 30" (30 cm to 75 cm)
Sun needed: Shade
Bloom color: Mostly white with green-and-purple striping
Planting space: 12" to 18" (30 cm to 45 cm) apart

Soil preferred: Wet organic soils in the spring; not swampy year-round; drier soils during the winter months
Propagation method: Seed is easiest, with some species dividing or producing offsets from the tubers

Recommended Varieties

Arisaema candidissimum

Arisaema candidissimum is a Chinese species now available through some specialist mail-order catalogs. It is a fragrant species and much sought after. Do not hesitate to purchase it if you see it in a catalog or garden center. It is marginally hardy here in my zone 4 garden if grown dry in the fall and winter. If you can't guarantee a dry winter soil, treat this plant as an annual and dig it up in the fall and store it.

Arisaema triphyllum

Arisaema triphyllum, the native jack-in-the-pulpit, is easy to grow and quite winter hardy well into zone 3. I have several in my front garden and enjoy its reliability and hardiness. It lends a touch of the exotic to my garden.

Arisaema sazensoo

In tender Japanese *Arisaema sazensoo,* the blooms droop over, resembling a monk bowed in prayer. The name comes from the Japanese *zazen,* or Japanese meditation. This plant is only marginally hardy, so you should treat it as an annual bulb in zone 4.

Arisaema ringens

Arisaema ringens is one of the largest blooms in the family and worth growing for sure. It's marginally hardy in zone 4, so it is safest to treat it as an annual bulb.

Arisaema serratum

Arisaema serratum is very tall—often over 3' (90 cm). It's usually hardy in zone 4, but I do lose them in a wet fall. It's safest to dig and store it if you have a cold garden.

Arisaema sikokianum

Arisaema sikokianum is an easy plant. It is marginally hardy here in zone 4. Treating it as an annual is the safest unless your soil is quite dry during the fall and early spring. *Arisaema sikokianum* is one of the showiest species of the *Arisaema* family.

Growing *Arisaema*

Many of the Asian species are entering our garden world (see Resources), and several are not hardy in my zone 4 garden. To grow well, they have to be treated as annuals—you will need to dig the tuber up in the fall and store it dry and cool for the winter. Treat the tuber much like a gladiola or dahlia. Excessive moisture—for example, leaving it in a pot with damp soil—will rot the tuber, and I note this from sad personal experience. These new species are worth the extra effort if you enjoy growing this family. I grow these tender species in clay pots in my front garden. They make an excellent pot plant, and the tubers can easily be removed or harvested in the fall to go into storage. Growers in warmer gardens should follow the growing directions provided below or in specialty garden catalogs.

I've had the best success with these plants by growing them in medium, dappled shade rather than full shade. On our sandy soils, I water them regularly all spring but increasingly let them dry out starting in August. Compost is all they get for feed. In hotter gardens, more shade will likely be called for.

Arisaema species are not showy plants in the same way that garden phlox is a showy plant, but in the shade garden, they are classic plants with a great deal of horticultural interest. "Horticultural interest" is a dedicated gardener's way of saying that the plants are great collector's plants and will impress other gardeners but not those who depend on gaudy blooms for their gardening enjoyment.

Arisaema triphyllum   DOUGLAS GREEN

From a gardener's point of view, these plants are expensive to purchase. However, they come easily from seed, so a few years of growing them will likely give you all the seed and babies you'd like to have. Then you can experiment with winter hardiness in your garden using your own plants rather than the original and expensive plants.

Potions and Poisons

There is some disagreement about *Arisaema* when it comes to both its medicinal value and its food value. I suspect that there may be some confusion about the specific plant family; herbal authors (both old and new) are using different genus names to describe this plant. For the record, some say natives would eat the tubers and others say it is a violent irritant to the mucous membranes. Personally, I don't eat the tubers and I would recommend that you do not either.

CORYDALIS

Common names: fumewort, rock harlequin

The name *Corydalis* comes from the Greek word *korydalis*, "lark," because the flowers were said to resemble the head of that bird. *Fume* comes from the Latin *fumus*, "smoke." Fumeworts apparently reproduced without seed—from smoke, as it were—in that the seed was not seen by the gardener. Given that *harlequin* comes originally from the Old French *hellequin*, "leader of a band of demonic horsemen," and is often used to refer to a classic comic role, I confess to not knowing how the name *rock harlequin* came into being.

Bloom time: Starting in late spring, many for an extended period
Height: 12″ to 24″ (30 cm to 60 cm)
Sun needed: Sun to part shade; the hotter the climate, the more shade required
Bloom color: Yellows and blues

Planting space: 18″ (45 cm) apart
Soil preferred: Well-drained and high in organic matter; not dry sand but good woodland soil
Propagation method: Seed; division with some species, but use seed if you're not sure

Recommended Varieties

Corydalis flexuosa

Corydalis flexuosa is one of the "blue"-flowering species and is well worth a spot in any garden. It does resent drying out and is still "on trial" in my own garden. There are many new varieties of this plant being brought to market.

'China Blue' has lacy blue-green foliage with sky-blue flowers all summer. If you can grow *Corydalis flexuosa*, you should grow this gem.

'Purple Leaf' is relatively new to cultivation. The purplish tinge to its foliage and fragrant flowers make this a winner. 'Purple Leaf' tends to go dormant in summer if it is unhappy but does reappear again, so do not dig it up thinking it is dead, unless it fails to reappear the following spring.

Corydalis elata

Corydalis elata is a little harder to find than *Corydalis flexuosa* varieties. It may grow better than *Corydalis flexuosa* varieties in the stress of a hotter—and interestingly enough, colder—garden. It's on trial in colder sections of my garden.

Corydalis lutea

Corydalis lutea is a wonderful little gem of a plant. It starts blooming in mid spring and continues for most of the summer until fall frosts knock it back. At 12″ (30 cm) tall and equally wide (taller and wider in shade), its bright yellow flowers are a real sight for winter-weary eyes. The only drawback with this plant is that it is a prolific self-sower. It will pop up all over your garden, reaching places you wouldn't think possible. Thankfully, it is easy to weed out.

Corydalis ophiocarpa

Corydalis ophiocarpa is often available in seed catalogs. This is an extremely weedy species with dull yellow flowers that are not attractive at all. It self-sows everywhere in my garden after only two years of growing it. I am now weeding it out to eliminate it from the garden. It is not worth growing, so save your money for good plants.

Growing *Corydalis*

Corydalis is grown as much for its fernlike foliage as the abundant show of flowers it produces. The taller species and varieties are best grown on the woodland edge, with moist or damp soils with good drainage (the soil can't be boglike with constant water and no drainage). High organic matter is important in full sun or light shade. In hotter climates, provide protection from that broiling noon sun. A mulch is useful to help hold the moisture levels constant and to offer some protection during the winter.

The shorter species, such as *Corydalis lutea*, also make excellent alpine or rock garden plants. This is especially true if the rock garden is shaded or the plants are tucked into the protected north side of large rocks. None of the family requires heavy feeding; they perform quite well in low-fertility areas. In our gardens, they are more likely to colonize the stone pathways than they are the fertile garden soil.

Potions and Poisons

Corydalis is used medicinally in traditional Chinese medicine, but because it contains alkaloids, it is not recommended for internal use or experimentation by the untrained.

Corydalis lutea DOUGLAS GREEN

DICENTRA

Common names: bleeding heart, heart's ease, Dutchman's breeches, staggerweed, turkey corn

*D*icentra derives from the Greek *dis*, meaning "twice," and *kentron*, which translates as "a spur." All Dicentra family flowers have two spurs. The reason for the name *bleeding heart* is immediately obvious to anyone who has grown this plant. *Staggerweed* may refer to the plant's reputation for producing alkaloids. (See Potions and Poisons.)

Bloom time: Late spring or throughout summer, depending on species; see notes on specific cultivars
Height: 12″ to 36″ (30 cm to 90 cm), depending on species
Sun needed: Shade to part shade, with some tolerance of sun; see notes on specific cultivars

Bloom color: White, pink, or red
Planting space: 18″ (45 cm) apart with smaller species; 24″ to 30″ (60 cm to 75 cm) apart with larger
Soil preferred: Well-drained but with good organic matter
Propagation method: Division; some self-sow

Recommended Varieties

It should be noted that there is some discussion in the trade about the parentage of some of the shorter hybrids. I really don't care about the genetic parentage; personally, I just want to grow delightful-looking plants. So I list the varieties as they are described in their originating nursery catalogs and as they grow in my garden.

Dicentra eximia

Dicentra eximia is a North American native (Northeast) with heavily indented leaves (quite fringed, actually) and small flowers. It is most charming in the shade garden or naturalized shade area with *Trillium* and other shade plants. The bloom time is quite long if the soil is kept damp but not waterlogged.

'Alba' is white.

'Stuart Boothman' is a soft pink with glaucous foliage.

Dicentra formosa

Dicentra formosa is the western North American native. This species is more drought tolerant than *Dicentra eximia* but not as tolerant of wet conditions. It is much showier and heavier-blooming than *Dicentra eximia*, and there are more garden varieties under development.

'Adrian Bloom' has ruby-red flowers and good growth.

'Alba' is a white-flowering variety, and while not as vigorous as 'Luxuriant' below, it gives a good flower show.

'Luxuriant' has cherry-red flowers carried above the 12″ (30 cm) foliage. It blooms for a very long time and is much admired in my part-shade garden. I planted several together in a clump, and it really is spectacular when it starts to bloom.

'Snowflakes' is an excellent white variety with larger white flowers than 'Alba.'

Dicentra spectabilis 'Alba'   DOUGLAS GREEN

Dicentra spectabilis 'Gold Heart'   DOUGLAS GREEN

Dicentra spectabilis

Dicentra spectabilis is the old-fashioned plant grown by everybody's grandmother. It still deserves a place in the garden. It self-sows in my garden and can make a bit of a nuisance of itself. My grandfather had a huge one so I give this plant some leeway in its invasiveness.

'Gold Heart' is a yellow/golden leaf form. It comes highly recommended, looks wonderful next to a dark yew, but is too young in my garden for me to report honestly on vigor and bloom.

'Alba' is a white form of the old-fashioned pink bleeding heart. It's not as vigorous as the pink in my garden but almost. It brightens up a shady garden with its masses of white blossoms.

Growing *Dicentra*

Dicentra is a woodland or woodland edge plant. It performs best in shade to part shade in well drained soils that are high in organic matter. If grown in the sun, *Dicentra spectabilis* will go dormant in midsummer to reappear the following spring. *Dicentra eximia* and *Dicentra formosa* varieties will tolerate more sunlight than *Dicentra spectabilis*. *Dicentra* performs the best in a moist yet well-drained soil (one high in organic matter). Allowing the soil to dry out limits both the number of blooms and length of the bloom time. To really grow *Dicentra* well, mulch with thick layers of compost. After a few years, the plant will be truly spectacular.

Potions and Poisons

Dicentra produces alkaloids and if eaten in large enough quantities is harmful. It is described as narcotic in the old herbals. This may be because it was used in the treatment of syphilis, scrofula, and skin infections as well as "female disorders." *It is not recommended for backyard medicine.*

Dicentra formosa 'Adrian Bloom'   Blooms of Bressingham North America, Barberton OH

Dicentra formosa 'Snowflakes'   Blooms of Bressingham North America, Barberton OH

PHLOX

Common names: ground phlox, creeping phlox, moss phlox

*P*hlox is Greek for "flame," an apt name for this colorful plant family. It is also used in Greek for "plant with flame-colored flowers." The common names *ground phlox* and *creeping phlox* come from their ground-hugging growth characteristic when compared to the later-blooming garden phlox. *Moss phlox* refers to a similar low-growing characteristic.

Bloom time: Late spring
Height: 2″ to 4″ (5 cm to 10 cm)
Sun needed: Full sun to part shade
Bloom color: Blues, reds/pinks, whites

Planting space: 24″ (60 cm) apart
Soil preferred: Sandy and well-drained
Propagation method: Division or cuttings

Recommended Varieties

Phlox subulata

Phlox subulata is commonly known as *ground phlox* and *moss phlox*.

'Emerald Blue' is a deep blue with open plant growth.

'Emerald Pink' is a clear pink with a tight growing habit—an excellent plant.

'Crimson Beauty' and 'Scarlet Flame' are both red with very open growth.

'Oakington Blue Eyes' has sky-blue foliage and is a heavy bloomer—an excellent plant.

'Snowflake' is white. Nobody said plant people were creative in naming plants.

You can probably guess the color of 'White Delight.'

Phlox stolonifera

Phlox stolonifera, commonly known as *creeping phlox*, is native to the northeast of North America and one of the most shade tolerant of the low-growing *Phlox* species. It is not as vigorous as other species and doesn't make the mat that is formed by *Phlox subulata*; it has a more open growth habit.

The most common variety of *Phlox stolonifera* is 'Sherwood Purple,' which is a purplish blue flower on a 6″ (15 cm) stem.

Phlox divaricata

Phlox divaricata is a bit taller than the other two species. It can grow to 12″ (30 cm) tall but slowly expands to fill a bed. The flowers tend to be shades of light blue. It grows best in a moist, part-shade garden soil. A hybrid cross of this plant with *Phlox pilosa* called 'Chattahoochee' is sometimes sold as *Phlox divaricata*. This is a bicolored form that has never lived in my garden for more than two years. I'm told that it is short-lived in warmer gardens as well. If you grow it, constantly make new plants by separating well-rooted divisions from the mother plant.

Growing *Phlox*

Ground phlox is an extremely easy plant to grow. Put a well-rooted bit in a loose, open soil, keep it watered for several weeks, and the deed is done. The only thing this plant does not appreciate is a heavy clay soil. Heavy soils or water-logged soils rot the roots. Keep the roots well

Phlox subulata 'Oakington Blue Eyes'
BLOOMS OF BRESSINGHAM NORTH AMERICA, BARBERTON OH

Phlox subulata   DOUGLAS GREEN

drained, and the plant will thrive. It is an excellent plant for installing between large rocks or in crevices on steep slopes. A light feeding of compost very early in the spring before blooming is all the feeding it requires for the season. Too-heavy feeding of garden fertilizer will promote soft, weak growth that is prone to winterkill.

There is no maintenance to this plant other than keeping it in bounds every few years with a sharp shovel.

Every now and then in a wet year, you may find that a section dies out and turns brown and a bit rotten. If this happens, do not worry. Simply dig out the dead patch and fill the area with a good soil from a nearby section of garden. Add a shovel of compost and allow the surviving patch to fill back in. It will likely do so immediately over the summer to rebloom the following spring.

It should be noted that this plant does not bloom all summer, but only for a month or so in mid spring. Many low-price catalogs sell it as an all-summer bloomer and mislead gardeners with their hyperbole.

Potions and Poisons

Apparently *Phlox* is safe to ingest—even for children. The *Phlox* family was used as an effective worm killer when prepared by herbalists. It is said to be particularly effective on roundworm—a fact I'm sure to retain. There is a dearth of instructions on exactly how to prepare these concoctions, so I'd suggest you not use it.

Phlox subulata 'Emerald Pink'   DOUGLAS GREEN

7

Early-Summer Bloomers

The plants listed in this chapter and the next are the backbone plants for the main season of bloom in the perennial garden. You can't escape them in any garden center, nor should you want to. I have also included a few that are not all that common but no garden is complete without.

Of course, there is a lot of overlap between early- and late-summer bloomers. While there is no difficulty saying that *Delphinium* blooms in early summer or that *Phlox* is a late-summer perennial, few plants are so easy to categorize. We get into trouble when we hit plants that tend to bloom around the very height of the summer. Each season brings something different to the bloom cycle in the garden. A long, cold, wet spring will delay the growth and flowering of many early summer perennials so that when the heat of summer finally arrives, so do the perennials— all at once. The garden resembles a crazy quilt of late spring and early- and mid-summer perennials all blooming their fool heads off at the same time.

I confess that my distinctions are arbitrary; they come from my interpretation of the season, my garden, and my idiosyncratic memory. Your summer will be different from mine, but by the end of the season you'll have a better idea of what to expect in your location.

ACONITUM

The Greek word *akoniton* (used by Theophrastus) given to these poisonous plants is the basis for the horticultural Latin. *Monkshood* comes from the shape of the individual flowers, resembling, well . . . monks' hoods. *Wolfbane* is derived from the use of the roots to poison wolves.

Bloom time: The starting bloom time of *Aconitum* varies from early summer through late summer, and most varieties bloom for extended periods of time. All are covered here for convenience.
Height: 48″ to 72″ (120 cm to 180 cm)

Sun needed: Full sun to light shade
Bloom color: Blues, violets, white
Planting space: 12″ to 18″ (30 cm to 45 cm) apart
Soil preferred: Humus-rich soil
Propagation method: Seed or division

Recommended Varieties

Aconitum bartlettii

'Blue Sceptre' is 48″ (120 cm) tall with mid-blue flowers. It has good weather tolerance, blooming from midsummer on.

'Bressingham Spire' is 48″ (120 cm) tall and is deep lavender/purple. It does not require staking and blooms over an extended period of time from midsummer onward.

Aconitum x cammarum

'Bicolor' is a delightful and older garden variety with bicolored (blue and white) flowers. Growing to 6′ (180 cm) in height, it blooms from early summer to midsummer and is one of the earliest to bloom in my garden.

Aconitum carmichaelii

This species is known as autumn monkshood because of its reliable late-summer- to fall-blooming period. It is a tall plant, easily reaching 6′ (180 cm) in height and throws multiple stems heavily laden with blooms.

'Arendsii' is one of the bright blue selections well worth searching out for fall garden blues.

Aconitum lamarckii

Aconitum lamarckii is a mid-summer bloomer only reaching 2′ to 4′ (60 cm to 120 cm) in height. It is unusual because of its creamy yellow flowers.

Aconitum napellus

Aconitum napellus is the old-fashioned garden plant beloved of cut-flower growers and flower arrangers. It grows to 5′ (150 cm) tall and is a mid-summer bloomer. The species with its bright blue flowers is most often grown, but there are new hybrids in development.

'Carneum' has a growth habit similar to that of the species but differs with its rose pink blooms.

Aconitum septentionale

'Ivorine' is found in the nursery trade more and more because of its reliable and excellent blooms. It is a short grower, only sending flower spikes to

Aconitum

Aconitum carmichaelii DOUGLAS GREEN

3′ (90 cm) in early summer to midsummer. I think it is one of the best of the white-flowering varieties in garden trials.

Growing *Aconitum*

The strong blue colors of *Aconitum* make it valuable in the summer palette. While some writers have suggested this plant is fine for the part-shade garden, in nature it is a plant of the moist meadow or woodland edge. The key is to keep the soil constantly moist; as the soil dries out, the performance of the plant deteriorates. This does not mean heavy clay is fine—the constant water will rot the root. The key to obtaining good blooms is to have a soil that is high in organic matter, and the easiest way to obtain both this and an even moisture supply is to mulch the plant heavily with leaves or other rapidly decaying organic matter. Do cut the plant down immediately after the first flush of blooms is finished; this will encourage the plant to rebloom. *Aconitum* grows best for me in the sunshine rather than the part-shade garden, and I would advise gardeners to start it out in their sunniest spot but ensure adequate water is available.

Potions and Poisons

The roots and leaves of this plant contain poisonous alkaloids and should be treated with caution. The concentration of poison is particularly high in the roots. When digging and dividing, take care not to leave the roots lying around. There are reports of people confusing these roots with horseradish—with disastrous results.

Aconitum

ACTAEA RUBRA

Common names: baneberry, snakeberry

The horticultural Latin name comes directly from Pliny, who used it to describe the plant. It may well have come from the Greek *aktea* meaning "elder" (as in plant, not person). *Baneberry* comes from the poisonous nature of the berries.

Bloom time: Early- to mid-summer blooms, mid- to late-summer berries
Height: 24″ to 36″ (60 cm to 90 cm)
Sun needed: Part shade to shade
Bloom color: White or tinged purple with red or white berries

Planting space: 18″ to 24″ (45 cm to 60 cm) apart
Soil preferred: Rich woodland soil
Propagation method: Seed or division

Recommended Varieties

Actaea rubra

Actaea rubra is the most commonly grown species. It's 24″ (60 cm) tall, with whitish flowers followed by dramatically red berries. This is a hardy plant for the woodland garden, found naturally from Alaska right down to New Mexico. This is an excellent plant and one that the plant breeders haven't yet discovered—such a pity.

Growing *Actaea*

Actaea is a plant of rich, damp, woodland soils. It is grown more for its bright red berries maturing in midsummer rather than its flowers. Its light green leaves are the perfect color to create dramatic contrasts with plants situated in front of it. *Actaea* is also excellent for the shady pond site, making a dramatic impact as the berries ripen to brilliant red.

Potions and Poisons

The berries are bitter tasting and reputedly poisonous. Crushed and mixed with water, they make a dye. They also have been used as a snakebite remedy, but as with all herbal remedies, care should be taken with the berries.

Actaea rubra   DOUGLAS GREEN

AGASTACHE

Common name: hyssop

*A*gastache comes from the Greek *agan*, or "very much," and *stachys*, "ear of wheat." This is a reference to the abundance of flower spikes. Discoroides, a Greek, gave us *hyssop* after *azob*, "holy herb," and it has been corrupted to hyssop.

Bloom time: Early summer to midsummer
Height: 24″ to 36″ (60 cm to 90 cm)
Sun needed: Full sun
Bloom color: Purples, white

Planting space: 12″ to 18″ (30 cm to 45 cm) apart
Soil preferred: Open, well-drained
Propagation method: Seed

Recommended Varieties

Agastache foeniculum

Agastache foeniculum is commonly known as anise hyssop and is an important herbal plant as well as a fine ornamental one. The color is variable in seed mixes, and selections can be made from deeper purples up to whites.

Growing *Agastache*

Agastache is a plant that loves to be grown in full sun in well-drained soils. It is an easy plant and if happy in its location will self-sow with abandon, becoming a bit of a pest in the process. It is, however, a delightful pest because of the fragrance of its leaves; if you have too much of it, make tea or potpourri.

Potions and Poisons

Agastache is quite edible, and the leaves are used in a variety of teas, liqueurs, and other aromatic preparations.

Agastache foeniculum DOUGLAS GREEN

ALLIUM

Common name: ornamental onion

*A*llium comes to us from *all* meaning "hot," the Celtic word for *garlic*. In ancient times *Allium* referred to garlic and not the entire family. But the famous botanist Linnaeus named the whole onion family *Allium*, and the rest—as they say—is history.

Bloom time: The shorter, the earlier; midsummer for tall varieties; fall for a few

Height: 24″ to 4′ (60 cm to 120 cm)

Sun needed: Full sun

Bloom color: Yellows, whites, mauves

Planting space: 3″ to 8″ (7.5 cm to 20 cm) apart

Soil preferred: Sandy, light

Propagation method: Seed or offsets

Recommended Varieties

Allium christophii

Known as star of Persia, species *Allium christophii* grows 24″ to 30″ (60 cm to 75 cm) tall and has one of the largest and most beautiful flowers in purple-violet (with a bit of a sheen to the flowers) of all the *Allium* species. As you might tell, it is one of my favorite ornamental onions.

Allium giganteum

Allium giganteum is also known as giant onion. While this is not a great name, it is a great plant. This species reaches 4′ to 5′ (120 cm to 150 cm) tall and is topped with an 8″ (20 cm) flower head. It is a showstopper when it comes into bloom in midsummer.

Allium x hybrida

More and more of these ornamental onions are coming into the gardening trade. The breeders are focusing on *Allium x hybrida* as a pest-free and easily grown plant for the garden. As a general rule, grow any of them that you find in your local garden centers or favorite mail-order catalog.

'Globemaster' is a flower stalk 3′ to 4′ (90 cm to 120 cm) tall with a massive flowering violet globe of a flower.

'Purple Sensation' is another huge-flowering variety with purple flowers.

Growing *Allium*

While *Allium* is more properly a bulb and not a herbaceous perennial, it cannot be refused a place in the summer garden because of this technicality. While some of the shorter species bulbs are perfect for the spring bulb garden (and are not listed here), the main season garden would be poorer without the taller species listed.

Grow *Allium* in full sun in a well-drained soil. Soils high in organic matter allow this shallow-rooted plant to feed and grow in optimum conditions. Compost is all the food it requires. While *Allium* is normally native to grassland and dry, rocky terrain, regular watering helps its summer-flowering bulbs up to their flowering season. But watering should be discontinued after flowering to allow them the dry time they require to recover and grow strong enough to

Allium   Douglas Green

flower in subsequent years. *Allium* does not do well at all on clay soils because of the excessive moisture.

Note that most of the taller plants make excellent cut or dried flowers and the seed heads are as ornamental as the flowers. For this reason, they have an excellent reputation in the garden for having season-long interest.

Potions and Poisons

As *Allium* is of the onion family, there is a great deal of folklore associated with the plant. Wearing it around the neck to ward off illness and plague and eating it daily for good health are better stories than fact. Actually, onions are rather high in vitamin C, so the last is probably a good idea.

Allium aflatunense 'Purple Sensation'
International Flower Bulb Centre

ARUNCUS

Common name: goatsbeard

Pliny used the name *Aruncus* for this family of herbs and Linnaeus simply agreed with him or copied him—and *Aruncus* it became. *Goatsbeard* is fairly easy to understand if you've ever seen one of the blooms, with its white spires. If you haven't gotten it yet, turn the flower upside down in your mind the next time you see it.

Bloom time: Early summer to midsummer
Height: 12″ to 6′ (30 cm to 180 cm)
Sun needed: Shade to part shade

Bloom color: Creamy white
Planting space: 24″ (60 cm) apart
Soil preferred: Damp, woodland soils
Propagation method: Division

Recommended Varieties

Aruncus aethusifolius

Aruncus aethusifolius is a Korean native and is only 12″ to 18″ (30 cm to 45 cm) tall; it is a very compact plant ideally suited to the front of the shade border. Its leaves are as finely cut as its taller cousin, *Aruncus dioicus*, but much more mounded, as you would imagine in a shorter species. I find that it does not do well in deep shade but prefers sunshine as long as it is protected from the noonday sun.

Aruncus dioicus

Aruncus dioicus, at 6′ (180 cm) tall, is a wonderful shade garden plant. Its creamy white blossoms make a good cut flower and dried flower, as well as garden centerpiece. The leaves are quite feathery in texture.

'Child of Two Worlds' is slightly shorter than the species at 4′ (120 cm).

'Kneiffii' is a shorter variety at 3′ (90 cm).

Note that some nurseries may still be selling *Aruncus dioicus* under the name *Aruncussylvester* or *Aruncus sylvestris*, an old and incorrect name.

Growing *Aruncus*

Aruncus is an excellent plant for the shade or part-shade garden, particularly in damp or slightly damp soils. It is originally a plant of the mountain woodland in damp areas. I've found that it takes about three years for a division to mature and throw flower stalks of the appropriate height. *Aruncus* propagates easiest by division, but this is the only plant that has broken my transplanting shovel when I tried to dig and divide it. It has a thick and well-anchored root system, and you have to work hard to divide it.

Aruncus dioicus   DOUGLAS GREEN

ASTRANTIA

Common name: masterwort

The origin of *Astrantia*'s name is a bit confused according to my sources. At best, they are guessing that it derived from the Latin *magister*, meaning "master," or *aster*, meaning "star." *Masterwort*, the common name, is derived directly from the Latin combination, and we already know that *wort* is Saxon for *plant*.

Bloom time: Early summer to midsummer
Height: 18″ (45 cm)
Sun needed: Full sun to part shade

Bloom color: Rose, pinks, whites
Planting space: 12″ (30 cm) apart
Soil preferred: Moist, rich
Propagation method: Seed or division

Recommended Varieties

Astrantia major

Astrantia major grows 24″ to 30″ (60 cm to 75 cm) tall. You'll sometimes see the species *Astrantia major* itself in garden centers.

'Lars' is a lighter red on stems 24″ (60 cm) tall.

'Rubra' is a light pink-red on stems 18″ to 24″ (45 cm to 60 cm) and is the most commonly available variety.

Astrantia minor

Astrantia minor grows 12″ to 18″ (30 cm to 45 cm) tall. The biggest difference between *Astrantia major* and *Astrantia minor* is height. *Major* is, as you might guess, the taller of the two.

'Rainbow' is a deeper wine red color on taller stems, up to 18″ (45 cm). It is excellent for cutting.

Growing Astrantia

Astrantia is naturally found in alpine meadows and sunny woodland spots. Grow it best in a fertile soil that is moisture retentive. In other words, it likes lots of water during the summer but resents wet feet during the winter. When found near streams, it is always in areas where the roots will dry out during the winter or not be waterlogged during the summer. *Astrantia* will take part shade, although it grows best in full sunshine.

Astrantia major 'Rubra' Douglas Green

BAPTISIA

Common name: false indigo

*B*aptisia comes from the Greek word *bapto*, which means "to dye." *False indigo* refers to the fact that the garden plant *Baptisia australis* is not the plant *Baptisia tinctoria*, which is used for creating the indigo (blue) color in dye. If it isn't the right plant, it's false, although there are some indications that *Baptisia australis* was used by American settlers as a substitute for the real thing.

Bloom time: Early summer to midsummer
Height: 24″ (60 cm)
Sun needed: Full sun
Bloom color: Intense blue

Planting space: 18″ to 24″ (45 cm to 60 cm) apart
Soil preferred: Open, sandy, and gravelly
Propagation method: Seed or division

Recommended Varieties

Baptisia australis

Baptisia australis is the most commonly grown species in gardens and wonderfully so. If growing from seed, try to sow each seed (or several) in its own pot. It resents transplanting as a small seedling, and many plants have died off for me after I disturbed the young roots. Keep the seedlings in the pot until they are large enough and the weather is warm enough for direct transplanting into the garden. Do so with as little root disturbance as possible.

Growing *Baptisia*

Baptisia is a plant of poor soils in dry locations. In the wild, it is often found on gravelly or sandy soils that are low in nutrients. Grow it in full sun, and it will do best in soils that are neutral to slightly acidic. You may have to stake the plant if it gets too tall—and if so you're feeding it too much.

Potions and Poisons

The family has a reputation for being a purgative (causing vomiting) and having antiseptic uses. It is not labeled as poisonous, but I suspect that eating the seeds would not provide a happy experience. Deadhead the plant for safety.

Baptisia australis   DOUGLAS GREEN

THE NAME GAME

*T*he game of naming plants is that the first person to name the plant wins. So if someone named a plant in 1784, then by our modern rules, his or her name for the plant is the name we should use. It doesn't matter if everyone in the world likes the name given to the plant by a second botanist in 1845; we agree to use the name originally given in 1784. In the past, name changes in the plant world have focused on historical research to discover who named what and when they did it. These changes trickled down into the gardening world slowly.

A recent development has been the examination of the gene structure of plants. Botanists are discovering that certain plants share more genetic material with other entire families of plants than they do with those with similar names. So, if a plant is genetically closer to another family, then its name gets changed. *Cimicifuga* becomes *Actaea; Chrysanthemum nipponicum* becomes *Nipponanthemum nipponicum.* It is a long list of changes and quite boring to the average gardener.

Botanists tell us that this is scientific progress and that as our understanding of the plant world changes, it is necessary to call things as they are, not as we want them to be called. Keep all this in mind when you read the plant descriptions for the *Chrysanthemum.*

Baptisia australis Douglas Green

CENTAUREA

The plant name has come from the Greek word *kentauros*, "centaur," the mythical half-man/half-horse. A related plant name, *centaury*, was a great healing herb used by Chiron the centaur healer, but healing properties are not ascribed to this plant. *Knapweed* is derived from *knobweed*, and this is a reference to the large flower bud or knob on top of the stem. *Bachelor's buttons* comes to us in two ways. The first is a good story but with little in the way of historical proof. Country boys would carry some of the flowers around in their pockets to help them divine their success with the girl of their dreams. The second, more likely derivation is that the flowers resembled the buttons or insignia worn by gentlemen in the seventeenth and eighteenth centuries.

Bloom time: Early summer to midsummer
Height: 24″ to 48″ (60 cm to 120 cm)
Sun needed: Full sun
Bloom color: Blues, pinks, yellow

Planting space: 12″ to 18″ (30 cm to 45 cm) apart
Soil preferred: Poor, well-drained
Propagation method: Seed or division

Recommended Varieties

Centaurea dealbata

Centaurea dealbata grows 30″ (75 cm) tall with rose red flowers. The plant flops around in my garden, and it does require staking or should be grown next to a supporting plant.

Centaurea montana

Centaurea montana is a classic plant 18″ to 24″ (45 cm to 60 cm) tall with bright violet-blue flowers. It spreads like mad around my garden, and I simply weed out any excessive plants.

Centaurea macrocephala

Centaurea macrocephala is one of the taller garden members of the family at 36″ to 48″ (90 cm to 120 cm). It is a strong, upright plant that requires no staking. The silvery brown flower buds are as

Centaurea macrocephala Douglas Green

Centaurea macrocephala buds   DOUGLAS GREEN

interesting as the subsequent mop-top yellow flowers. It makes an excellent cut flower.

Growing *Centaurea*

If you grow this plant family in the full, hot sun in soils that are sandy, well-drained, and indeed poor in fertility, you'll soon be swamped with self-sown plants. *Centaurea* grows much better when abused in this way than when grown in more gardenlike conditions. I have some out in a sandy soil bed. In fact the soil was originally ditch enlargement soil and gravel from some roadwork, and I used it to fill in a low section next to my driveway. With no water or feed, *Centaurea* has taken over the entire area.

CHRYSANTHEMUM

Common names: chrysanthemum, mum, pellitory

*C*hrysanthemum is derived from two Greek words, *chrysos*, "gold," and *anthemon*, "flower." For the past fifteen years, or forever it seems to confused gardeners, botanists have been arguing about the naming of this plant family. *Mum* is an obvious derivative of *Chrysanthemum*. *Pellitory* comes from the Latin *parietarus*, meaning "belonging to the walls." Some old species of *Chrysanthemum* were typically found growing in cracks in rocks and in the cracks of stone walls. Gardeners still call it *Chrysanthemum*, but botanists have now separated the *Chrysanthemum* family into *Leucanthemum*, *Tanacetum*, and other more scientifically appropriate names. I'll describe them according to the most recent information I have, but botanists will likely find another reason to rename the entire family by the time you read this. However it is named, *Chrysanthemum* is a garden favorite.

Bloom time: Early summer to midsummer (see Chapter 9 for fall bloomers)
Height: 12″ to 40″ (30 cm to 100 cm)
Sun needed: Full sun to light shade
Bloom color: Yellows, whites, and shades of red

Planting space: 12″ to 24″ (30 cm to 60 cm) apart
Soil preferred: Well-drained but high in organic matter
Propagation method: Division, cuttings, or seed

Recommended Varieties

Leucanthemum x superbum

Formerly known as *Chrysanthemum superbum*, *Leucanthemum x superbum*'s common name is shasta daisy. It is the white-flowering daisy that we all love to have in our gardens. If it is kept reliably deadheaded (the blooms removed as soon as they start to wilt), then it is the longest-blooming daisy in the garden. It will tolerate more shade than most of the other plants described here, so a bit of experimentation is in order. The shorter varieties will take more shade than the taller, but if the blooms are not heavy or the stalks are flopping, then the plant is not receiving enough sunshine. It is important to deadhead or shear *Leucanthemum x superbum* after

blooming to encourage a second or third flush of blooms.

'Alaska' is the old 36″ (90 cm) standard variety, which is easy to grow and reliable.

'Little Miss Muffet' and 'Little Princess' are both 12″ to 18″ (30 cm to 45 cm) tall and heavy bloomers.

'Snowcap' is a 14″ (35 cm) plant with mounds of beautiful white blossoms from early to late summer. It is a classic plant and well worth growing.

'Summer Snowball' is a tall 30″ (75 cm) variety, with double white flowers from early to late summer if you deadhead. Even though it is tall, it tolerates winds and heavy rain quite well, unlike some other fully double flowers that fall over.

Leucanthemum x superbum 'Alaska'   DOUGLAS GREEN

Tanacetum parthenium   DOUGLAS GREEN

Tanacetum coccineum

Formerly known as *Chrysanthemum coccineum*, the common name of *Tanacetum coccineum* is painted daisy. This old-fashioned flower brightens up any cottage garden. It can be floppy, so it is best planted in masses or next to other flowers that will hold it upright. If you deadhead this species regularly, it will be encouraged to produce extra flowers. The one disadvantage to this plant is that it can be short-lived. Some gardeners say that regular dividing and encouraging new growth keeps the plant alive much longer. This plant is easily grown from seed even for beginning gardeners. The Robinson hybrids and 'James Kelway' are the most commonly available varieties both in nurseries and in seed catalogs.

Tanacetum parthenium

Formerly *Chrysanthemum parthenium*, *Tanacetum parthenium*'s common name is feverfew. This small-flowered daisy has large numbers of blooms in bunches on the ends of tall stems. The plant is quite aromatic, and like many of the *Chrysanthemum* family, it will be much more bushy and attractive if it is pinched back to half its height in mid to late June. The rule of thumb in my garden is that when the plant gets to 1′ (30 cm) in height, pinch. This might be early June in a warm year or late June in a cooler year. The rule of 1′ (30 cm) works no matter where you garden. In my garden, this has been a short-lived perennial, but with any luck at all, it self-sows. A well-drained soil is absolutely essential if you want this plant to overwinter; clay is a killer. Varieties include the following:

'Aureum' has yellow-tinged green foliage with white flowers containing a yellow eye.

'Double White' has small pom-pom buttons of flowers.

'Golden Ball' has a yellow button flower and a compact growth habit. It is one of the better varieties.

Growing Chrysanthemum

Most of the *Chrysanthemum* plant family does best in full sun. While some of the shorter- and thicker-stalked plants will grow in light shade,

Leucanthemum x superbum   Douglas Green

Leucanthemum x superbum 'Summer Snowball'
Blooms of Bressingham North America, Barberton OH

they do tend to get floppy in shadier gardens. They are plants of the open meadows and resent standing water. They resent it so much that their lifespans are much shorter in clay soils than in sandier ones. Overfeeding tends to produce floppy plants, so a single spring application of compost is adequate for the season's growth.

Potions and Poisons

In his herbal, Culpepper tells us that this plant is a fine purge for the brain (whatever that does). It has also been used for toothache and as a snuff to clear the head, and when used as a gargle, it is reputed to ease the partial paralysis of the tongue. This is not likely going to hurt you, but it is not recommended for use without a physician's supervision.

DELPHINIUM

Common names: larkspur, delphinium

*D*elphinium comes to us from the Greek *delphinion*, which in turn is derived from *delphis*, "dolphin." This is an allusion to the flower form—it resembled a dolphin to the ancient Greek botanists—of the annual species of *Delphinium* we know as larkspur. *Larkspur* comes from the resemblance of the individual flowers to—what else?—the head of a lark.

Bloom time: Early summer to midsummer
Height: 18″ to 96″ (45 cm to 240 cm)
Sun needed: Full sun
Bloom color: White/blue, violet/pink
Planting space: 12″ (30 cm) apart for

short plants, 18″ to 24″ (45 cm to 60 cm) apart for taller plants
Soil preferred: Well-drained but rich
Propagation method: Mostly by seed; cuttings and division are possible

Recommended Varieties

Delphinium x 'Connecticut Yankee'

Mid-blue *Delphinium x* 'Connecticut Yankee' has graced my garden on and off for fifteen years. It has been short-lived for me, but its open growth habit and ability to inject a good mid-blue color into a perennial border have earned it its place. It does not resemble a perfectly formed delphinium spire but is more open, like the annual larkspurs.

Delphinium elatum x hybrida

Millennium series is a new taller hybrid series from breeders in New Zealand and is available through the Internet (see Resources). The seed is hand-pollinated. It is available in excellent colors and is taller than the more common Pacific hybrid series. Pacific hybrids are the typical plants found in garden centers with names from the King Arthur legends.

'King Arthur' is royal violet with a white bee.
'Guinevere' is lavender-pink with a white bee.
'Galahad' is (what else?) pure white.
'Black Knight' is a very deep violet with a dark bee.

'Blue Jay' is medium blue with a dark bee.
'Blue Bird' is a medium blue with a white bee.
'Summer Skies' is light blue with a white bee.

Delphinium x belladona

Delphinium x belladona is a more loosely branched plant, and the flowers are not as large or intensely colored as *Delphinium elatum* hybrids. It makes a wonderful addition to the mixed cottage border but does not resemble what we think of when we think of tall delphinium spires.

Delphinium grandiflorum

Short *Delphinium grandiflorum*, at 8″ to 12″ (20 cm to 30 cm) tall, is a heavy bloomer and is literally covered with bright, electric blue flowers for most of the summer. It blooms itself to death and you'll have to replace it regularly. Look for 'Blue Elf' or 'Blue Mirror,' and try them at the front of the border.

Delphinium nudicaule

Delphinium nudicaule is a tender species of reddish delphinium that is native to California. It is not

Delphinium elatum 'Blue Jay' and 'Galahad'
Douglas Green

Delphinium nudicaule 'Beverly Hills Scarlet'
Douglas Green

expected to be reliably hardy in my zone 4 garden, and it's not. Having said that, this plant has self-sown the odd year and produced an open-flowering plant—much like the *belladona* and larkspur types—that is a conversation piece. It did its best growing in a sandy, well-drained soil in full, hot sunshine.

Growing *Delphinium*

All species and hybrids require a full-sun garden spot and a rich garden soil. Well-drained but moist is the familiar mantra for soil, and clay soils will shorten the lifespan of this plant.

There is no doubt that to obtain the maximum height of the flower bloom, regular feeding is required. The problem comes after you hit this bloom height and overfeed the delphinium. Then it becomes quite floppy and falls over in the slightest breeze. Now, having overfed, you have to stake your plant if you want it to stay upright. There's a thin line between feeding for great

blooms and feeding to create work for yourself. I confess that I don't feed *Delphinium* any heavier than a single application of compost to its location first thing in the spring. After that, it's on its own. I'm sure my plants are not as nice as yours are; but then again, I don't stake mine either, and they seem to do quite nicely in the garden.

If you cut your *Delphinium* bloom off as soon as it has finished and is starting to wither, it will justify this timely tidiness by producing another set of blooms for later in the summer. Also, *Delphinium* makes wonderful cut flowers.

Potions and Poisons

This plant is not to be eaten by children. If eaten the seeds will cause vomiting. The rest of the plant is also an irritant and possible poison. The injury to the child will depend on the amount eaten and the size of the child. When used medicinally, the seed is made into a tincture for killing head lice.

DIANTHUS

Common names: Sweet William, pink, carnation

This is a plant of the gods. The Greek word *di* means "of Zeus" or "of Jove," and *anthus* means "flower." *Dianthus* is also a plant of great folklore. *Sweet William* comes to us from the Latin *ocellus*, "eye," referring to the light-colored patch in the middle of the flower. The Latin became *oeillet* in French and was slurred by the English to *willy*, then to *William*. *Sweet* comes from the fragrance or perhaps from the ballad "Fair Margaret and Sweet William," which dates back to the 1700s, when the plant was first grown in gardens.

Pink as a name is even less clear. One author suggests that *pink* meant "eye" in Dutch, but there is no apparent word in that language. There are also confused references to a season called *pinksten* (in German), which was apparently when one of the family members bloomed. For all I know, the flower color is predominately pink, so perhaps that's the origin of the name. And if you thought the preceding two derivations were interesting, try this one:

> *Bring coronations and sops in wine*
> *Worn of paramours*
> Spenser, "Shepherd's Calendar"

Coronations were chaplets, or decorative, woven flower strings worn on the head often by young maidens like a headband. Coronae, the Latin word for "coronations" gave us carnations—the flowers that were used in the chaplets.

Bloom time: Early summer to midsummer until late summer
Height: 4″ to 24″ (10 cm to 60 cm)
Sun needed: Full sun to light shade

Bloom color: Reds, pinks, whites
Planting space: 12″ (30 cm) apart
Soil preferred: Light, well-drained
Propagation method: Seed or cuttings

Recommended Varieties

Dianthus barbatus

Known as Sweet William, *Dianthus barbatus* is a biennial plant that sometimes behaves as a short-lived perennial. At 18″ to 24″ (45 cm to 60 cm) tall and coming in a wide range of fragrant, colored blossoms, it has been a garden favorite for over three hundred years. It is most easily started from seed scattered on the garden or into individual pots and transplanted to where they should bloom. Self-sown seedlings will ensure the garden will never lack for fragrant blooms.

Dianthus caryophyllus

Dianthus caryophyllus is the wild plant that is the ancestor of most modern garden carnation-type hybrids. You won't find it as a species in the garden center, but you might find plants labeled with that name and then a variety name.

Dianthus barbatus   DOUGLAS GREEN

Dianthus deltoides 'Tiny Rubies'   DOUGLAS GREEN

Dianthus chinensis

Dianthus chinensis is often sold in garden centers as a perennial, but they have never been reliably hardy for me. Treat it as a hardy annual, and you'll be much better off unless you live in a warm zone 6 or 7.

Dianthus deltoides

Dianthus deltoides is a common plant in garden centers because of the ease of starting it from seed. It should not be used in the main perennial border because it grows flat to the ground and will be smothered by taller border plants. Use it in the rock garden.

'Tiny Rubies' is a bright red.

Dianthus grataniapolitensis

Also known as Cheddar pink, *Dianthus grataniapolitensis* grows to 12″ (30 cm) and is delightfully fragrant and soft pink in color.

Dianthus x hybrida

There are simply too many *Dianthus x hybrida* to list them all, and these are mostly the carnation types. Unfortunately, many of these hybrids are not commonly available in North America.

'Grenadin' is a commonly found hybrid in garden centers because it is easy to grow from seed, but it is not reliably hardy here in my zone 4 garden.

'Double Rainbow Blend' is a simple seed blend that usually gives at least a few good colors and sturdy plants. It is commonly available from seed catalogs.

Dianthus knappii

Dianthus knappii is also called *yellow pink* if you can imagine the contrast. At 24″ (60 cm) tall with soft yellow flowers that bloom for several weeks, it is worth a place in the garden. It usually lives only three to four years for me before it fades away over the winter and I have to replace it with a new seed-generated plant.

Dianthus plumarius

Dianthus plumarius is the plant we call *pink* and is worthy of most garden spaces. It is shorter than many carnation-type *Dianthus* and so does best

Dianthus grataniapolitensis   Douglas Green

Dianthus plumarius 'Oakington'

Blooms of Bressingham North America, Barberton OH

in rock garden sites or protected from aggressive plants in the border.

'Oakington' is 4″ (10 cm) tall by 10″ (25 cm) wide with soft pink blooms. Deadhead regularly to encourage extra blooms. This makes an excellent rock garden plant or container plant as well as border plant.

Growing *Dianthus*

Dianthus grows best in full sun in slightly alkaline soils. It prefers well-drained soils that are high in organic matter. Clay kills *Dianthus* plants, and unless you want to grow them as annuals in this soil type, don't bother wasting your time.

DICTAMNUS

Common names: gas plant, burning bush

The name *Dictamnus* comes to us in a roundabout fashion. It is named after Mount Dikte in Greece, but the name was not originally applied to this herbaceous perennial but rather to a species of oregano, *Origanum dictamnus*. At some point, the name was transferred from the oregano over to the plant we know and love today. The name *gas plant* (and *burning bush*) comes from the very strong fragrance and oil produced by the plant. It is said that if you put a match near this plant on a calm but sunny day, its vaporous oil is strong enough to ignite. I must not be doing it on calm or sunny enough days because I've never gotten so much as a tiny spark. I have heard other gardeners say that it did work for them, so perhaps I'll keep trying. Whatever my failings, it is a delightful plant in the sunny border.

Bloom time: Early summer to midsummer
Height: 36″ (90 cm)
Sun needed: Full sun
Bloom color: White or soft pink

Planting space: 18″ (45 cm) apart
Soil preferred: Fertile, well-drained
Propagation method: Seed or division

Recommended Varieties

Dictamnus albus

Dictamnus albus is a white-flowering species.

'Purpureus' is soft pink. Other than flower color, there is no cultural difference from *Dictamnus albus*.

Growing *Dictamnus*

Dictamnus is an excellent perennial for the general flower border. It makes a good cut flower as well if you can bear to sacrifice the bloom. It is quite slow to establish itself, taking two to three years after a move to recover, so do not unnecessarily move it about the garden. I note that while it is sulking (recovering) there are few sadder looking plants in the garden. Once established it will bloom summer after summer with little or no care, and having a little patience is well worth the wait. It resents division, going immediately into a major setback and taking several years to recover. The easiest way to obtain new plants is to encourage the young seedlings at the base of the plant. Handle the seedlings with great care so as not to disturb the roots, but they are easier to move than established plants. Old seed is almost useless for germination, but fresh seed will germinate well.

Potions and Poisons

The leaves of *Dictamnus* have been used in the distant past as a substitute for tea and given for "nervous complaints." It is no longer used and not recommended.

Dictamnus albiflorus   Douglas Green

DIGITALIS

You have to imagine that each individual flower of this plant resembles the finger of a glove. If you've got that in your mind, then you'll have no trouble with the derivative from the Latin word *digitus* (finger). It is also said that the Germans called the plant "*Fingerhut*" which translates as "thimble" and the botanists simply Latinized the name, using finger and *digitus* as common ground. Again, though, we come around to the word *digitus*. *Foxglove* is a corruption of the older name "Folks Glove," the flower used by the *folks* or *fairies* for gloves.

Bloom time: Starts early summer to midsummer
Height: 24″ to 36″ (60 cm to 90 cm)
Sun needed: Part sun to shade; will adapt to sun
Bloom color: Whites/yellows/browns with variations and pinks and purples

Planting space: 12″ to 18″ (30 cm to 45 cm) apart
Soil preferred: Moist but well-drained, high in organic matter
Propagation method: Seed

Recommended Varieties

Of the twenty species of *Digitalis*, the following are the best garden plants.

Digitalis grandiflora

Digitalis grandiflora has a yellow-blooming flower and is perennial rather than biennial. It blooms a second time in the fall if deadheaded as soon as the blooms start to fade. It's long-lived and also does well in sunshine.

Digitalis x mertonensis

Digitalis x mertonensis's common name is strawberry foxglove. This is a good tall hybrid with pinkish flowers and is one of the best. If you only allow the blooms of the colors you like to set seed (there's a wide color variation of different shades of pink in the plant genes), you can slowly create a uniform patch of flowers in your customized color scheme.

Digitalis purpurea

Digitalis purpurea is the common foxglove and is very showy in bloom. It does best in uniformly moist soils. The different hybrid seed strains usually revert back to species after a few years as they self-sow and the older plants die off. To maintain the color you prefer, let only the colors you want to maintain set seed. Cut all other blooms off before the seed matures so the remaining seed heads will be the color you want.

Growing *Digitalis*

Digitalis is a plant of woodland clearings and one of the earliest colonizers of newly cleared forest areas. It prefers moist part shade as a prime habitat. Note that this plant is a biennial, although in warmer climates it might live for more than two years. The easiest way to start this plant is to scatter seeds in the place where you want the plant

Digitalis x mertonensis DOUGLAS GREEN

Digitalis purpurea DOUGLAS GREEN

to become established. If sown in the fall, they will germinate the following spring and flower the subsequent year. Self-sown seedlings will keep the patch going from then on. Some gardeners purchase a plant and allow it to self-sow to start the cycle a year earlier. If you do this, do not overfertilize the plant. If it goes into the winter in a soft or lush state, it will be prone to winterkill.

The plant will establish itself in shade or part-shade spots, but with damp soil, it can be con-vinced to establish itself in sunshine as well. The species grow better in sunshine than lush-leaved hybrids.

Potions and Poisons

The leaves and seeds of *Digitalis* are active med-icinally and are not for consumption. Luckily they are quite bitter in taste and unpleasant in smell. Do not consume or allow this plant to be consumed.

GERANIUM

Common names: cranesbill, Herb Robert

The long beak of its flower carpels gives *Geranium* both its official name and one of its common names. *Geranion* is the derivative in classical Greek from the common name for *geranos*, "crane." *Herb Robert* comes to us from the Middle English word *herbe*, which is derived from the French *erbe* or Medieval Latin *herba*, meaning "plant or herb." *Robert* is simply the derivative of *Robertus*, and I confess to not knowing who Robertus was.

Bloom time: Early summer and again in fall if pruned
Height: 12″ to 48″ (30 cm to 120 cm)
Sun needed: Full to part sun
Bloom color: Violet through red tones to whites and pinks

Planting space: 18″ (45 cm) apart
Soil preferred: Moderately fertile and well-drained
Propagation method: Seed, division, or cuttings

Recommended Varieties

Should you grow *Geranium* plants? Yes, *almost* every one of them. These are wonderful plants for perennial gardens, and I admit to sprinkling them liberally throughout mine. No matter how many *Geranium* plants I list, there will always be one more that is irresistible. This is one of the most popular perennials and deservedly so; which is why there are entire books written about it. Collect *Geranium* plants and fall in love with them because they are one of the easiest, hardiest, and most carefree plants in the border. Some of the best include the following:

Geranium x cantabrigiense

Geranium x cantabrigiense is low growing, 12″ (30 cm) tall, and is only suited for the front of the border.

'Biokovo' is getting a lot of publicity for its largish white flowers. I had it and took it out of the garden because I didn't like it. Mind you, many gardeners will disagree with me on this plant.

'Cambridge' has bright pink, showy flowers. Get it.

Geranium cinereum

Geranium cinereum is another low-grower, 6″ (15 cm) tall, that is almost purely an alpine plant, although I confess I have it tucked in among some *Trillium* plants in a part-shade bed and it is doing well.

'Ballerina' is the most often found variety, and it has smallish purple-pink flowers on a smoky foliage.

'Laurence Flatman' has deep pink flowers with darker veining and earns its spot in the garden. Grow it.

'Splendens' has bright magenta flowers (a shocking color, really) with darker centers. Grow it, particularly if you need a spot of cheer in your alpine garden.

Geranium psilostemon 'Bressingham Flair'
BLOOMS OF BRESSINGHAM NORTH AMERICA, BARBERTON OH

Geranium macrorrhizum 'Bevan's Variety'
BLOOMS OF BRESSINGHAM NORTH AMERICA, BARBERTON OH

Geranium clarkei x collinum

Hybrid *Geranium clarkei x collinum*, 18″ (45 cm) tall, is a good choice for the perennial border; it grows in a mound shape and has rather large flowers compared to the rest of the family.

The most commonly found varieties of *Geranium clarkei x collinum* in garden centers are the 'Kashmir' plants: 'Kashmir Purple,' 'Kashmir White,' 'Kashmir Pink,' and 'Kashmir Blue.'

Geranium endressi

The leaves on *Geranium endressi*, which is 18″ (45 cm) tall, will be evergreen in warmer zones but are quite tattered by spring here in zone 4. The flowers are very showy.

Geranium himalayense

Geranium himalayense is a perennial border type with large leaves that turn red in the fall and a good clumping growth habit.

'Plenum' (also called 'Birch Double') has fully double, lavender-violet flowers. The flowers are sterile, and this cultivar is described in some catalogs as not as vigorous as other geraniums. This

makes me feel much better because I have lost it twice and had it struggle along most poorly while it was alive.

'Gravetye,' 12″ to 18″ (30 cm to 45 cm) tall, is a mat-forming cultivar. The flowers are deep blue with an interesting center. The center of the flower is white surrounded by a reddish zone fading into the blue, and it is quite attractive in the garden.

Geranium x hybrida

'Ann Folkard' is 12″ to 18″ (30 cm to 45 cm) tall with magenta blooms from early to late summer. This is an outstanding plant, but it does like to grow.

'Ann Thompson' is more compact than 'Ann Folkard.'

'Johnson's Blue' is the classic 12″ to 18″ (30 cm to 45 cm) tall perennial *Geranium*, found in every garden center. Large lavender-blue flowers grace a hardy and strong-growing plant. The plant is easy to grow in full sun or part shade. It is certainly one of the better *Geranium* plants, and it is deservedly well known.

Geranium cinereum 'Laurence Flatman'

Geranium cinereum 'Ballerina'

'Rozanne' is 20″ (50 cm) tall with violet-blue flowers that have a light yellow center. This plant flowers for a very long time to produce a stunning display of blooms. It is a wonderful plant and is highly recommended. (See photograph in Chapter 10.)

Geranium macrorrhizum

Geranium macrorrhizum was the first *Geranium* I ever grew, and I confess I fell in love with the fragrance of its leaves. I'd wander past it and give its leaves a whap with my hand just to release the fragrance into the garden. It didn't hurt that its pinkish flowers were abundant, that if sheared, it would flower again in the fall, or that it was rock hardy in the garden. While I grew the species first, there are now good varieties available including the following:

'Bevan's Variety' has deep magenta-pink blooms.

'Ingwersen's Variety' is the most widely grown cultivar, named after Mr. Will Ingwersen, one of the leading perennial and alpine nurserymen of England. Its pale pink flowers are excellent.

Geranium maculatum

Species *Geranium maculatum* has deeply cut leaves and is a good strong grower. Its early-summer blooms are always a welcome addition to the garden.

With its pale, lilac-pinkish flowers, lovely 'Chatto' is named after one of England's premier plantswomen of the twentieth century, Beth Chatto.

Geranium x oxonianum

Geranium x oxonianum is another species that is 18″ (45 cm) tall. The flowers tend to be pink with darker veins, and the foliage is a glossy green. This species likes to grow and makes an excellent ground cover as well as border plant. Use it both ways in your garden.

'A. T. Johnson' has bright pink flowers and a long bloom time.

'Bressingham's Delight' has soft pink blooms and a long bloom time. (See photograph in Chapter 10.)

'Claridge Druce' has dark pink flowers and a long bloom time.

Geranium psilostemon   DOUGLAS GREEN

Geranium sanguineum 'John Elsley'

BLOOMS OF BRESSINGHAM NORTH AMERICA, BARBERTON OH

Geranium phaeum

Geranium phaeum, the mourning widow *Geranium* (nice name!), has heavily cut leaves and does better than most other varieties in a shade location. Most of the species are 18″ to 24″ (45 cm to 60 cm) tall.

'Album' has large white flowers.

'Lily Lovell' has large mauve flowers, and the foliage is a lighter green than other Geranium species.

Geranium pratense

Geranium pratense is 18″ (45 cm) tall with big leaves. It tolerates shade a bit better than many other Geranium species.

You'll often see 'Himalayanum' listed in catalogs. It is unfortunately variable in growth and flowering because the name itself is not registered (and hence not valid), so plants sold under this name are not necessarily the same plant. Note that this is *not Geranium himalayense*.

'Mrs. Kendal Clark' is medium violet with lighter veining. It is a good grower and a garden delight.

Geranium psilostemon

Geranium psilostemon is my favorite member of the family. This is a taller species—it can reach 3′ to 4′ (90 cm to 120 cm) tall—and it has outrageous magenta flowers that shout across the garden. Mine is protected from the wind by some stronger-growing plants so it doesn't need staking; if your garden is open, either get ready to stake it or lean it up against some other plant as I do.

'Bressingham Flair' has blooms that are a slightly softer color than the loud magenta of the species.

Geranium sanguineum

Geranium sanguineum, commonly known as bloody cranesbill, makes a good plant to edge the border with, with its finely cut leaves and 12″ (60 cm) height. It is reasonably drought-tolerant.

'Alan Bloom' has bright pink flowers.

'Album' has white flowers, but the foliage is more open than other varieties.

'John Elsley' has bright pink flowers. It is more of a trailer than an upright plant and is good for the rock garden but perhaps not the border. You'll see it in catalogs.

'New Hampshire' has deep magenta purple flowers. It is not quite as tall as the species but not as short as 'John Elsley.'

Geranium sylvaticum

Species *Geranium sylvaticum* is more of a clump grower than a ground cover, and at 18″ (45 cm) tall, it makes a good border plant.

'Album' has large white flowers and an excellent growth habit to 24″ (60 cm) tall.

'Mayflower' has violet-blue flowers with white eyes.

'Silva' has bright pink flowers.

Geranium thunbergii

Geranium thunbergii is a tiny white-flowering plant that spreads with the speed of the wind. It colonizes every bit of soil it can find and then wanders over to visit the neighbors. It is not worth growing unless you have a wild area where it can wander. Keep it away from good gardens. There are also pink and purple varieties appearing in plant lists, but the same warning applies to them as well. I have a purplish variety that escaped the nursery and now resides in the adjoining field and lawn. It's a pretty thing, but I do weed it out of the gardens to prevent a total takeover.

Growing *Geranium*

Geranium will grow in any moderately fertile soil. It does particularly well when the moisture level is even but not soggy or waterlogged. It is an excellent plant for part-sun locations and for use as a ground cover. Once established it will tolerate a drier location, but dry shade is not its favorite spot. If the earlier-blooming plants are sheared after their initial bloom, they will recover to produce another flush of blooms in early fall.

Potions and Poisons

The root is quite bitter-tasting and was given to patients to induce sweating or as a sedative. I found nothing of concern about the top growth of the plant itself.

GYPSOPHILA

Common name: baby's breath

As some members of this plant family like lime soils, the Greeks used *gypsos*, "lime," and *philos*, "loving," to describe *Gypsophila*. *Baby's breath* is a romantic description of the masses of delicate white flowers.

Bloom time: Early summer to midsummer
Height: 36″ to 48″ (90 cm to 120 cm)
Sun needed: Full sun
Bloom color: White, pink
Planting space: 24″ to 36″ (60 cm to 90 cm) apart

Soil preferred: Alkaline, well-drained, high in organic matter
Propagation method: Seed, division, or cuttings

Recommended Varieties

While there are approximately one hundred species of this plant worldwide, only four species are grown in most gardens. Two, *Gypsophila repens*, a low-growing plant suited for the rock garden and not the perennial border, and *Gypsophila elegans*, an annual species, are not described here.

Gypsophila paniculata

'Bristol Fairy' is 36″ (90 cm) tall and has double white flowers. It is excellent for cutting.

'Schneeflocke,' sold as 'Snowflake' in North America, is 36″ (90 cm) tall with double white blooms.

'Viette's Dwarf' is 18″ to 24″ (45 cm to 60 cm) tall, with double flowers in a pink blush color.

Gypsophila pacifica

Gypsophila pacifica is 36″ (90 cm) tall with single pink blooms. It is more tolerant of acidic soils than *Gypsophila paniculata*.

Gypsophila paniculata 'Schneeflocke'
Douglas Green

Growing *Gypsophila*

Grow *Gypsophila* in well-drained soils in full sun-light. One way to make use of its billowy flower stalks is to plant it next to earlier-blooming plants that will be finishing off as *Gypsophila* starts to expand its flowers. Allow it to fill in and expand over the top of the other plants that are ending their bloom time. This is another way of saying you can crowd this plant between two other earlier bloomers without creating many problems.

The open nature of the flower display allows adequate sunshine to reach the leaves of neighboring plants.

Potions and Poisons

The plant roots are quite bitter, and the plant has been used medicinally in the treatment of syphilis and jaundice. *Gypsophila* is not reported to be poisonous.

HEMEROCALLIS

Common name: daylily

*H*emera is Greek for "day," and *kallos* means "beauty." Need I say more? *Daylily* is an easy name to understand, as each one of the lilylike flowers of this plant lasts for only one day before it dies.

Bloom time: Early summer to midsummer
Height: 18″ to 48″ (45 cm to 120 cm)
Sun needed: Sun to part shade
Bloom color: Yellows, reds, white, pinks

Planting space: 18″ (45 cm) apart
Soil preferred: Well-drained and high in organic matter
Propagation method: Division or seed

Recommended Varieties

There are literally thousands of registered names for this plant, and hundreds more come onto the market every year. I have several hundred varieties in my collection, and I haven't even begun to scratch the surface of what is available. I describe the Lovely Lady series below, as they are quite good plants, with up-to-date breeding, and are easily available through mail-order and at better garden centers. At many garden centers you will find *Hemerocallis* labeled only by the generic colors, *red*, *pink*, and so on; these are much older varieties—usually imported from Holland at discount prices. You get what you pay for, and if you want repeat blooming and spectacular flowers, stay with named varieties. Once you see the color pictures and descriptions in catalogs, I suspect you'll be as lost in the wonder of this plant as I am.

Hemerocallis x hybrida

'Lady Elizabeth' is 18″ (45 cm) tall with single clear white blossoms in early summer and repeat bloom later in fall.

'Lady Eva' is 24″ to 30″ (60 cm to 75 cm) tall with violet petals with darker center sections.

This is a semievergreen plant in warmer areas and may bloom twice there.

'Lady Emily' is 16″ (40 cm) tall and lavender-pink with lighter veins.

'Lady Florence' is 18″ (45 cm) tall with double golden yellow blooms that come in midsummer and bloom twice in warmer climates. (See photograph in Chapter 10.)

Hemerocallis 'Lady Elizabeth'
BLOOMS OF BRESSINGHAM NORTH AMERICA, BARBERTON OH

Hemerocallis Lovely Lady™, 'Lady Eva'
BLOOMS OF BRESSINGHAM NORTH AMERICA, BARBERTON OH

Hemerocallis 'Lady Emily'
BLOOMS OF BRESSINGHAM NORTH AMERICA, BARBERTON OH

Hemerocallis Lovely Lady™, 'Lady Jackie'
BLOOMS OF BRESSINGHAM NORTH AMERICA, BARBERTON OH

Hemerocallis 'Lady Lucille'
BLOOMS OF BRESSINGHAM NORTH AMERICA, BARBERTON OH

Hemerocallis 'Lady Scarlet'
BLOOMS OF BRESSINGHAM NORTH AMERICA, BARBERTON OH

Hemerocallis Lovely Lady™, 'Miss Amelia'
BLOOMS OF BRESSINGHAM NORTH AMERICA, BARBERTON OH

Hemerocallis Lovely Lady™, 'Miss Mary Mary'
BLOOMS OF BRESSINGHAM NORTH AMERICA, BARBERTON OH

Hemerocallis Lovely Lady™, 'Miss Tinkerbell'
BLOOMS OF BRESSINGHAM NORTH AMERICA, BARBERTON OH

Heuchera 'Harmonic Convergence'
BLOOMS OF BRESSINGHAM NORTH AMERICA, BARBERTON OH

Heuchera 'Charles Bloom'
BLOOMS OF BRESSINGHAM NORTH AMERICA, BARBERTON OH

Heuchera 'Bressingham Bronze'
BLOOMS OF BRESSINGHAM NORTH AMERICA, BARBERTON OH

Heuchera 'Rosemary Bloom'
BLOOMS OF BRESSINGHAM NORTH AMERICA, BARBERTON OH

Heuchera 'Strawberry Swirl'

Heuchera 'Cherries Jubilee'

Heuchera 'Purple Sails'

Heuchera 'Champagne Bubbles'

HEUCHERELLA

Common names: none

Heucherella is a modern garden hybrid, a cross between *Heuchera* and *Tiarella*. The original cross was made in France around 1912, but the most popular flowering cross is *Heucherella alba*, made by Alan Bloom of Bloom's Nursery in the 1950s.

Bloom time: Early summer to midsummer
Height: 12″ to 24″ (30 cm to 60 cm)
Sun needed: Part shade
Bloom color: Pink, white
Planting space: 12″ to 18″ (30 cm to 45 cm) apart

Soil preferred: Well-drained, high in organic matter
Propagation method: Division

Recommended Varieties

Heucherella x hybrida

'Burnished Bronze' has large leaves. A bronze tone to the dark leaves makes this plant a good garden show all summer long. (See photograph in Chapter 10.)

'Dayglow Pink' has brilliant pink flowers as well as cut leaves with a darker-vein inlay. It is a good performer.

Imagine a leaf with silver, purple, and greens— that's 'Kimono.' The plant starts small in the spring, but later the new leaves are huge. It has an evergreen metallic winter color. This is a winner in my garden. (See photograph in Chapter 3.)

'Ninja' has large, well-formed white flowers on well-cut green leaves. The leaves have a darker vein.

'Quicksilver' has a good silvery "overlay" on the leaf. It has white flowers on darker-colored stems. It enjoys a longer blooming season than many.

'Bridget Bloom' has soft pink flowers and semievergreen foliage in warmer climates. It is a very heavy bloomer.

Heucherella 'Bridget Bloom'
BLOOMS OF BRESSINGHAM NORTH AMERICA, BARBERTON OH

Heucherella 'Dayglow Pink'
TERRA NOVA NURSERIES

Heucherella 'Quicksilver'
BLOOMS OF BRESSINGHAM NORTH AMERICA, BARBERTON OH

'Viking Ship' offers delightful silver-green leaves in spring and then the most amazing show of pink blooms on *Heucherella* I've ever seen. It's one of the longest bloomers in this family—an excellent plant all around. (See photograph in Chapter 10.)

Growing *Heucherella*

Heucherella is a plant for the semishade in moist but well-drained soils. It tolerates more shade than *Heuchera* does, and it tends to bloom for a longer time. Otherwise, grow it the same as *Heuchera*.

LATHYRUS

Common names: perennial sweet pea, everlasting pea

*L*athyros is Greek for "pea" or "pulse." The perennial sweet pea is *Lathyrus odoratus*, with *odoratus* meaning "smell" or "fragrance." Note that this is a different plant family than the edible garden pea that is in the *Pisum* family.

Bloom time: Early summer to midsummer
Height: Vinelike: unsupported, 2' (60 cm) tall in large twining clumps; supported, 6' to 8' (180 cm to 240 cm)
Sun needed: Sun to part shade

Bloom color: Violets, reds
Planting space: 24" (60 cm) apart
Soil preferred: Well-drained but with adequate water
Propagation method: Seed

Recommended Varieties

There are approximately forty species of this plant grown in gardens around the world. The plant you'll most often find in garden centers is *Lathyrus latifolius*. There are varieties of this species, but again, you'll likely only find one separate color, 'Rose Queen,' a rose pink, while the rest will be a seed mix and of undetermined color. The easiest thing to do is purchase the seeds yourself and then weed out the colors you don't like when the plant starts blooming in its second year in shades of white, rose, and pink. Do this and allow your chosen color to set seed.

Other species are available only through seed companies and plant societies. (See Resources.)

Growing *Lathyrus*

This rambling, vinelike grower is excellent for banks and waste spaces or perfect for scrambling up the trunks of flowering shrubs and shrub roses. It thrives in dampish soils in part shade but will grow almost anywhere if you take the time to establish it. One of the biggest clumps of *Lathyrus* I've ever seen lived in the waste soil of a neighbor's ditch, and it endured baking summer heat, no watering, and roadside salt—you couldn't kill it if you tried.

Lathyrus will self-sow in the garden but is not invasive. And like its namesake, it makes a good cut flower, but unlike the annual sweet pea, the perennial plant is not fragrant.

Lathyrus latifolius DOUGLAS GREEN

LILIUM

Common name: The word *lily* is ubiquitous.

The lily is one of our most storied plants, and the origin of its name is shrouded in the mists of time. There is a story (a good one but not necessarily true) that originally the word *lily* meant "flower" in Illyrian. Our word *lily* is derived from the Latin *lillium*, and if our first story is true, then the Romans adopted the word in their turn. However, they probably adopted it from the Greek word *leirion*, making our story of the Illyrians somewhat suspect.

The next time you look at old paintings, look for the lilies represented in them. You'll often see them as cut flowers standing in a jar. This representation is twofold. The lily is the symbol of purity and is most often associated with Mary, mother of Jesus. The jar is the symbol of womanhood, and together they stand for Mary, the ultimate mother-woman figure.

Bloom time: Early summer to midsummer

Height: 2′ to 6′ (60 cm to 180 cm)

Sun needed: Sun or light shade

Bloom color: Full range

Planting space: 6″ to 8″ (15 cm to 20 cm) apart, except for Orientals at 12″ (30 cm) apart

Soil preferred: Well-drained, high in organic matter

Propagation method: Seed, aboveground bulbils, division, or scaling depending on species

Recommended Varieties

Just over one hundred species of lily grow around the world, but only a few of these are important garden plants. I note that the botanists are currently arguing over the naming of this family as well, but for our purposes, we'll simply proceed with traditional names found in nurseries worldwide. A delightful fact is that wonderful new lily varieties are constantly being introduced to the market. The opposite side of this coin is that these varieties often disappear as fast as they arrive, the dictates of fashion, color, and price determining which bulbs appear in your local garden center. While specialist catalogs offer a good range of bulbs, the bulbs listed here will most often be available locally. These are the tried-and-true varieties, the ones that gardeners demand from year to year. You can't go wrong starting with any bulb on this list.

Lilium candidum

Lilium candidum is known as *Madonna lily*. At 4′ to 6′ (120 cm to 180 cm) tall and with pure white blooms, this is the storied lily of antiquity and fables. The one thing you might want to remember about this plant is that it throws a rosette of leaves in the fall that overwinter aboveground; do not pull out this rosette thinking it is a weed. *Lilium candidum* is a delightful plant and should be in every perennial garden.

Lilium x hybrida

Asiatic Lilies Asiatic lilies are a mixed bag of breeding as well as flower forms. It sometimes

Asiatic lily 'Chivalry' DOUGLAS GREEN

Asiatic lily 'Sunray' DOUGLAS GREEN

seems that the breeders put every lily here that doesn't fit into the following classes. Pay attention to flower descriptions in catalogs as the flower form, height, and fragrance will vary widely between varieties. As a rule of thumb, the sizes of Asiatic lilies fall somewhere between the small Martagon lilies and the large Trumpet lilies, but they are, as a rule, very heavy blooming and weather resistant. They make good garden performers, and their only weak spot is that their fragrance is nonexistent. They are usually the lowest-priced lily in a catalog and so are fine for mass planting or even naturalizing.

'Connecticut King' is gold yellow.
'Mont Blanc' is white with irregular spots.
'Red Carpet' is red.
'Rosita' is mauve pink.
'Déjà vu' is deep pink.

Trumpet and Aurelian Lilies Trumpet and Aurelian lilies have trumpet-shaped blooms with the classic flower form. These are the tallest of garden lilies, 4′ to 6′ (120 cm to 180 cm) tall, and they tower over the rest of the garden. They have outward-facing horizontal flowers and put on one of the brightest shows in the garden.

They tend to be damaged by summer storms, so staking or providing support by nearby plants is a good idea. The fragrance of these depends on the variety but is generally not overly powerful.

'Golden Splendor' is deep, rich golden yellow.
'Midnight' is darkish purple.
'Moonlight' is chartreuse yellow.
'Pink Perfection' is fuschia pink.

Oriental Lilies Oriental lilies are plants 3′ (90 cm) tall blooming in midsummer. They are a hybrid lily characterized by huge flowers and heavy fragrances. They are susceptible to fungal attack, so a bit wider spacing is suggested. Most of the flowers are upward-facing, but a few are downward-facing, so do read catalog descriptions to obtain the form you want.

'Casa Blanca' is white.
'Paramount' is magenta with darker veining.
'Pink Paramount' is light pink.
'Stargazer' is crimson red with white margins.

Martagon Hybrids Martagon hybrids are also called *Turk's cap lilies*, and it is easy to tell them from the other lily classes. The flowers of this class are smaller, and there are many more of them, upwards of forty blossoms 1″ to 2″ (2.5 cm to 5 cm) wide, on each stem. Also, each flower hangs facing straight down. The long stamens hang down from the flower, and the pollen is a bright yellow. The flowers are generally fragrant but not as much as the Oriental hybrids. Plant in full sunshine in well-drained soils, and the bulbs will last for years.

'Dalhansoni' is reddish brown with vibrant gold centers.

'Paisley Hybrids' is yellowish brown with mottled purple spots.

'Terrace City' is a gold-pink combination.

Lilium regale

Lilium regale is a Chinese lily that is sometimes in garden catalogs. This is a showy, white lily that is well worth a place in your garden. It is 4′ (120 cm) tall. After the Madonna lily, it is my favorite lily.

Growing *Lilium*

For the most part, lilies enjoy an open, free-draining, loamy type of soil. To achieve heavy blooming, try to grow them in soils that are high in organic matter and for the most part slightly on the acidic side. If you have clay soils, then raised beds constructed of good soil are the only way you'll grow this plant. They do prefer to be deeply planted, so the best results are to be had if the soil is well dug and compost is incorporated throughout the planting area. An old and still sound bit of advice is to keep the roots of this plant in the shade while the tops are grown in the sun.

Potions and Poisons

These plants are not poisonous. They have a very long history of being used for cosmetics and cooking.

LOBELIA

Common names: Indian tobacco, eyebright, gagwort

The plant was named in honor of Mathias de l'Obel (1538–1616). He was a Flemish botanist born in Lille, France, and court physician to King James I of England. The plant was named *Indian tobacco* because for a while it was shipped to Europe (by the Shakers) and used as a chewing tobacco. When chewed, it apparently tastes like tobacco. *Eyebright* comes to us from Lobelia's use as an infusion applied to the eyes to remedy a multitude of problems. *Gagwort* (remember, *wort* means "plant") comes from its use as an expectorant, making the patient gag or cough up phlegm.

Bloom time: Midsummer to late summer
Height: 24″ to 36″ (60 cm to 90 cm)
Sun needed: Shade to full sun depending on soil moisture
Bloom color: Blue, white, or red

Planting space: 12″ (30 cm) apart
Soil preferred: Damp soils
Propagation method: Seed, division, or cuttings

Recommended Varieties

Lobelia cardinalis

Lobelia cardinalis is commonly known as cardinal flower. This plant, 24″ to 30″ (60 cm to 75 cm) tall, is marvelous for its bright red flowers shrieking across the shade garden. There is no brighter red flower in the garden than this one. It does prefer part shade, and to grow properly, it does need constantly moist soils. In the wild, I've seen cardinal flowers growing underwater when water levels were high. Plant them in clumps of at least three for best effect in the garden.

'Queen Victoria' is bronze-leaved, and while it is a nice flower, it is not hardy in zone 4.

Lobelia x hybrida

'Monet Moment' is 30″ to 36″ (75 cm to 90 cm) tall and is a very large-flowering clear pink plant with masses of blooms. Each blossom is also huge by normal *Lobelia* standards.

'Summit Snow' is a tall plant, 30″ to 36″ (75 cm to 90 cm), blooming clear white.

Lobelia syphilitica

Lobelia syphilitica's common name is Indian tobacco. There are both blue and white varieties of this plant, and they come highly recom-

Lobelia 'Monet Moment'   TERRA NOVA NURSERIES

Lobelia 'Summit Snow'   TERRA NOVA NURSERIES

mended. I've grown both, and while they grow well in damp shade, the blue variety has grown very well in dry shade for me. The white disappeared after a few years of this dry treatment, but the blue has persisted. It is not as tall or showy in the dry shade as it is in damp ground, but it does live. The blue also lives in full sun where the soil is dampish, and this year I saw a white variety self-sow out in the sun garden as well. I have to emphasize that if you grow this plant in full-sun locations it will require watering. The plant does not grow in full sun when combined with dry soils. Water it well and this plant will reward you with magnificent blooms.

Growing *Lobelia*

Lobelia is a native plant of shade and damp soils. If given these two conditions, the plant will show off with a brilliant display of flowers worthy of any garden. It does self-sow—particularly the *Lobelia syphilitica*—so you'll never want for it once you establish it in the garden.

Potions and Poisons

This plant can be considered poisonous, although most herbalists will say different. It is a matter of degree: if enough is eaten by a child, then sweating and convulsions may occur. The child needs to eat the bark of the mature stem or the roots to obtain this amount or concentration of the active ingredients, so it is not likely to be a problem. The flowers and leaves are not considered to be a problem—remember the leaves were used as chewing tobacco.

Lobelia cardinalis   DOUGLAS GREEN

Lobelia syphilitica   DOUGLAS GREEN

LYSIMACHIA

Common name: yellow loosestrife

The plant is reputed to be named after King Lysimachos of Thrace, who was the first to identify *Lysimachia* as a healing plant. I should emphasize the word *reputed*, as the following explanation has more current support. The Greek word for "ending strife" is *lysimachos*, and this gives us the common name *loosestrife*. One small bit of surviving folklore says that if this plant is laid on the yoke of struggling oxen, it will cause them to cease fighting each other or "loose their strife." This may be because the plant also has the reputation of repelling flies and fleas. If laid onto the yoke, it was said to keep these insects from bothering cattle, thus ending the strife between the oxen. It was also burned in houses in medieval times for its ability to repel flies.

Bloom time: Early summer to midsummer
Height: 24″ to 48″ (60 cm to 120 cm)
Sun needed: Full sun to part shade
Bloom color: Yellows, whites
Planting space: 18″ to 24″ (45 cm to 60 cm) apart

Soil preferred: Damp
Propagation method: Seed, division, or cuttings

Recommended Varieties

Lysimachia ciliata

The species *Lysimachia ciliata* is a North American native and is seldom seen in garden centers.

'Firecracker,' 24″ (60 cm) tall, has bronze-purple leaves with nodding yellow flowers. It is one of the least invasive of the garden cultivated varieties.

Lysimachia clethroides

Gooseneck *Lysimachia* is 36″ (90 cm) tall and a white-flowering species. The white flowers are much prized by florists, and their nodding characteristic is quite attractive. The foliage develops a good red fall color in my garden, so it has some fall interest as well. This is one of the more aggressive spreaders in the family, able to swamp shorter or slower-growing perennials "in a single bound."

'Lady Jane' has a pale pink eye in the flower and good fall coloring.

Lysimachia punctata

Lysimachia punctata is the tallest species in my garden, growing at least 36″ (90 cm) tall and sometimes reaching 48″ (120 cm) tall depending on how kindly I treat it. If I give it the rich, moist soil it so clearly craves, it will throw tall spires and spread with wild abandon. I contain its enthusiasm for territorial expansion by potting it and plunging the pot.

'Alexander' is a variegated variety of *Lysimachia punctata* that differs from the species only in its leaf variegation. The new shoots and leaves in the spring are heavily tinged with pink and are

Lysimachia punctata 'Alexander'   DOUGLAS GREEN

Lysimachia clethroides   DOUGLAS GREEN

quite attractive. This coloring fades as the leaves begin to mature. I have it potted and plunged.

'Golden Glory' is a brand-new introduction with random variegation of yellow markings and dense yellow flower clusters.

Several ground-hugging species of *Lysimachia* are suited for rock gardens but not the main border. *Lysimachia nummularia*, both the species and a golden-leaved variety called 'Aurea,' are strong growers and bloom for long periods of time. *Lysimachia japonica* is similarly a low grower with a good long bloom time. It is slightly better behaved than the previous two short varieties but not by much. I find these are easily controlled with a firm hand on an edging tool or shovel.

Growing *Lysimachia*

Lysimachia never met a garden it didn't like and will prove it to every unwary gardener who allows it free access to good garden soil. These plants are, for the most part, rampant spreaders in a decent soil, and the only thing that will slow them down is to grow them in the heaviest of clay soils. Grow them in full sun to light shade in

almost any soil. They prefer soils that are fertile and evenly moist but well-drained. I've grown them in sandy, shallow, dry soils in an attempt to slow them down, but they simply wilted in the heat of a summer's day, recovered in the evening, and kept growing.

I now grow several good varieties in large nursery containers plunged into the ground next to pond areas. The plants put on a good show, and the containers make a valiant effort to hold these rampant spreaders in check. I do not allow them to set seed. When I fill up the ponds with the hose, I ensure the pots get well watered. *Lysimachia* also will grow quite nicely as a potted plant (big pot) with its feet standing in a few inches of water on the shelf of a pond.

All the taller varieties of *Lysimachia* make excellent cut flowers.

Potions and Poisons

Besides being used as an insect repellent, this plant was used as an expectorant and to stop bleeding of any kind. It is not seen to be poisonous and has a bitter taste, in any case.

OENETHERA

Common names: sundrop, evening primrose

As with some other plant names, the name *Oenethera* has absolutely nothing to do with the family of plants it now describes. The entire family (mostly North American natives) in no way is described by the name. However, in case you're interested, here's the background. There are two theories. The first is that the name derives from the Greek *oinos*, "wine," and *thera*, "booty." The second is that it is a corruption of *onotheras*, which is a combination of *onos*, "ass," and *thera*, "hunting," which gets combined and translated as "chasing a wild beast." I'm afraid none of my reference texts describe how we got from chasing a wild beast to yellow-flowering perennials, although they do say that Theophrastus was the person to use the name—likely referring to an *Epilobium* species and not this plant at all.

Sundrop is easily understood because once you see the bright yellow of the blossoms, you'll understand how the sun could have dropped a bit of light in your garden. *Evening primrose* is another easily described name, as the flowers open later in the day. Some of the varieties indeed open at night rather than the day.

Bloom time: Midsummer
Height: 3″ to 3′ (7.5 cm to 90 cm)
Sun needed: Full sun
Bloom color: Mostly yellow, one pink, one white

Planting space: 18″ (45 cm) apart
Soil preferred: Well-drained
Propagation method: Seed or, more rarely, cuttings

Recommended Varieties

Oenethera fruiticosa

Oenethera fruiticosa is a much taller species, 24″ to 36″ (60 cm to 90 cm) tall, with bright yellow flowers.

'Fireworks' is also sold as 'Fyrverkeri.' This plant has bronze foliage, a floppy growth habit, and delightful yellow flowers. It is a good pondside plant if you contain it.

Oenethera fruiticosa subspecies *glauca* has blue-green leaves.

'Erica Robin' is 18″ (45 cm) tall. The early foliage is an apricot-orange shade, and the plant has good yellow flowers in season.

'Sonnenwende' grows to 24″ to 30″ (60 cm to 75 cm) tall with purplish brown leaves and gold-yellow flowers.

Oenethera macrocarpa

Oenethera macrocarpa, formerly *Oenethera missouriensis*, is a good, ground-hugging, bright yellow species with large flowers 2″ to 3″ (5 cm to 7.5 cm) wide. This plant flowers quite prolifically. Grow it in full sun in well-drained soils for best results.

Oenethera pallida

Oenethera pallida has a white and extremely fragrant flower that fades to a light pink overnight

Oenethera fruiticosa   DOUGLAS GREEN

when it is open. It is an excellent plant for nighttime viewing but has been rather short-lived for me. It is quite ground-hugging and demands excellent drainage. I suspect that if happy, this could become a bit of a pest through self-sowing. Unfortunately, it's not happy yet.

Oenethera speciosa

'Siskiyou' was formerly known as *Oenethera berlandieri*. Whatever the name, this is a gorgeous rose-pink bloomer with good up-facing flowers. It is very drought tolerant and forms a low mat. It is marginally hardy for me (in zone 4), and I've lost it more than once owing to wet winters. It is likely going to be more successful for me in a rock garden setting with perfect drainage rather than in the main border.

Growing Oenethera

Oenethera will grow almost anywhere there is full sunshine and a bit of ground to spread its roots. It prefers a well-drained site and average soil drainage instead of heavy clay and wet feet. If you stay away from the extremes of wet or dry, you can grow this plant. Most of the flowers open up in the afternoon or evening and then fade and wither in the morning sun; this makes them ideal for nighttime gardens, and they should be sited where they are visible in the evening. The taller species, such as *Oenethera biennis*, are rampant self-sowers and will quickly try to colonize a good garden soil. The shorter, prostrate species, such as *Oenethera macrocarpa*, are best put in rock gardens or at the front of borders.

Potions and Poisons

This plant's seeds were and are used medicinally. The young shoots of some species are eaten raw in salads. It is not likely to be a problem unless huge amounts of seed are eaten—this being difficult to do given the podlike method of seed production on the plant (you'd have to find and eat a lot of pods to get enough seeds).

PAEONIA

Common name: peony

The name *Paeonia* comes from classical Greek and is said to commemorate Paeon, physician to the gods, who reputedly discovered the medicinal properties of the plant. Another possible derivation is that Paeon was in fact Apollo in disguise when he cured the wounds Pluto, Ares, and Hades suffered in the Trojan wars. There is also a possibility that the name is derived from the Greek *paio*, "I strike." This is part of an incantation used by the medical practitioners in classical Greek times; whether it is referring to striking themselves or striking out the disease is not clear. It is also possible that the name comes from *paeon*, or "song of praise," originally sung as a hymn to Apollo.

Bloom time: Late spring to early summer
Height: 24″ to 36″ (60 cm to 90 cm)
Sun needed: Full sun
Bloom color: Variable from yellows through reds/whites

Planting space: 30″ (75 cm) apart
Soil preferred: Sandy, well-drained soil high in organic matter
Propagation method: Division or seed

Recommended Varieties

Increasingly, specialist garden centers are growing species peonies. These are quite delightful plants and the most commonly available ones are the following:

Paeonia tennuifolia

Paeonia tennuifolia is called the *fernleaf peony* for its finely cut foliage that resembles a fern more than it resembles the average garden peony. It has quite delicate bright red single flowers and is the earliest of the peonies to bloom in my garden.

Paeonia lutea

Paeonia lutea is a yellow species also now available. It too is wonderful as an early-blooming garden show.

Paeonia lactiflora

Paeonia lactiflora is the common garden peony we all know and love so dearly. The list of widely available varieties goes on and on, and it is almost impossible to pick and choose favorite plants. Most of us will pick from neighbors' or grandmothers' yards if given half a chance. My favorite plant came from a churchyard where it was planted over one hundred years ago to mark the wedding day of a friend's great-grandmother. The dark blood-red blossoms are delightful every early summer. Seek out specialist catalogs for the newest and best hybrids in a full range of colors. The single, or Japanese, plants are also included in this class, and indeed the Asian breeders have produced some amazingly beautiful plants. I confess to having a small love affair with these single bloomers, and I'm in the process of collecting ever more of them.

Paeonia suffruticosa

Paeonia suffruticosa is the tree peony ancestor, and all modern tree peonies are descended from this species. The same advice holds true for tree

Paeonia tennuifolia   Douglas Green

peonies as it does for the garden peonies; there are so many listed varieties that it is best to consult a specialist catalog for the colors and forms that appeal to you. I do find here in zone 4 that in a hard winter, our tree peonies will die to the ground. Luckily, I planted them quite deep—graft is 8″ (20 cm)—to protect the tender graft area, and they regrow and produce flowers in the same year even when frozen to the ground.

Growing *Paeonia*

Peonies are relatively easy to grow if a few simple rules are followed. Plant them in the full sunshine. For every bit of reduction in sun you make, you'll lose a bit of flowering potential. Plant them in a good, compost-enriched soil. They will stay in one spot quite happily for a very long time, so the richer the soil to begin with, the faster the plant will establish itself and the happier it will be. Note that sometimes

peonies sulk for several years after transplanting before starting to bloom again.

Plant them so the "eyes," or growing points of the plant, are no more than ½″ to 1″ (1.25 cm to 2.5 cm) deep in the soil. If you plant these growing points (you'll recognize them as reddish-colored, sharp, spearlike points) too deep, the peony will grow well and lushly but the flower will not.

Water them deeply several times a month during the growing season. Remember that peonies are genetically mountain meadow plants and would receive full sun and lots of spring water (melting snow) along with periodic downpours throughout the summer. The mountain meadow soil would also be enriched with the dying grass leaves, which is why organic matter is recommended for this plant.

Do take care not to break the brittle roots. These can easily be snapped and broken, so handle them gently. If moving a big old plant, allow it to sit in the shade for an hour or so if possible before handling or dividing it. This sitting seems to toughen up the root and reduce brittleness.

Do deadhead the spent flowers unless you want to grow the plant from seed. Obtaining new plants from seed is quite possible and not too difficult. The tricky part is remembering that the seed germinates in the first year and produces a small root but *no* aboveground leaves. The second year it produces a small aboveground shoot and leaves. Thus germinating peonies is a two-year project. The easiest way to do this is to sink a nursery pot in the ground, fill it with a sterilized potting soil, and sow the seed. Cover it with ½″ (1.25 cm) of soil and leave it alone for several years. It will freeze during the winter (not a problem) and grow during the summer months. (Don't forget to keep the soil damp.) If nothing happens after three years, you have lost the seed and can gently excavate to ensure nothing is happening. As long as the seed is hard, it is alive.

Staking some of the modern hybrids is necessary because they tend to flop over—their blossoms being too large for the stem to support. The easiest way to stake a peony is to make hooks in the ends of a piece of wire (coat hangers work well) and then wrap the wire around the plant about two-thirds of the way up the foliage. Use the hooks fastened together to keep the wire in place, and note that the length of wire will be variable depending on the size of the plant. This extra support keeps the plant from flopping over and holds the peonies upright in a natural way. The wire disappears into the foliage so the plant appears quite natural-looking, unlike with other systems where strings and stakes are used.

Potions and Poisons

Peonies have a long history of use in tonics, particularly for convulsions and "nervous afflictions." Older herbals also recommend *Paeonia* for liver problems. Note that this is not recommended today.

TO STAKE OR NOT TO STAKE

*P*roper feeding reduces the need for staking. I rarely stake my perennial gardens. I try very hard to put plants that tend to be floppy next to more sturdy plants that will help support them. My delphiniums were planted amid some bush roses and did quite nicely there when I had them in the main perennial garden.

When I do stake, it is most often for peonies or other perennials I'm experimenting with. For the peonies, I use a straightened-out coat hanger with a small loop at each end. When the plant starts sending up buds, I wrap the coat hanger around the plant about two-thirds of the way up the plant, locking the looped ends together to hold the wire in a circle. The circle of wire holds the plant upright and is invisible against the foliage. I find that holding the foliage upright will also hold the blossoms upright in all but the most extreme winds and weather. True, heavy blossoms do tend to bend the stalks of some varieties, but this is a fault of the variety, not the technique. These are the same varieties that bend with more traditional stick-and-string staking. The older and thicker the peony clump, the better this looped wire technique works.

For perennials that might need some staking, I use old Christmas tree branches. When the needles fall off the Christmas tree, there is a perfect latticework arrangement of branches that are well suited to supporting wayward perennials. The branches are cut 24" to 30" (60 cm to 75 cm) in length and then stuck into the ground quite early in the spring next to the plants that will require staking. The plants grow up to cover the branches, and the branches, with their fine fingers of support, cushion the perennials from wind damage. I particularly like stakes of this kind because they are easily cleaned up in the fall, can be composted, and do not leave lost chunks of string, old posts, or metal pieces around to foul up garden machinery, tools, or knees.

PAPAVER

Common name: poppy

The Anglo-Saxon word for the poppy plant was *papig*, while the Romans called it *papaver*, and that is how we got to *poppy*. The names of different kinds of poppies usually describe an aspect of their growth or habitat; for example, the Oriental poppy is named after its geographical origins. (In case you were wondering, the word *opium* is derived from the Greek *opos*, "juice.")

Bloom time: Early summer
Height: 8″ to 36″ (20 cm to 90 cm)
Sun needed: Full sun
Bloom color: Reds, pinks, orange, white

Planting space: 8″ (20 cm) apart for short, 18″ (45 cm) apart for tall
Soil preferred: Well-drained
Propagation method: Seeds or root cutting

Recommended Varieties

Some shorter, alpine-type poppies are appearing in the nursery trade, but for the most part, they are more suited for the rock garden than the main perennial border.

Papaver alpinus

Papaver alpinus is a short variety at 6″ to 8″ (15 cm to 20 cm) and is a good self-sower if grown in well-drained, almost rocky soils.

Papaver atlanticum

Papaver atlanticum is short-lived but a prolific self-sower, blooming its orange heads away during the early summer.

Papaver nudicaule

Papaver nudicaule, beloved of garden centers (it blooms the first year from seed), is a biennial, and its happy blooms of orange, red, and yellow might self-sow if the garden soil is well-drained and a bit on the gravelly side. If purchased in bloom, they will last only a single year in the homeowner's garden.

Papaver orientale

Papaver orientale, commonly known as *Oriental poppy*, is the plant we think of when we think *poppy*.

'Allegro,' 18″ (45 cm) tall, is a seed-raised variety, popular in the trade because of the ease of starting seeds. It is good only if you want a shorter variety.

'Beauty of Livermere' is a deep red, grown from seed.

'Brilliant' is one of the most commonly sold varieties. It is medium red and is grown from seed.

'Cedar Hill' is a soft pink.

'Helen Elizabeth' has crinkled petals and salmon-pink flowers with a black spot.

'Perry's White' is a large white flower with a darker center spot.

'Picotee' is a salmon-pink flower with a large white center. Or you could describe it as a white flower with a wide salmon-pink edge. Either way, it is an attractive combination.

'Turkenlouis' is a bright, fiery red with a dark eye and crinkled, fringed petals.

Papaver orientale 'Turkenlouis'   DOUGLAS GREEN

Papaver orientale 'Turkenlouis'   DOUGLAS GREEN

Papaver somniferum

Papaver somniferum is sometimes sold in garden centers but is mostly sold as double poppy seed in catalogs. While technically an annual and easily grown from seed, it self-sows with abandon in my garden, and I routinely weed 90 percent of the seedlings out every year. It does come in a color range from red through pinks and off-whites with some bicolor streakings.

Growing *Papaver*

Grow *Papaver* in the full sun in average garden soil. Well-drained soils are best; average garden watering will produce excellent plants with little care. A yearly application of compost is adequate for nutrition. It does tend to die back and become ugly after flowering. For this reason, it is often planted behind a medium-height perennial that will allow it to flower over the top but hide the subsequent foliage deterioration during the rest of the summer. *Papaver* blooms early and prolifically and puts on a massive flower show, but then it is finished and no further bloom or color can be coaxed from it.

Potions and Poisons

One of these plants, *Papavar somniferum*, is one of the most important of medicinal and culinary plants (the source of morphine). The seeds are used in baking, and the sap from the flower buds is a powerful drug. Do not experiment with this plant.

PENSTEMON

Common name: beard tongue

The name *Penstemon* comes without glory or legend, being merely a botanical description, from the Greek words *pente*, "five," and *stemon* "stamen." *Penstemon* has five stamens and the most prominent of them is sterile. *Beard tongue* refers to the shape of the bottom flower petal and its resemblance to human anatomy.

Bloom time: Early summer to midsummer

Height: 6″ to 36″ (15 cm to 90 cm)

Sun needed: Full, hot sun

Bloom color: Whites, pinks, shades of violet

Planting space: 12″ to 18″ (30 cm to 45 cm)

Soil preferred: Well-drained

Propagation method: Seeds or cuttings

Recommended Varieties

Penstemon barbatus x hybrida

Penstemon barbatus x hybrida is one of the hardiest and easiest classes of *Penstemon* to grow and makes an ideal beginner plant. It typically forms a mound of foliage and then in early summer to midsummer, it produces flower spikes that shoot up out of the mound.

'Elfin Pink' is 18″ (45 cm) tall with clear pink flowers.

'Prairie Dusk' is 18″ to 24″ (45 cm to 60 cm) tall with bright purple flowers. It is one of the longest-blooming varieties.

Penstemon digitalis

'Husker Red' was Perennial Plant of the Year in 1996 and is also a good beginner plant. It has purplish foliage and the palest of pink flowers (some would call them white). It is a good plant for mass planting or taking cut flowers for the kitchen table.

Penstemon fruiticosa

'Purple Haze' is 18″ to 24″ (45 cm to 60 cm) tall and is technically a subshrub rather than a perennial. This means its woody stems act like shrub stems rather than dying back to the ground every winter. It has wonderfully bright lilac-purple flowers. Do not install this plant where it will receive irrigation water or on anything but extremely well-drained soils. It is suited for rock gardens more than perennial borders.

Penstemon x hybrida

You'll sometimes find very tender *Penstemon x hybrida* in garden centers, and many salespeople will say they are hardy because *Penstemon* is native to North America. Don't believe it—these hybrids are tender (hardy in zone 7 or warmer) and that is why they are included here.

'Garnet' has wine-red flowers on 20″ (50 cm) stems.

'King George' is salmon-red with a white throat on 24″ (60 cm) stems.

'Mother of Pearl' is soft lilac-pink on 24″ (60 cm) stems.

'Purple Passion' is rich violet-purple on 24″ (60 cm) stems. It is worth growing just for the single year it lives.

'Ruby' has bright red flowers on 20″ (50 cm) stems.

Penstemon 'Purple Passion'

Penstemon 'Mother of Pearl'

'Sour Grapes' is one of the larger blooms, in pale purple, and is 24″ to 30″ (60 cm to 75 cm) tall.

'Snowstorm' is snow white and 18″ to 24″ (45 to 60 cm) tall.

Growing *Penstemon*

The single most important thing to remember when growing *Penstemon* is that it cannot tolerate any kind of wet feet. It requires perfect drainage (particularly during winter) if it is to thrive and grow. This is not a plant for wet or clay soils. The second thing to consider is that *Penstemon* demand full, hot sunshine. Remember, these are plants of alpine meadows and dry land areas. Even if the rest of your garden is struggling, the *Penstemon* plants will be fine without extra water. Well, most of them will. A few hybrids that are crosses between *Penstemon hartwegii* and *Penstemon cobaea* will tolerate high humidity but not winter wet. Unfortunately, as already stated, most of these hybrids are quite tender and will require a zone 7 to 8 garden to reliably overwinter. They are beautiful, but I consider them an annual in my zone 4 area.

Do note that the taller varieties of *Penstemon* all make excellent cut flowers.

Penstemon 'Ruby'

Polemonium caeruleum 'Brise d'Anjou'
BLOOMS OF BRESSINGHAM NORTH AMERICA, BARBERTON OH

Polemonium reptans   DOUGLAS GREEN

Grow it in a moist, fertile soil in part sun for best results. While the plant will tolerate sunshine, it will not when combined with dry soils. It responds well to high levels of organic matter.

Potions and Poisons

Polemonium was used by herbalists as a cough remedy. There are no indications that the plant is poisonous.

POLYGONUM

Common names: knotweed, smartweed

The name *Polygonum* is derived from the Greek words *polys*, "many," and *gonu*, "joint," and this just about sums up this plant's stem appearance. *Knotweed* refers to the same thing, while *smartweed* might indeed refer to the plant's amazing tendency to travel great distances in a single bound—outwitting unwary gardeners with its speed of travel.

Bloom time: Early summer
Height: 48″ (120 cm)
Sun needed: Sun or part shade
Bloom color: White

Planting space: 24″ (60 cm) apart
Soil preferred: Moisture-retentive but not overly fertile
Propagation method: Rhizomes

Recommended Varieties

You have to be careful with plants with this name. Some, such as *Polygonum japonicum*, are pernicious weeds and very difficult to eradicate once established. I'm not recommending any of the shorter, fast-spreading plants for the garden. Most are simply weeds, but there is one that is suited (with care) for the main perennial border:

Polygonum alpinum

Polygonum alpinum is 3′ to 5′ (90 cm to 150 cm) tall and blooms white. It thrives in full sun or part shade and puts on a magnificent show of white blooms. It's not overly aggressive, but it does spread by underground rhizomes.

Growing *Polygonum*

Polygonum does not like overly fertile soils, in which it will become floppy. Although moisture-retentive soil is good, bogs are not, as the plant does not appreciate standing water. A soil high in organic matter is excellent, and the blooms will be outstanding. Full sun is good, but grow it in part shade if the soil will dry out in midsummer to any extent. Keeping it moist in midsummer will extend the bloom time. Keep your shovel sharp to edge this plant every year or so to keep it in bounds.

Potions and Poisons

There are no concerns with growing this plant. Other family members have been used medicinally as gargles and to prevent children's diarrhea.

Polygonum alpinum DOUGLAS GREEN

PRIMULA JAPONICA

Common name: Japanese primula

See Chapter 5 for a description of *Primula*. *Japanese primula* is fairly straightforward in that this plant is a native of Japan.

Bloom time: Early summer to midsummer
Height: 24″ to 30″ (60 cm to 75 cm)
Sun needed: Part shade
Bloom color: Whites, pinks, reds

Planting space: 12″ (30 cm) apart
Soil preferred: Moist woodland soils
Propagation method: Seed or division

Recommended Varieties

Primula japonica

'Miller's Crimson' is medium red and readily available.

'Postford White' is the white most often found in catalogs.

Growing *Primula japonica*

This plant grows best in part shade in a moist soil that is high in organic matter. I have seen it growing in the sun in damp soil and in part shade in normal garden soil, but I have not seen it thrive in hot and dry conditions. It is a plant of the damp woodland forest. It will self-sow if happy, or it can be divided either after flowering is done or first thing in the spring.

Primula japonica   DOUGLAS GREEN

Primula japonica 'Glowing Embers'   DOUGLAS GREEN

162

THERMOPSIS

Common names: false lupin, golden pea

The name comes from the Greek *thermos*, a name for the lupin plant, and *opsis*, meaning "appearance." Combining them we get *Thermopsis*—"appearing to be a lupin." *False lupin* clearly refers to the fact that while this plant looks like a lupin, it is not. *Golden pea* describes the golden color of the flower and the fact that this plant is in the same botanical family as the common garden pea.

Bloom time: Early summer to midsummer
Height: 36″ to 48″ (90 cm to 120 cm)
Sun needed: Full sun
Bloom color: Yellow

Planting space: 24″ (60 cm) apart
Soil preferred: Open, sandy
Propagation method: Seed

Recommended Varieties

Thermopsis lanceolata

Thermopsis lanceolata, 12″ (30 cm), is a lemon-yellow plant that is extremely drought tolerant. It does resent being moved, so plant it where you want it to live.

Thermopsis villosa

Thermopsis villosa is 48″ (120 cm) tall, a golden-yellow-flowering plant with stout stems that never need staking.

Growing *Thermopsis*

If you can't seem to grow regular lupins, this is the plant for you. Both short and tall varieties are available, and they are drop-dead easy to grow. Put them in the full sun in any average garden soil with decent drainage (they don't like wet feet), and you'll succeed. The only warning is that they seem to resent being transplanted, so if you like to move your plants around, this is one plant that should wear a Do Not Disturb sign.

Thermopsis caroliana DOUGLAS GREEN

TIARELLA

Common name: foamflower

*T*iarella comes from the Greek word *tiara*, meaning "crown." This is an obvious reference to the shape of the fruit of this plant.

Bloom time: Early summer
Height: 12″ (30 cm)
Sun needed: Sun to shade
Bloom color: White, pale pinks

Planting space: 12″ to 18″ (30 cm to 45 cm) apart
Soil preferred: Well-drained but moist
Propagation method: Cuttings or seed

Recommended Varieties

Tiarella x hybrida

'Iron Butterfly' has fragrant white flowers. Its heavily cut leaves are green with a darker center, making this an excellent garden plant. The blooms make for good cut flowers.

'Heronswood Mist' has green leaves flecked with cream and pink tones that will make this introduction stand out in your garden. Its pinkish stems are unique, but this variety grows more slowly than other hybrids.

'Ninja' has coral-tinted white flowers and a heavily cut green leaf with a darker center, making this a good garden performer. The winter color is outstanding—it is close to dark purple.

Growing Tiarella

Tiarella thrives in damp soils (but not waterlogged or heavy clay) that are well drained. In the wild, it is most often found on the steep sides of stream banks where moisture is freely available but where there is no winter flooding or wet feet. It grows well in sunlight if kept damp, but if allowed to dry out in midsummer, it would prefer a shadier spot. It is the heat of the midday sun that does the damage, and if possible, plant it where it is protected from the extreme heat. I have several different varieties planted around a small pond in a dappled-shade location under an ornamental crabapple tree.

Tiarella 'Iron Butterfly'   TERRA NOVA NURSERIES

Tiarella 'Heronswood Mist'   Terra Nova Nurseries

Potions and Poisons

The plant family was used as a general tonic and for "diseases of the bladder" as well as an aid for digestion. There are no concerns with the garden growing of this plant.

Tiarella 'Ninja'   Terra Nova Nurseries

TRADESCANTIA

Common name: spiderwort

The plant is named for John Tradescant (1608–1662), a British naturalist, traveler, plant collector, and gardener. The name *spiderwort* is given to plants with the ability to cure the poisonous bite of a spider. Originally, the name was given to another plant—now unknown. How did *Tradescantia* come to be called *spiderwort* as well? Who knows, but you have to agree that it's an interesting name. And no, *Tradescantia* has no effect on spider bites.

Bloom time: Early to late summer
Height: 24″ to 36″ (60 cm to 90 cm)
Sun needed: Full to part sun
Bloom color: Purples, violets, pink, white

Planting space: 18″ to 24″ (45 cm to 60 cm) apart
Soil preferred: Moist
Propagation method: Division or seed

Recommended Varieties

Tradescantia virginiana

Tradescantia virginiana is the hardy North American native that provides a solid genetic base of hardiness and constant blooming. Some tender species are grown as houseplants, but we need not concern ourselves with them.

'Concorde Grape' is a bright purplish pink and shines out over the garden.

'Iris Pritchard' is a pale blue.

'Karminglut' is carmine red and a very attractive plant.

'Osprey' is pure white, although some plants with this name may have some violet flecks in the flowers.

'Zwanenburg Blue' is a rich blue color.

Growing Tradescantia

Tradescantia is a plant for moist soil if it is to be allowed to bloom for a long time. If you reduce the moisture, you reduce the bloom time. It seems to prefer full sun as long as the moisture needs are met. If soil water is limited, it will flower better in dappled shade where it is protected from the heat of the noonday sun. It does not appreciate bog conditions nor clay but does like a soil with high organic matter.

Tradescantia virginiana 'Concorde Grape'
Douglas Green

VERONICA

Common name: speedwell

Veronica is supposedly named after St. Veronica (1660–1727), a nun who received a very visible impression (along with corresponding pain) of the crown of thorns of Jesus. Medical treatment did no good, and she is normally represented with a crown of thorns and hugging a cross. Another theory is that the name comes from the Greek *phero*, "I bring," and *nike*, "victory," reputedly for its ability to fight disease. Say the two words together fast to get a sense of this possible derivative. *Speedwell* comes from the fact that the blossoms were said to fall off immediately after cutting. The term *speedwell* was synonymous with *farewell* or *good-bye*, and the speed with which the flowers say "good-bye" apparently gave the plant its name.

Bloom time: Early summer to midsummer
Height: 4″ to 36″ (10 cm to 90 cm)
Sun needed: Full to part sun
Bloom color: Lavenders, pinks, intense blues

Planting space: 18″ (45 cm) apart
Soil preferred: Well-drained, high in organic matter
Propagation method: Cuttings, division, or seed

Recommended Varieties

Most plants of the *Veronica* family make excellent flowering plants. Unfortunately, many of those available in the trade are on the short side. This makes them excellent for rock gardens, but their lack of stature is a problem in the mixed perennial border. So, while some of the newer varieties are heavily advertised, for example 'Noah Williams,' a variegated hybrid variety, do make sure you read the tag and install them in the appropriate space. There are few things sadder than watching a wonderful plant lose the battle for space to a taller and more aggressive garden neighbor.

Veronica gentianoides

I truly enjoy this plant because even at only 6″ to 12″ (15 cm to 30 cm) tall, it is cast-iron hardy. The flowers are the most wonderful light sky blue you can imagine. I have it tucked next to a pathway into the main garden so I can enjoy it without its being overtaken by aggressive neighbors. There is a variegated variety as well, and it too is quite lovely. I find the variegated variety appreciates and grows more successfully in areas with better drainage. This is a polite way of saying that my poor plant died because of overwatering and overcrowding in the main perennial border.

Veronica x hybrida

'Sunny Border Blue' is one of the longest blooming of the family, and its short, deep violet-blue spikes are worth a place in any garden. Its flowers are 18″ to 24″ (45 cm to 60 cm) tall, and this is a good cutting variety if you can bear to part with it from the garden. It has excellent mildew resistance considering it has a dense, compact growing habit when compared to other *Veronica* plants.

Veronica spicata 'Blue Peter'   Douglas Green

Veronica spicata 'Icicle'   Douglas Green

Veronica longifolia

Veronica longifolia is the best *Veronica* for cutting, with very well-formed flower spikes of lavender-blue with nodding tips that are a bonus in mid-summer for a flower designer. At 30″ (75 cm) tall, it may need staking to ensure the flowers grow straight and tall. It is a mid-summer bloomer.

'Alba' is a white flower.

'Blue Giant' is a good lavender-blue color. It has very fat flower spikes.

'Lavender Charm' has light lavender-blue flowers. It is a heavy bloomer.

Veronica spicata

Veronica spicata's common name is spike speedwell. And although it is on the short side at 12″ (30 cm), its bushy shapes and longlasting, upright flower spikes make it a good garden performer. This is one of the most heavily hybridized species and most commonly available in garden centers. Do understand that it is short before you place it in your garden.

'Icicle' is a white variety that grows 12″ to 18″ (30 cm to 45 cm) and is the very best-blooming white.

'Blue Peter' is also excellent at 18″ (45 cm) tall in dark violet.

Growing *Veronica*

In general, *Veronica* is a plant of sun or part-shade locations. It does best when the soil is amended with compost and the soil moisture is constant (but not boggy) and well-drained. The taller forms are plants of the meadow or woodland edge. They do grow best if lifted and divided every three to five years. Cut them back to the ground in fall. *Veronica* is quite susceptible to

Veronica longifolia 'Alba'   DOUGLAS GREEN

powdery mildew, so good air circulation is a must for success, particularly if it is grown in shadier conditions.

Potions and Poisons

Veronica was and is used as a general tonic and for cough relief. While not recommended as a culinary herb—it has a very bitter taste—it is not considered a problem in the garden.

Veronica longifolia 'Lavender Charm'
DOUGLAS GREEN

8

Late-Summer Bloomers

Late-summer bloomers are some of the finest and hardiest of the perennial plants found in gardens. The fragrances are strong on still nights when the breeze sends their subtle messages over to my big patio chair, and I have to confess a quiet summer night in the garden is as close to heaven as I'll likely be until I get to the real thing. You can hear the night insects buzzing by, the moths fluttering, and the nightjars swooping overhead.

The high to late summer is also the time when our kitchen table groans under the weight of the cut-flower garden. It seems that two of my daughters have formed a bond with cut flowers as a form of artistic expression, and this has caused some upsets in the household. There is an inherent conflict built into the relationship between a gardener who loves plants in the garden and daughters who love cut flowers in the house. The gardener's wife seems to support the daughters, so the gardener has built them their very own garden bed and filled it with all the cutting and fragrant flowers they could wish for. Peace has once again settled onto the garden kingdom, but the gardener keeps a wary eye out for interlopers carrying pruning shears.

ACHILLEA

Common names: sneezewort, yarrow

*A*chillea is named for that great warrior of the Trojan War, Achilles. It is said that Achilles learned the incredible wound-healing value of this plant from Chiron, his boyhood tutor. You'll remember that Chiron was a centaur (half man/half horse) and a great herbal teacher. You'll also likely remember that Achilles had absolutely no need of *Achillea* because he was invulnerable except for his heel. His mother, Thetis, dipped him into the River Styx as a baby, and the only part of him that wasn't wet was the heel that she used to hold onto him. That heel eventually was his downfall, as Apollo directed the arrow of Paris to that spot to end Achilles' life. I ruefully note that *Achillea* was of no use to Achilles in this particular case.

Sneezewort comes from the use of *Achillea ptarmica* as a form of snuff—hence *sneeze*—and *wort* is, as you already know, the Saxon word for "plant." *Yarrow* is a corruption of the Anglo-Saxon name for the plant *gearwe*. The Dutch called it *yerw*. There are literally hundreds more common names for this plant along the lines of *soldier's woundwort, knight's milfoil, nose bleed, carpenter's weed, staunchweed,* and *bad man's plaything*. Bad man's plaything apparently comes from the use of the plant in divination and sorcery spells and may indeed have been dedicated to who was known in medieval times as the Evil One. *Nose bleed* comes from a rhyme recited in the eastern counties of the United Kingdom, where the plant was called *yarroway*.

> *Yarroway, yarroway, bear a white blow,*
> *If my love me, my nose will bleed now.*

The rhyme was recited as a shoot of *Achillea* was shoved up the nose. If the nose bled, the divination was a success. Other sources say that rolling up a shoot of *Achillea* and packing it into the nostril would stop a nosebleed, while yet others say that a shoot of *Achillea* would start a nosebleed and thus relieve a headache.

Bloom time: Midsummer
Height: 24″ to 36″ (60 cm to 90 cm)
Sun needed: Full sun
Bloom color: Yellows, whites, pinks

Planting space: 18″ (45 cm) apart
Soil preferred: Open, well-drained
Propagation method: Cuttings, division, or seed

Achillea 'Credo'   DOUGLAS GREEN

Achillea 'Anthea'

BLOOMS OF BRESSINGHAM NORTH AMERICA, BARBERTON OH

Recommended Varieties

Achillea x hybrida

'Anthea' is one of the longest blooming varieties on the market. It's 30″ (75 cm) tall and a pale yellow color.

'Apple Blossom' is 36″ (90 cm) tall with lilac-pink blooms.

'Cerise Queen' is 24″ to 30″ (60 cm to 75 cm) tall and mid red. It is seed-generated, so there is a variation in the color; luckily it is easy to start from seed.

'Coronation Gold' is 36″ (90 cm) tall and bright yellow.

'Credo' is 30″ (75 cm) tall in sunset tones of warm orange and yellow.

'Heidi' is 24″ (60 cm) tall and clear pink.

'Moonshine' is one of the early hybrids and remains one of the best, with canary yellow flowers held over silvery foliage. Its height is 24″ (60 cm).

'Paprika' is 30″ (75 cm) tall and is cherry red with lighter golden centers.

'Red Beauty' is 30″ (75 cm) tall and has deep crimson-red blooms.

Although seed-generated mix 'Summer Pastels' won a major plant award and comes up looking good in other people's gardens, it has never given me a bloom color that I would keep in my garden.

Achillea 'Coronation Gold'   DOUGLAS GREEN

Achillea 'Terra Cotta'   DOUGLAS GREEN

'Terra Cotta' is 30″ (75 cm) tall with salmon-pink blooms.

Achillea ptarmica

Achillea ptarmica is a native species. It grows 36″ (90 cm) tall and is quite weedy. I grew it in the garden, but it properly belongs in the wild garden area.

Achillea tomentosa

There are several varieties of *Achillea tomentosa*. It is called *woolly yarrow* because of its silvery, hairy leaf. It is best suited to the rock garden, as it tends to be the short, 12″ to 18″ (30 cm to 45 cm) size.

Growing *Achillea*

Achillea is a plant of full sunshine and meadows. It prefers a well-drained, light soil, and it does best when not overly fed in a lush garden setting. Grow it on the poor side for best results. Clay soils and standing water are to be avoided with this plant. Other than those concerns, put this plant in the ground, and it grows. Do try to avoid allowing the plant to set seed—deadhead carefully. Its reputation as a roadside weed and a copious producer of seed is well deserved. The hybrids need to be deadheaded, as the seeds may not resemble the parent plant. Propagate hybrids by division or cuttings.

Potions and Poisons

The herb has the reputation for stanching wounds when applied as a poultice. The ancient Scots made it into an ointment for spreading on wounded humans and animals. It has already been noted that the pungent leaves have been used as a snuff. It is also used as a tea—a remedy for colds and the relief of melancholy. I'm also told by a reputable source that if men shampoo with it, the plant will prevent baldness. My kids would say it does not work. It should also be noted that Linnaeus wrote that beer brewed with *Achillea* was more potent than beer brewed using hops. There are no concerns associated with the growing of this plant unless the gardener is bald or needs beer badly.

ANTHEMIS

Common names: stinking chamomile, false chamomile

*A*themon is Greek for "flower," and the heavily flowering habit of this plant makes the name truly appropriate. The pejorative use of "stinking" and "false" when applied to this flowering plant is easily explained because the true herbal chamomile was named *Anthemis nobilis* until it was reclassified by the botanists.

Bloom time: Midsummer to late summer
Height: 18″ to 24″ (45 cm to 60 cm)
Sun needed: Full sun
Bloom color: Yellow to orange

Planting space: 18″ to 24″ (45 cm to 60 cm) apart
Soil preferred: Loose, well-drained
Propagation method: Seed

Recommended Varieties

Anthemis tinctoria

Species *Anthemis tinctoria* is sometimes available, but most of the time the variety 'Kelwayi' will be used.

'Kelwayi' is the most easily obtained variety of *Anthemis tinctoria* and one of the heaviest bloomers. It is easy to grow from seed, and once planted its bright yellow blooms will never again be a stranger.

Anthemis sancti johannis

Anthemis sancti johannis is a more orange member of the family. Its bright golden orange blossoms are a hit in any mid-summer garden.

Growing Anthemis

Anthemis loves full sun and well-drained soils. Once you have it established, you can forget to water it, and it will still thrive and flower. It makes a good cut flower and will self-sow with abandon so you'll never lack for seedlings to transplant to other parts of your garden or to give to friends. Each plant is relatively short-lived, two to three years being common, but because of the huge number of seedlings produced, you'll never lack for it. One trick to keeping the plants alive a bit longer is to cut them back almost to the ground in the early fall; this will force them to form rosettes, which are the basis for the following year's growth. If this plant is grown in too fertile a soil, it can grow too sparse and tall and flop over.

Anthemis 'Kelwayi'   Douglas Green

175

ASTILBE

Common name: false goatsbeard

The word *Astilbe* comes from the Greek, and it means "without brightness." This is a reference to the dull nature of the species' leaves or flowers, depending on which resource you consult. It is no longer important to modern gardeners, as both the leaves and flowers of modern varieties are quite bright. The plant is sometimes called *false goatsbeard* because it resembles goatsbeard (see *Aruncus* in Chapter 7) in both leaf and flower form, but it obviously isn't that plant; therefore, it's false.

Bloom time: Midsummer to late summer
Height: 12″ to 36″ (30 cm to 90 cm)
Sun needed: Shade to part shade
Bloom color: Whites, pinks, reds, mauve

Planting space: 18″ to 24″ (45 cm to 60 cm) apart
Soil preferred: Moist but well-drained
Propagation method: Division

Recommended Varieties

Astilbe x arends or *Astilbe arendsii*

The famous German plant breeder George Arends is responsible for giving us this family of hybrid plants that now bears his name. It is a large family, and breeders are adding to the total every year.

'Amethyst' grows to 36″ (90 cm), with lilac flowers tinged with pink.

'Anita Pfeiffer' grows to 30″ (75 cm), with salmon-pink flowers.

'Bressingham Beauty' is 40″ (100 cm) tall with bright pink blossoms. It has long-lasting flowers.

'Cattleya' is 36″ to 40″ (90 cm to 100 cm) tall with lilac-pink blooms. It is late-flowering.

'Diamant' grows to 30″ (75 cm) and is white.

'Elizabeth Bloom' is 24″ (60 cm) tall and has pink blooms. It is a vigorous grower.

'Fanal' grows to 30″ (75 cm) and has dark crimson flowers. It is an old favorite.

'Glut' (also sold as 'Glow') grows to 30″ (75 cm) and has bright red flowers that are late in coming.

Astilbe 'Elizabeth Bloom'

BLOOMS OF BRESSINGHAM NORTH AMERICA, BARBERTON OH

Astilbe 'Diamant'   Douglas Green

Astilbe 'Sprite'

Blooms of Bressingham North America, Barberton OH

'Granat' is 36″ (90 cm) tall and has deep ruby red flowers that fade to a pink shade. It has large blooms.

'Juno' is 24″ to 30″ (60 cm to 75 cm) tall, with shocking bright pink blossoms. It is a heavy bloomer.

'Kriemhilde' is 30″ (75 cm) tall with light pink flower spikes that are quite large.

Astilbe chinensis

Generally, species *Astilbe chinensis* and its varieties are shorter than the *arendsii* hybrids. The leaves are quite fernlike.

'Finale' is 12″ (30 cm) tall and bright pink.

'Pumila' is 8″ to 12″ (20 cm to 30 cm) tall, the foliage is dark red-green, and the pinkish flowers are quite late for a short plant.

'Purple Lance' (or 'Purpurlanze') is 36″ (90 cm) tall and has bright purplish red blooms.

'Serenade' is 12″ to 18″ (30 cm to 45 cm) tall, with pink-red blooms.

Astilbe chinensis taquetii 'Superba'

Don't let the name of *Astilbe chinensis taquetii* 'Superba' turn you off—this is good plant with

flower height to 30″ (75 cm) and purplish pink flowers. Some nurseries sell it as *Astilbe chinensis* 'Superba.'

Astilbe x rosea hybrida

Astilbe x rosea hybrida may be difficult to find in garden centers, but there are specialist nurseries that carry these wonderful plants. The flowers tend to be pyramid-shaped and large, and they are mid-summer bloomers.

Astilbe arendsii 'Bressingham Beauty'

Blooms of Bressingham North America, Barberton OH

Astilbe arendsii 'Juno'   Douglas Green

Astilbe arendsii 'Anita Pfeiffer'   Douglas Green

'Peach Blossom' is 20″ (50 cm) tall and covered with soft peach-pink blooms. It has good glossy green foliage. This may be one of the easiest varieties to find in nurseries.

'Queen Alexandra' is another 18″ to 24″ (45 cm to 60 cm) plant but with dark salmon blooms. It is an excellent plant.

Astilbe simplicifolia x hybrida

'Aphrodite' is 12″ (30 cm) tall and covered in rose red blossoms. The foliage is a bit coarse when compared to others in the family.

'Sprite' is 10″ (25 cm) tall and has shell pink blooms held well above the bronzy foliage. This is a good variety that was a Perennial Plant of the Year.

'William Buchanan' is 8″ to 12″ (20 cm to 30 cm) tall, with creamy white flowers held over crimson-tinged foliage.

Astilbe thunbergii x hybrida

Astilbe thunbergii x hybrida typically blooms later than most of the rest of the *Astilbe* family. The flowers are quite tall and tend to arch. Big patches take on a sweeping look in the garden.

'Professor van der Weilen' has massive plumes of white on a mounding type of foliage. The flowers grow to 48″ (120 cm) tall.

Growing *Astilbe*

Astilbe is a plant for the shade or part-shade garden in soils that are moist. It can be grown in direct sunlight as long as the soil is not allowed to dry out. It is an excellent plant for the pondside garden. It does appreciate organic matter, so either allowing the leaves of sheltering trees to compost naturally or giving it a covering of compost every spring will result in superior plants.

It is necessary to contain this plant, or it will expand and become a nuisance. I regularly dig and trim the edges of the plant mass to restrain their enthusiasm for expansion. Many perennial texts recommended digging up the entire plant every three to five years to divide it and encourage new flowering growth. Mind you, I have plants that have stayed undisturbed for ten years with only regular edging to contain them. They do quite well, and I don't often dig up entire plants just because a text recommends it.

CAMPANULA

Common names: bellflower, rampion

*R*ampion comes from the specific epithet for one of the *Campanula* species, *Campanula rapunculoides*. This is derived from the Latin *rapa*, "turnip." This plant was used as a food source. The roots were boiled or eaten fresh with vinegar, while the young shoots were used as spinach or cooked and blanched like asparagus. As a literary note of interest, it is said that the original Grimm's story of Rapunzul (she's named after the plant) revolves around the theft of rampions from the magician's garden. Modern garden wags would suggest that *rampion* comes from the English word *rampant*, which perfectly describes the spreading nature of the plant. *Bellflower* comes directly from the shape of the flowers, as does *Campanula*, which is the diminutive of *campana*, Latin for "bell."

Bloom time: Midsummer to early fall

Height: 8" to 40" (20 cm to 100 cm)

Sun needed: Sun to part shade

Bloom color: Blues, whites

Planting space: 12" to 18" (30 cm to 45 cm) apart

Soil preferred: Open, well-drained, high in organic matter

Propagation method: Seed or division

Recommended Varieties

Campanula is a large family of desirable plants for specific garden purposes such as rock gardens as well as general garden use. The only negative feature about some of them is their spreading or invasive nature. The other feature that needs to be recognized by gardeners is that the different species can be difficult to identify, and in fact some of the worst of the spreading varieties are masquerading as other plants in the nursery trade. The way to avoid this last problem is to purchase only named varieties from reliable nurseries and avoid growing the species of the taller plants.

Campanula carpatica

Campanula carpatica is a 12" (30 cm) species that starts blooming in my garden in early summer and doesn't finally quit until late summer or early

Campanula rotundifolia   DOUGLAS GREEN

Campanula lactiflora 'Pouffe'
BLOOMS OF BRESSINGHAM NORTH AMERICA, BARBERTON OH

Campanula lactiflora 'White Pouffe'
BLOOMS OF BRESSINGHAM NORTH AMERICA, BARBERTON OH

fall. Two varieties come easily from seed, 'White Clips' and 'Blue Clips.' While 'White Clips' is easily seen to be white, 'Blue Clips' is a mid blue with violet tones. The species is slightly darker than 'Blue Clips.'

'Chewton Joy' is a slightly later blooming variety with a darker blue flower.

Campanula glomerata

At 12″ to 18″ (30 cm to 45 cm) tall, 'Purple Pixie' is a compact growing variety with huge masses of upturned, deep purple flowers. It gives a stunning flower display and is well appreciated in the garden.

Campanula x hybrida

'Dickson's Gold,' 6″ to 8″ (15 cm to 20 cm), has a gold-yellow leaf and mid-blue flowers. The leaves are an excellent contrast to surrounding rocks or other foliage plants. It is not as heavy in blooming as *Campanula carpatica*.

'Elizabeth' is 18″ (45 cm) tall with arching stems and dark pink bell-like flowers.

'Kent Belle' is 24″ (60 cm) tall with tall, arching stems of large violet-purple bells.

'Samantha' started out as a chance seedling in a rock garden. With its 8″ (20 cm) stems covered

with 1″ (2.5 cm) wide, upward-facing, cup-shaped blooms, it is a winner. Look for it on the Internet or at specialty nurseries.

Campanula lactiflora

Species *Campanula lactiflora* is taller than most of the family, and some of these plants are classic garden backbone plants suitable for any perennial border.

'Loddon Anna' is 48″ (120 cm) tall with light pink flowers.

'Pritchard's Variety' is 36″ (90 cm) tall and lavender blue.

'Pouffe' is 24″ (60 cm) tall with light blue flowers.

'White Pouffe' is 24″ (60 cm) tall with white flowers.

Campanula latifolia

'Gloaming' has light blue flowers on tall 48″ (120 cm) stems. It is a wonderful border plant.

Campanula medium

Campanula medium is the old-fashioned Canterbury bells or cup-and-saucer plant. This is technically a biennial and comes as a seed mix in a range of colors. It's so easy to grow yourself as a

Campanula glomerata 'Purple Pixie'

Campanula persificolia 'Chettle Charm'

self-sowing plant that it is almost a crime to pur-chase it from a garden center or nursery.

Campanula persificolia

The peach-leaved bellflower, *Campanula persifi-colia* tends to have midsized flowers and is one of the easiest perennials to grow. It self-sows like mad if happy.

'Chettle Charm' is a 30″ (75 cm) variety with extremely pale porcelain blue flowers flecked with darker violet along the petal edges.

Campanula poscharskyana

This mouthful of a plant (sometimes called *Ser-bian bellflower*) is a classic rock garden plant. It has a prostrate growing habit—usually 6″ (15 cm) high—and as one catalog euphemistically puts it, "spreads rather quickly." This plant spreads so fast it could win horse races. It does do well in shade—or at least shade restricts its growth a bit. Besides the species, you may be able to find 'E. H. Frost,' a white variety with a very pale blue center eye.

Campanula punctata

'Wedding Bells' is a double-flowering variety traditionally known in the flower world as "hose

in hose." This refers to the bloom's having one fully formed flower inside another fully formed flower. At 24″ (60 cm) tall, it is quite attractive with its white outer bloom and red inner bloom. However, and I quote from a plant catalog, "This species is inclined to spread." A word to the wise is sufficient.

Campanula rotundifolia

Campanula rotundifolia, 8″ (20 cm) tall, is perfect for the front of the border or a rock garden. It blooms pale blue flowers over a long period start-ing in midsummer.

Campanula takesimana

Campanula takesimana is sometimes available in catalogs and nurseries. There is no gentle way of

Campanula poscharskyana   DOUGLAS GREEN

Campanula carpatica 'White Clips'   DOUGLAS GREEN

putting this: while the other *Campanula* plants have spreading tendencies and sometimes come with a warning, this is a thug even by *Campanula* family spreading standards. The flowers are attractive with their pale blue bells and darker-spotted inner petals. It took me over four years to get rid of it from my garden after its being there just two years, and I suspect there are still seeds under the mulch just waiting for their chance.

Growing *Campanula*

If you want to see *Campanula*'s growth explode, give it a moist but well-drained soil and stand back. A regular garden soil is fine, although clay is not recommended. Most of the members of this family tolerate part shade and make a fine addition to this part of the garden. The plant self-sows abundantly and can make a nuisance of itself. Some of the species, such as *Campanula rapunculoides* also grow by underground shoots and are considered quite invasive. The advantage of their spreading nature is that they will ulti-

Campanula 'Samantha'   TERRA NOVA NURSERIES

mately colonize places where they are happy. I have several clumps of *Campanula carpatica* that have made themselves charmingly at home in the gravel pathway leaving the garden bed that is for more delicate plants.

CEPHALARIA

Common name: giant scabious

The plant's Greek name comes from *kephale*, "head," referring to the rounded head-shaped flowers it produces. The common name certainly doesn't recommend this plant, but it likely refers to the flower resemblance to the common annual *Scabiosa*, which in turn refers to an itch (Latin for "itch" is *scabies*) caused by the rough leaves.

Bloom time: Midsummer to late summer
Height: 6′ (180 cm)
Sun needed: Full sun
Bloom color: Soft yellow

Planting space: 24″ (60 cm) apart
Soil preferred: Moisture-retaining
Propagation method: Seed or division

Recommended Varieties

Cephalaria gigantea

Cephalaria gigantea is the species most often found in gardens, and at 6′ (180 cm) tall, it is a magnificent specimen for the back of perennial borders in large gardens. Soft yellow blooms contrast nicely with the dark foliage.

Growing *Cephalaria*

Grow *Cephalaria* in full sun in a soil that is moisture-retentive. It is adaptable to a wide range of soils, from good garden soils to clay, as long as it has adequate water to support its huge growth. Even though it is tall, it rarely requires staking because of its tough stems.

Cephalaria gigantea   Douglas Green

CIMICIFUGA

Common names: bugbane, black snakeroot

I list this plant under *Cimicifuga*. Although the official plant name is likely to be changed to *Actaea*, most nurseries will continue to sell it as *Cimicifuga* for some time. In case I'm wrong, simply check under both names in your specialist nurseries to find it.

This name is relatively straightforward. *Cimex* is Latin for "bug," and *fugo* is Latin for "drive away." This name comes from using the plant (specifically *Cimicifuga foetida*) as a bug repellent. *Black snakeroot* comes from the color and shape of the underground-spreading rhizome.

Bloom time: Late summer
Height: 4' to 6' (120 cm to 180 cm)
Sun needed: Prefers shade, tolerates sun
Bloom color: White
Planting space: 18" to 24" (45 cm to 60 cm) apart

Soil preferred: Damp woodland soils high in organic matter
Propagation method: Division; possibly seed

Recommended Varieties

Cimicifuga racemosa

North American native *Cimicifuga racemosa* grows 4' to 5' (120 cm to 150 cm) tall and has white flowers in late summer. I note that the fragrance is not something you'll want to take into the house. This one belongs outside. It is commonly called *bugbane*, and it is well named.

Cimicifuga ramosa

The foliage of *Cimicifuga ramosa* 'Atropurpurea' is a dark purplish color and very attractive. It makes an excellent contrast with the white flower spikes. It can reach 7' (210 cm) in height. 'Brunette' grows to the same height, has even darker foliage, and is highly recommended.

Cimicifuga racemosa   DOUGLAS GREEN

Cimicifuga ramosa 'Atropurpurea'   Douglas Green

Growing *Cimicifuga*

Cimicifuga is a lover of woodland shade and damp sites. It is not for the dry shade but rather does best in moist soils. I have seen it growing out in the main sunny perennial border, and as long as it is not allowed to dry out, it performs reasonably well in the sun.

Potions and Poisons

Cimicifuga was an important medicinal plant to early settlers. It was reputed to be good for snakebite. In small doses it was supposed to be an antidote for children's diarrhea. While not rec-

Cimicifuga ramosa 'Brunette'   Douglas Green

ommended in current medicine, it is unlikely to be a problem unless the roots are dug up and eaten fresh and raw. I note that while I haven't eaten them, the literature says they are quite bitter and not something anybody would want to eat.

CLEMATIS

Common name: clematis

*C*lematis is a straight derivative from the Greek word *klematis*, which was used to refer to climbing plants.

Bloom time: Midsummer to late summer
Height: 36″ to 48″ (90 cm to 120 cm)
Sun needed: Full sun
Bloom color: Blue, violets, white

Planting space: 24″ to 30″ (60 cm to 75 cm) apart
Soil preferred: Rich, organic soils
Propagation method: Cuttings or seed

Recommended Varieties

The *Clematis* family is heavily hybridized in Europe, but unfortunately many of the finer plants have been slow to cross the Atlantic. Even the bush species have multiple listings in European catalogs, yet even the species themselves are hard to find and expensive in nurseries here in North America. I list the species here, but if you find new varieties, simply purchase them, as they'll have better colors or form than the species. I know I'll be doing exactly that.

It is important to emphasize that these *Clematis* are mid- to late-summer bloomers and that they are not vines but rather sprawling bushlike perennials.

Clematis heracleifolia

With blue-violet flowers, *Clematis heracleifolia* is a bush 3′ (90 cm) tall that acts like a perennial flower—it dies to the ground here in zone 4. It might act a little more like a shrub, staying partially alive, in warmer gardens. This staying alive only means you'd have to prune it down to live wood in the spring or cut it to the ground every few years to renew the growth and get rid of old stems. Let me suggest you plant this *Clematis* near another sturdy perennial that can help hold it upright. It does tend to flop a bit, particularly if

the soil is quite fertile. A variety that is available in catalogs is 'Wyevale,' with deeper violet-blue flowers than the species.

Clematis integrifolia

Clematis integrifolia is another bush-type *Clematis* that forms a sprawling clump here in zone 4. The flowers are a really deep violet-blue and nodding. The flowers are followed by wonderfully fluffy seed heads. Plant it next to supporting perennials and cut it to the ground in the fall.

Clematis x jouiniana

Clematis x jouiniana is another of the sprawling bush-type *Clematis*. While perfectly hardy into zone 3, it will tend to be more evergreen in warmer gardens. It does die to the ground here in zone 4. I note that a variety, 'Mrs. Robert Brydon,' is available from nurseries. The flower is off-white with a blue tint. 'Mrs. Robert Brydon' will benefit from staking or being allowed to lean on something quite sturdy.

Clematis stans

Sprawling bush-type *Clematis stans*, 3′ (90 cm) tall, has pale blue starry flowers in midsummer to late summer and is quite attractive in a cottage-style garden. I have several leaning against species roses, and together they create a blue and red show that delights my gardening sense of color.

Growing *Clematis*

Full sun is the preferred garden location, although light shade does not seem to deter either the flowering or survival. The short perennial *Clematis* species and varieties listed here are less upright in the shade than they are in full sunshine; although to be candid, they can be pretty floppy in both situations. They prefer a regular garden soil that is high in organic matter with adequate water. *Clematis* is not a plant of dry lands or heavy clay soils.

Potions and Poisons

Clematis has an extensive use in homeopathy, but it is not recommended for home use. The leaves and flowers can irritate both eyes and skin. Some species, such as *Clematis recta*, are said to contain an alkaloid (clematine) that is a poison. Generally, the data is unclear as to negative effects, but what is clear is that casual contact is not a problem but no part of the plant should be eaten.

Clematis integrifolia © GRAHAM RICE/GARDENPHOTOS.COM

COREOPSIS

Common names: butter daisy, tickseed

Coreopsis comes from the Greek *koris*, "bug," and *opsis*, "like"—buglike. This refers to the shape of the seedhead. And to finish off this name stream, *tickseed* is used because the seed looks like a bug—the tick. *Butter daisy* comes to us from the butter-yellow flower color.

Bloom time: Midsummer to late summer into fall
Height: 18″ to 72″ (45 cm to 180 cm)
Sun needed: Full sun
Bloom color: Shades of yellow, pinks

Planting space: 18″ (45 cm) apart
Soil preferred: Open sandy soil with no clay content
Propagation method: Seed, division, or cuttings

Recommended Varieties

Coreopsis grandiflora

The varieties of *Coreopsis grandiflora* are more short-lived than other species. They depend on self-sowing to increase in the garden. They are also extremely easy to grow from seed, and serious gardeners would never dream of purchasing them when they can be so easily found in seed catalogs.

'Baby Sun' is 18″ (45 cm) high and has a good yellow flower, making it a good summer container plant.

'Double Sunburst' is usually a double flower, although some seeds produce semidouble blooms. It's 36″ (90 cm) tall with golden yellow blooms.

'Early Sunrise' is a semidouble that grows to 24″ (60 cm). It's easy to grow from seed.

Coreopsis rosea

Coreopsis rosea resembles *Coreopsis verticillata* in growth and flower habit. The only difference is that the flowers are a light pink. This plant does best in a moist soil. This is an excellent garden plant.

Coreopsis verticillata

Coreopsis verticillata is a classic perennial flower and rightfully so, with its finely cut leaves, masses of longlasting flowers, and slowly spreading growth habit. It blooms for most of the summer and is rock hardy. The small daisy flowers

Coreopsis grandiflora 'Double Sunburst'
DOUGLAS GREEN

Coreopsis verticillata 'Golden Gain'

BLOOMS OF BRESSINGHAM NORTH AMERICA, BARBERTON OH

Coreopsis verticillata 'Moonbeam' DOUGLAS GREEN

brighten up any garden. *Coreopsis verticillata* tolerates dry ground more than any other *Coreopsis* but still grows well in moist soils.

'Golden Showers' (also called 'Grandiflora') is a gold-yellow bloomer and one of the more vigorous members. It spreads more quickly than other *Coreopsis*, but has never been a problem in my garden.

'Golden Gain' has heavy-blooming, golden flowers that make a good show. It blooms over an extended period of time. Shear it after its first flush of bloom to encourage a second flush.

'Moonbeam' with its pale yellow flowers is one of the most popular perennial flowers, deservedly near the top of any gardener's list. It

is late to appear in the spring; most years it is one of the last flowers to appear, and it is easy to believe it dead. It has a reputation of being short-lived but I have never seen that in my gardens.

Compact 'Zagreb' has very bright yellow flowers and a long flowering period.

Growing *Coreopsis*

Grow *Coreopsis* in full sun in a moist but well-drained soil for best results. Light shade is acceptable for most species, but full sun clearly produces more flowers. This plant produces large numbers of flowers, and if kept deadheaded, it blooms for extended periods of time.

ECHINACEA

Common names: coneflower and variations, such as purple-leaf coneflower

*E*chinacea is named after its seedpods; the Greek root word *echinos* means "sea urchin," in reference to the spiky seedheads on matured flowers. *Coneflower* also refers to the shape of the flower.

Bloom time: Midsummer to late summer into fall
Height: 36″ (90 cm)
Sun needed: Full sun but will tolerate light shade
Bloom color: White, pinks with mauve tones

Planting space: 18″ (45 cm) apart
Soil preferred: Well-drained but fertile
Propagation method: Seed, division, or root cuttings

Recommended Varieties

Echinacea purpurea

'Magnus' is a deeper shade of purplish pink than the species. It has large flowers.

'White Swan' has white blooms 4″ (10 cm) wide on typical upright stems.

Growing *Echinacea*

Grow this large, daisylike plant in full sun in reasonably dry soils. It will need to be watered to

Echinacea purpurea 'Magnus'   Douglas Green

Echinacea purpurea 'Magnus'   Douglas Green

Echinacea purpurea 'White Swan'   Douglas Green

become established, but after that you can ignore the irrigation hoses with this plant. While it doesn't do particularly well in shade, it will tolerate light shade. It makes an excellent cut flower. Let its colorful blossoms grace your kitchen table.

Potions and Poisons

The root of this plant is used medicinally, but its use is not recommended without first seeking medical supervision.

Echinacea purpurea 'White Swan'   Douglas Green

ERYNGIUM

Common name: sea holly

Theophrastus used the Greek word *eyringion* for this plant, and we are stuck with it today even though we have no idea why it was given. *Sea holly* is clear, given the spiny or hollylike leaves and their blue coloring.

Bloom time: Midsummer to late summer
Height: 24″ (60 cm)
Sun needed: Full sun
Bloom color: Steel blue
Planting space: 12″ to 18″ (30 cm to 45 cm) apart

Soil preferred: Well-drained
Propagation method: Seed or careful spring division

Recommended Varieties

Eryngium planum

Eryngium planum is one of the more common species found in gardens. While the species itself is not a superior garden plant (I'm still weeding it out of my garden), some of the varieties are quite showy.

'Sapphire Blue' has a good clear blue coloring to the flowers.

'Roseum' has a flower head that is tinted a rose shade.

'Blauer Zwerg' ('Blue Dwarf' in North America) is a shorter, 18″ (45 cm), plant with an intense blue color.

Eryngium giganteum

This plant, commonly known as Miss Wilmott's ghost, is sometimes found in garden centers. Miss Wilmott, an eccentric English gardener, used to surreptitiously spread seeds of this, her most favorite plant, in the gardens she visited. They would pop up in the unsuspecting host's garden, I'm sure much to their consternation and her

Eryngium planum 'Sapphire Blue'
BLOOMS OF BRESSINGHAM NORTH AMERICA, BARBERTON OH

Eryngium planum   DOUGLAS GREEN

delight. It is relatively short-lived but taller, at 48″ (120 cm), than most other species.

Growing *Eryngium*

If given full sun and well-drained soil, *Eryngium* can become a bit of a nuisance. It self-sows with abandon, and the deep roots make digging it up a bit of a chore. The one single thing that characterizes all species of this plant is the demand for perfect drainage if they are to survive—no clay for this one. *Eryngium* plants make excellent cut and dried flowers. If the garden soil is damp in

the fall and tends to stay wet in the winter, try clearing away all the foliage around the crown of the plant so it doesn't rot—and subsequently spread that rot to the crown.

Potions and Poisons

The roots of *Eryngium maritinum* were considered to be an aphrodisiac, so gardeners should be careful when transplanting it. Other species have been used as flavorings and tonics, so there is no concern with growing this plant—assuming you don't go messing about with the roots.

FILIPENDULA

Common name: meadowsweet

Filipendula comes from the Latin word *filum*, "thread," and *pendulus*, "drooping," referring to the way the tubers of some of the species appear when dug up. Dr. Prior says "Meadowsweet—an ungrammatical and ridiculous name, a corruption of mead-wort from Anglo Saxon." Mead was honey wine and wort is our old friend—"plant."

Bloom time: Midsummer to late summer
Height: 36″ to 60″ (90 cm to 150 cm)
Sun needed: Part shade
Bloom color: White, pink

Planting space: 18″ (45 cm) apart
Soil preferred: Moist
Propagation method: Division or seed

Recommended Varieties

Filipendula hexapetala

'Kakome' is 12″ (30 cm) tall and topped with rosy pink flowers from midsummer to late summer. It's an excellent dwarf variety, does very well in damp ground next to ponds, and is suited for full sunlight in damp soils.

Filipendula ulmaria

Filipendula ulmaria is one of the taller species, growing up to 6′ (180 cm) in height. While it prefers damp soils, it will tolerate sunshine as long as the soils are moist.

The leaves on 'Aurea' are golden yellow in the spring fading to green in the summer. It's 36″ (90 cm) tall.

'Rosea' is 36″ (90 cm) tall with lovely pinkish flowers.

'Variegata' has fully variegated leaves—a yellow stripe down the middle. It has white flowers and grows to 36″ (90 cm) tall.

Growing *Filipendula*

Filipendula is best suited for streamside or bog gardens or any garden where damp soils are present. It does best in a cool, semishaded site. Specific species may have different sunlight needs, as already mentioned. This plant has been advertised in some nurseries as being a full-sun border plant, and I believe that to be a mistake. It thrived in my garden in the shade of other, taller plants but did much better when I moved a division to damper soil and protected it from the midday sun.

Potions and Poisons

Filipendula is a plant with a long and storied herbal history. It is one of the fifty ingredients in a drink called *save* that is mentioned by Chaucer

---

1. R. C. A. Prior, M.D., *On the Popular Names of British Plants* (London: Williams and Norgate, 1863), page 149.

Filipendula hexapetala 'Kakome'   Blooms of Bressingham North America, Barberton OH

in "The Knight's Tale" from *The Canterbury Tales*. It has been added to wines and beers for its aromatic powers. *Gerard's Herbal* says, "It is reported that the floures boiled in wine and drunke do take away the fits of a quartaine ague and make the heart merrie."[2] Flowers or wine— take your pick, I suppose, as to which one makes you merry. There are no special concerns with growing this plant in the garden, although qualified advice should be sought before trying to use it.

---

2. M. Grieve, *Gerard's Herbal*, in *A Modern Herbal*, 3rd ed. (London: Tiger Books, 1992), page 524.

GAILLARDIA

Common name: blanket flower

The plant was named in 1786 by botanist Fougeroux de Bondaroy after a French magistrate and patron of botany, Gaillard de Charentonneau. *Blanket flower* escapes my historical sleuthing.

Bloom time: Midsummer to late summer
Height: 12″ to 24″ (30 cm to 60 cm)
Sun needed: Full sun
Bloom color: Warm oranges, reds, yellows

Planting space: 12″ to 18″ (30 cm to 45 cm) apart
Soil preferred: Well-drained, medium fertility
Propagation method: Seed

Recommended Varieties

Gaillardia x grandiflora

Gaillardia x grandiflora is the most commonly available hybrid range and the best overall garden performer.

'Mandarin' is 24″ (60 cm) tall and a good bicolor. It is a very long bloomer in flower, from early to late summer.

'Royal Monarch Blend' is a seed-generated blend that you should grow from seed yourself, as they are quite easy to grow, rather than buying the plants.

Growing *Gaillardia*

Grow *Gaillardia* in the full sunshine in moderately fertile but well-drained soils. It's very tolerant of heat and drought. This plant will die out over the winter in clay soils or with poor drainage. The only problem with this plant is that it blooms itself to death; heavy bloom production often leaves it weakened and susceptible to winter death. Luckily it produces copious amounts of seed, and you'll seldom be without them if they like your garden. They do tend to wander about the garden, so get used to the look of the seedling so you don't weed all of the new crop. It doesn't hurt to cut *Gaillardia* back when it is finished flowering, and during the winter, protect it from crown rot by placing evergreen boughs over it to stop ice formation on the crown. If you stop the ice from forming on the crown, the plant has a much-improved winter success rate.

Gaillardia x grandiflora 'Mandarin'
BLOOMS OF BRESSINGHAM NORTH AMERICA, BARBERTON OH

GAURA

Common name: butterfly gaura

The name *Gaura* comes from the Greek word *gauros*, meaning "superb," referring to the flowers. The flowers superficially resemble butterflies, hence the common name.

Bloom time: Midsummer to late summer
Height: 24″ to 36″ (60 cm to 90 cm)
Sun needed: Sun or very light shade
Bloom color: White, pink

Planting space: 18″ (45 cm) apart
Soil preferred: Well-drained, sandy
Propagation method: Seed

Recommended Varieties

Gaura lindheimeri

The species *Gaura lindheimeri* is fine in the garden if you can find it in a local garden center. Otherwise purchase the seed (widely available) and start your own.

'Corries Gold' is a variegated leaf selection; its flowers are white. Frankly, this plant looks sick to me. I know leaf variegation is supposed to be garden-sexy, but on this plant it merely makes the plant look diseased. This plant must be propagated from cuttings rather than seed, and this, thankfully, will reduce its availability.

'Siskiyou Pink' is a light pink variety and well worth growing in the garden. It does best on well-drained sites. Note that clay will kill this plant.

'Whirling Butterflies' is a shorter variety at 24″ (60 cm), and it flowers for a longer time than the other two varieties listed. It is worth growing in any garden.

Growing Gaura

Plant *Gaura* in a light soil (sandy) with excellent drainage. Clay kills this plant. It prefers full sun but will tolerate a bit of shade during the midday heat or later on in the day. If it gets too floppy, you're not giving it enough sunlight. Once established, it can tolerate drier soils. Save the seed; you can grow lots more of your own.

Gaura lindheimeri 'Siskiyou Pink'   Douglas Green

GENTIANA

Common name: gentian

Gentiana is said to be named for Gentius, an ancient King of Illyria (180–167 B.C.). He is reputed to be the discoverer of the medicinal uses of the *Gentiana* roots.

Bloom time: Late summer
Height: 12″ to 60″ (30 cm to 150 cm)
Sun needed: Shade
Bloom color: Electric blue

Planting space: 18″ (45 cm) apart
Soil preferred: Constantly moist
Propagation method: Seed or careful division

Recommended Varieties

I get quite grumpy when I see the lists of this plant that are available in Europe that have not yet made their way to my gardens. The flowers of *Gentiana* are the most electric blue, colors that almost defy description. I installed a garden pond in a shady area of my garden simply to provide a habitat for this plant family. Does this sound like I'm encouraging you to find some of these plants? Well, I am if you follow the rules for growing them below. If you don't follow the rules, you'll have miserable luck with them and you will never be able to become as enthusiastic as I am about this plant.

Gentiana gelida

Gentiana gelida grows to 18″ (45 cm) and does well for me even in part sun and drier soils. There is a white variety as well as the more common blue. There are hybrids available in Europe, but I have never seen them here in North America.

Gentiana linearis

Gentiana linearis is a good blue color and grows to 18″ (45 cm).

Gentiana lutea

Gentiana lutea is a strong grower, reaching 48″ to 60″ (120 cm to 150 cm) with yellow flowers.

Gentiana septemfida

Gentiana septemfida is commonly available in nurseries, but it is a plant of rock gardens and not perennial borders. You might grow it in the front of a shady border, but it seems to do best when its roots can hide down in the cool protection under rocks.

Growing Gentiana

There are approximately four hundred species of *Gentiana*, and not all are available for gardens. There are two distinct uses for them in the garden: in the alpine or rock garden and in the shadier late-summer-blooming garden. Luckily for our purposes, the taller plants do tend to be a bit easier to grow as long as they are given the conditions they demand. And for the most part, those that grow in our gardens are either Japanese or North American plants of shade and damp soils. This is not a plant to grow in dry

Gentiana angustifolia   Douglas Green

Gentiana gelida   Douglas Green

shade; it will not survive those conditions. It is also a plant of cool summers; it does not appreciate high, baking temperatures.

Potions and Poisons

During the Middle Ages, *Gentiana* was used as an antidote to poisoning. Every part of the plant—from root to flower—is bitter and was much used for this reason as a general tonic. This bitterness also led to its use in brewing alongside the more traditional hops. This herb is reputed to be one of the best when used for general exhaustion and strengthening of the immune system. Even though it has such a bitter taste, caution is recommended with small children.

INULA

Common name: elecampane

Inula is supposedly a corruption of *Helenium* (see Chapter 9). *Elecampane* is a little more complicated. Botanist Vegetius Renatus in the fifth century called the plant *Inula campana*, and St. Isidore, writing in the seventh century, shortened that to *Inula*. Medieval writers wrote it as *enula* changing the *i* to *e*. After Linnaeus finished his masterwork of codifying plant names, the plant became *enula campana* and was simply shortened by common usage to *elecampane*.

Bloom time: Midsummer to late summer
Height: 24″ to 36″ (60 cm to 90 cm)
Sun needed: Full sun to very light shade
Bloom color: Yellow

Planting space: 18″ (45 cm) apart
Soil preferred: Well-drained, regular soils
Propagation method: Seed or division

Recommended Varieties

Inula helenium

Inula helenium grows 24″ to 36″ (60 cm to 90 cm) tall, with large gold-yellow daisy flowers. This is the plant referred to as *elecampane* by herbalists.

Inula ensifolia

The species *Inula ensifolia* grows to 24″ (60 cm), with some good shorter varieties available.

'Compacta' is only 12″ (30 cm) tall with gold-yellow blooms.

'Gold Star' is 12″ (30 cm) tall with bright gold-yellow blooms.

Inula royleana

Inula royleana is 24″ (60 cm) tall with a flat, stiff, yellow daisy flower. It makes an excellent cut flower. It is a bit hard to start from seed but is long-lasting in the garden. It is one of my favorites.

Inula helenium   DOUGLAS GREEN

Growing *Inula*

Inula is a bright yellow daisy for the summer border. Grow it in full sun or very light shade for a wonderful display of daisy blooms. It prefers well-drained soils that are medium in fertility (a soil too high in fertility makes them floppy and ugly) and medium in moisture availability. *Inula helenium* will tolerate more sun and damp soils than other species—you can almost grow this one in a bog. If you grow *Inula* in fertile or well-watered soils, it may become invasive, so it is a good idea to keep a sharp shovel handy in the spring to prevent it from overtaking less vigorous plants.

Potions and Poisons

The roots of *Inula* are well regarded in herbal medicine as a gentle tonic. Do not use *Inula* unless under competent medical advice, but there are no concerns to growing the plant in the garden.

KNIPHOFIA

Common names: torch lily, red hot poker

The plant was named for J. H. Kniphof (1704–1756), a German botanist. *Torch lily* is pretty clear—if you've ever seen one bloom with the spikes of reds and oranges, it does look like a flowering torch. *Red hot poker* comes from the same line of thinking.

Bloom time: Midsummer to late summer
Height: 18″ to 36″ (45 cm to 90 cm)
Sun needed: Full sun
Bloom color: Reds, oranges, yellow
Planting space: 12″ to 18″ (30 cm to 45 cm) apart

Soil preferred: Well-drained, fertile, high in organic matter
Propagation method: Seed or division

Recommended Varieties

There are approximately sixty-eight individual species of *Kniphofia*, and most are from South Africa. Most of the species plants are available only from specialist growers. Luckily there are a good many hybrids in the nursery trade. This is a plant that is marginally hardy for me. I'm still experimenting with different species and locations to find some truly hardy ones. The best are below.

Kniphofia x hybrida

'Bressingham Comet' is 24″ (60 cm) tall with yellow and orange flowers. It flowers in midsummer to early fall.

'Primrose Beauty' is 30″ to 36″ (75 cm to 90 cm) tall, and the flowers are a softer yellow. This may be one of the hardier hybrids.

'Royal Castle' is 36″ (90 cm) tall and comes in a range of colors (from seed). You can start them yourself.

'Shining Sceptre' is 36″ (90 cm) tall and has golden orange flowers in midsummer to late summer. It is an excellent plant.

Growing *Kniphofia*

Grow *Kniphofia* in full, hot sun in a rich, fertile soil. The soil should be well-drained but contain large amounts of organic matter to provide regular moisture levels—particularly during flowering, as if the plant dries out while flowering, the blooms fade quickly. If growing this plant in zone 4, it helps to put evergreens over the crown in the winter to prevent ice forming on it (ice kills the crown and rots the plant). Then add a deep layer of mulch (leaves are perfect, as they can be swept away from the crown in the spring and left to decompose) to protect the root from temperatures below 5° F (−15° C). *Kniphofia* does not like having its roots disturbed, so do plant it where you want it to stay.

Kniphofia 'Bressingham Comet'   Blooms of Bressingham North America, Barberton OH

LAVANDULA

Common name: lavender

*L*avender is simply derived from the Latin *lavo*, meaning "to wash." This comes from the common use of the plant for bath and in toiletries.

Bloom time: Midsummer until late summer
Height: 12″ to 24″ (30 cm to 60 cm); to 36″ (90 cm) in mild climates if unpruned
Sun needed: Full, hot sun

Bloom color: Blues, violets, pale pinks, and whites
Planting space: 18″ (45 cm) apart
Soil preferred: Sandy, well-drained soils
Propagation method: Seeds or cuttings

Recommended Varieties

There are two different types of *Lavandula* found in garden centers. The first is the English-type: *Lavandula angustifolia*, *Lavandula latifolia*, and increasingly *Lavandula x intermedia*. These are the hardier plants that I grow in my garden. The second is a more tender type, called the French lavenders, and these are more suited for a zone 6 or 7 garden or indoor pot-culture in cooler areas; these include *Lavandula stoechas*, *Lavandula dentata*, and *Lavandula lanata*. I have tried all the French types outdoors at one time or other over twenty years of gardening, and while the dream is sound, the practical side of it has the plants dying with every effort. They will start to die when the temperatures near 20° F (−5° C). Increasingly larger numbers of the hardier types are available in garden centers and catalogs, but the more tender plants are not appearing in the same way.

Lavandula angustifolia

Lavandula angustifolia is the plant we call English lavender and is the classic lavender of gardening lore.

'Blue Cushion' is 12″ to 18″ (30 cm to 45 cm) tall, with deep blue-violet flowers on a compact-mounding plant.

'Hidcote' is 18″ to 24″ (45 cm to 60 cm) tall and deep violet.

'Jean Davis' is 18″ (45 cm) and pale pink.

'Lavender Lady' is a mid lavender-blue. It blooms the first year from seed.

'Loddon Blue' is a more compact grower than 'Hidcote,' but its deep violet flower color and form are comparable.

'Munstead,' also known as 'Compacta Nana,' is 18″ (45 cm) tall with a blue-lilac flower. The name 'Compacta Nana' is no longer used for any lavender plant, and if you see it, you're getting either the 'Munstead' plant or one of the *Lavandula x intermedia* plants called 'Twickle Purple.'

Lavandula dentata

The species *Lavandula dentata* is 24″ to 36″ (60 cm to 90 cm) tall, and its flowers are lilac with a tinge of purple. There is a silver-leaved variety called 'Silver Form,' with soft leaves that are silverier than the species and with large blue-violet flowers.

Lavandula angustifolia 'Blue Cushion'

BLOOMS OF BRESSINGHAM NORTH AMERICA, BARBERTON OH

Lavandula angustifolia   DOUGLAS GREEN

Lavandula latifolia

You can sometimes find the seed of species *Lavandula latifolia* in specialist catalogs. It can grow to 36″ (90 cm) tall in milder or protected gardens. The flowers are dark purple. With all the good varieties available, I wouldn't recommend you take the time with this species unless you are hopelessly addicted to lavenders and have collected all other varieties.

Lavandula x intermedia

Lavandula x intermedia are mostly hybrids between *Lavandula angustifolia* and *Lavandula latifolia*. Some are tender in my garden, but all are wonderful.

'Grosso' offers deep violet blooms on a thickly branched plant. One of the most fragrant hybrids, it is the main variety used in commercial production in both France and the United States.

'Hidcote Giant' grows to 24″ (60 cm) with a deep, rich purple flower. The plant has "open coarse" growth—that is, it is not compact and the stems become woodier more quickly than other varieties.

'Provence' is 24″ (60 cm) tall and has dark purple flowers. It is one of my favorites.

'Twickle Purple' (also known as 'Twinkles' and 'Twickes') is 24″ (60 cm) tall with purple flowers. It has broad, flat leaves flushed purple in winter. The plant needs heavy pruning after blooming to thicken it up, or it can become leggy. This is one of the best culinary varieties.

Lavandula stoechas

Lavandula stoechas is the classic French lavender plant. The leaf is a grayish color, and on the species the flowers are reddish purple. It will not survive in my garden outdoors, but I have overwintered it in well-protected containers buried under several feet of straw.

'Alba' is a white variety.

'James Compton' has deep purple flowers.

'Papillon' is a bright purple variety.

Lavandula lanata

Lavandula lanata, 24″ (60 cm) tall, is one of the more easily found tender varieties.

'Richard Gray' has gray-tinted leaves and purple flowers.

Growing *Lavandula*

Lavandula is a plant for the full, hot sun in well-drained soils. Gardens that are too fertile will have poorer-scented plants than those that are "tough," with sandy or gravelly soils. Excessive moisture, particularly over the winter, will kill this plant. Clay soils are not for this plant—you'll be running a mortuary rather than a garden.

Commercially, growers find that a plant lasts approximately five years before it starts to "run out" and decline in health. They take cuttings and propagate the plant so that there are always new ones coming along to replace those that die. Some garden experts say that you can expect a garden plant to last up to ten years before it starts to wither away. Mine have tended toward the five- or six-year mark, but it is hard to say whether it is winter doing the killing or simply the plants getting weaker, or even a combination of the two factors. Whichever is the case, I too take new cuttings every year.

Potions and Poisons

There are no concerns at all about growing *Lavandula*. At times in the past it was used to ease stomach discomfort. I note that it is still used in cooking, and recipes crop up now and again for its use.

LAVATERA

Lavatera was named in honor of J. R. Lavater, a seventeenth-century Swiss physician and naturalist. *Tree mallow* comes from the plant's woody nature and the fact that the flowers look like those of the Malva, or mallow, family.

Bloom time: Midsummer to late summer
Height: 48″ to 60″ (120 cm to 150 cm)
Sun needed: Sun to light shade
Bloom color: Pinks and white
Planting space: 24″ to 30″ (60 cm to 75 cm) apart

Soil preferred: Good garden soil, even moisture
Propagation method: Seed, division, or cuttings

Recommended Varieties

Lavatera arborea

Lavatera arborea has not been hardy here in zone 4 yet. I've tried it two times, and it has been so much mush the following springs. It should be hardy in zone 5 but unfortunately not here. There are a few good varieties, including a variegated variety 'Variegata' and an excellent pink 'Rosea.' If you can grow it, it will reach 8′ to 9′ (240 cm to 270 cm) and flower profusely in midsummer to late summer, covering itself with literally hundreds of pink flowers. In truly benign climates, the stems will overwinter and the plant behaves like a woody shrub rather than dying to the ground as a perennial does.

Lavatera cachemiriana

Lavatera cachemiriana is 4′ to 6′ (120 cm to 180 cm) and has been more than hardy in my garden; it has been downright weedy. But I love it all the same for its clear pink blooms and mid-summer to late-summer explosion of color. It is a thin, rangy plant and so belongs in a tall mixed-perennial border. I note that it will tell you

where it is happy because it will self-sow there. It is not fussy, having survived in my garden in full, hot sun in good soil, hot sun in poor sandy soil, and part shade in fertile, sandy soils. Even though it's tall, it is not blown over or otherwise damaged by winds or weather.

Lavatera thuringiaca

Known as tree lavatera, *Lavatera thuringiaca* is hardy as a perennial in zone 4. It dies to the ground over winter but makes up for it by being smothered in blooms starting in midsummer and lasting for a good six to eight weeks. It does not self-sow (the seeds are hard to start—even in a greenhouse) rampantly like *Lavatera cachemiriana*, but new plants do pop up from time to time. It pains me to say, but there are few of these plants available in North America as compared with Europe, but I'm quite hopeful that this situation will change. You should be able to find the following varieties:

'Barnsley' has a whitish flower with a red eye that fades to pink. The four varieties are a touch more tender than the species plant gracing my garden, but this one has overwintered here for

Lavatera thuringiaca DOUGLAS GREEN

Lavatera cachemiriana DOUGLAS GREEN

me. Mind you, I've also lost it in a harsh, cold winter. Prune off any branches that produce pure pink flowers—you may get one or two a season. It hasn't been a problem for me.

'Candy Floss' has pale pink flowers, even paler than the species.

'Pink Frills' has ruffled flowers and soft pink blooms with a darker veining.

'Rosea' has flowers of a pinky mauve.

Growing *Lavatera*

Each one of the hundreds of flowers produced by *Lavatera* plants is short-lived, but their sheer profusion compensates for their lack of durability.

The reference texts say to grow this plant in full sun, in sandier soils (clay will kill them), under moderate fertility. If you overfeed, they'll grow foliage like mad but slow down on flower production. They tend to self-sow in places where they shouldn't grow and manage to exist and bloom. Start them in the correct place and then let them wander around until they are happy.

Potions and Poisons

The leaves of *Lavatera arborea* have been steeped in hot water and applied as a poultice to sprains and strains. There is no indication that they are poisonous.

MACLEAYA

Common name: plume poppy

*M*acleaya was named after Alexander Macleay (1767–1848). He was colonial secretary to New South Wales, Australia, and once occupied the position of secretary to the Linnean Society of London. The plant is a member of the *Papaveraceae* family (the botanic poppy family), so the common name *plume poppy* comes from its long, flowering plumes and its family connection.

Bloom time: Midsummer to late summer
Height: 8′ (240 cm)
Sun needed: Full sun to part shade
Bloom color: White to pinkish red

Planting space: 24″ to 36″ (60 cm to 90 cm) apart
Soil preferred: Moist but well-drained
Propagation method: Division, but seed works

Recommended Varieties

Macleaya cordata

Macleaya cordata is the main plant in this family to be grown in the garden. The flowers are a beige-pink color with white in tall plumes or racemes.

'Flamingo' grows the same as the species but has more pinkish flowers.

Macleaya microcarpa

Macleaya microcarpa is the same height as *Macleaya cordata*, and the main difference is that the flowers are more flushed with pink. Its reputation as a spreader is that it is slightly less invasive than its cousin *Macleaya cordata*.

The flowers on 'Kelways Coral Plume' variety are a deep coral color.

Growing *Macleaya*

Macleaya is a tall plant that makes quite a statement in the garden. Its large, bold leaves and towering plumes ensure it will be the central focal area wherever it is sited in the garden. It loves slightly dampish but well-drained soils but will gladly grow in regular garden soil. The plant does spread quickly by underground runners, so its enthusiasm will have to be contained with a sharp shovel every spring. I regularly have to pull runners out of a nearby *Monarda*, and these two plants have been jostling for many years for a bit of extra garden space. Some authorities recommend staking the plant, but I have never found this necessary.

Macleaya MICK HALES

MALVA

Common name: mallow

*M*alva is Latin and means "mallow." It was derived from the Greek word *malache*, which is a derivative of *malachos*, meaning "soothing." The soothing part refers to its medicinal use.

Bloom time: Midsummer to late summer
Height: 24″ to 36″ (60 cm to 90 cm)
Sun needed: Full sun
Bloom color: Rose, purples, white, pink

Planting space: 12″ to 18″ (30 cm to 45 cm) apart
Soil preferred: Well-drained
Propagation method: Seed

Recommended Varieties

Malva moschata

Known as *musk mallow*, *Malva moschata* is a roadside weed in both pink and white varieties, but sometimes you will find it offered in nurseries. I let the less common white form into my garden fifteen years ago, and I'm still weeding it out.

Malva sylvestris

Known as *tall mallow*, *Malva sylvestris* is commonly found in garden centers or seed catalogs. It comes in a wide range of reds and red-purples; some wander over into pinks and whites. It self-sows with abandon, and you'll never want for it if you grow it one year. It is much more attractive than the common musk mallow, so I allow one variety to live in my garden. It is a historical plant that a friend's grandmother grew on their hundred-year-old farm, and he shared a seedling with me. 'Lloyd's Red' is not available in the nursery trade, but Lloyd and I share the plant. You could do the same by selecting a color you like and then only allowing this color to set seed. Pull up all others you don't like.

'Zebrina' is a lightly striped variety in shades of rose-purple that is worth growing.

Growing *Malva*

Malva will grow where it wants. Normally, it prefers full, hot sun on well-drained soils and is found mostly on gravel soils beside roads. Plant it in this kind of spot and let it wander around your garden as it will.

Potions and Poisons

Malva's foliage is edible, and herbal teas made from it are reputed to be a remedy for colds.

Malva sylvestris 'Lloyd's Red'   Douglas Green

MECONOPSIS

Common names: Himalayan blue poppy, blue poppy, Asiatic poppy

*M*econopsis's name comes directly from the Greek *mekon* for "poppy" and *opsis*, meaning "likeness" or "appearance." *Blue poppy* is rather obvious to those who have seen the pale blue flowers, and *Himalayan* merely describes one of its native habitats, as does *Asiatic*. It is also a member of *Papaveraceae*.

Bloom time: Midsummer to late summer
Height: 6″ to 36″ (15 cm to 90 cm)
Sun needed: Shade to part shade
Bloom color: Yellow, blue shades

Planting space: 12″ (30 cm) apart
Soil preferred: Woodland soils, high in organic matter
Propagation method: Seed

Recommended Varieties

Meconopsis cambrica

Known as *Welsh poppy*, *Meconopsis cambrica* is a free-blooming yellow species that gets to only 6″ to 8″ (15 cm to 20 cm) in height. It will grow almost anywhere and is most often found in poorly fertilized, well-drained soils in rock gardens. It will self-sow and if happy in its location, will become a delightful nuisance.

'Flore-Pleno' is a semidouble- to double-flowering orange-yellow variety.

'Frances Perry' has a much redder bloom than the species.

Meconopsis betoncifolia

Meconopsis betoncifolia is one of the two species that is most commonly available in catalogs and garden centers. It can hit 4′ (120 cm) tall in a suitable climate and its sky blue flowers are a gardener's delight. There is a white flowering variety, 'Alba,' which differs in growth habit and cultivation in the color of its flowers.

Meconopsis x sheldonii

Meconopsis x sheldonii hybrids are sometimes available through specialty catalogs, and if you can grow this plant, these are the varieties to search for. They tend to be more perennial than other species and hybrids. These also grow best on acidic soils.

'Blue Ice' has intense electric blue flowers.

Meconopsis betoncifolia 'Jean Brown'   DOUGLAS GREEN

211

Meconopsis betoncifolia   Douglas Green

Meconopsis cambrica   Douglas Green

'Crewdson' are light sky blue hybrids, with some variation in coloring.

'Lingholm' has flowers that are medium sky blue and 2″ (5 cm) across. Bright yellow anthers stand out.

Growing *Meconopsis*

With one exception, *Menconopsis cambrica*, *Meconopsis* is a plant of the high summer humidity and mild winters of Himalayan Asia. It grows in part-shade conditions (the more sunlight you give, the paler the blossoms will be). The soil has to be fertile, constantly moist but not waterlogged, and have good drainage in the winter so the plant does not rot. Water collecting around the crown of the plant will kill any species. The soil should be lime-free—of an acidic nature.

If you try to grow it without high humidity and cool summer temperatures, you are bound to be disappointed. Cold winters will kill it particularly, as already stated, if the plant is allowed to stay damp. The trick in growing *Meconopsis* is to find a place next to a source of humidity in part shade and create a miniclimate specifically for this plant. This is not a plant for the main perennial border, and it will die if planted out in the hot sun.

Meconopsis is *monocarpic*. This means that it will die after it flowers. It may take several years for the plant to get large enough to produce a flower crop, but once it does this, the main plant will die. Gardeners have experimented with removing flower blossoms from this plant to force it to grow quite large and strong. In other words, stop it from blooming for several years, and the resulting accumulated strength will enable it to bloom for several years in a row. In effect, this turns it into a tender and short-lived perennial rather than a biennial or monocarpic plant.

MONARDA

Common names: beebalm, bergamot, Oswego tea

*M*onarda was named for Nicholas Monardes (1493–1588), a physician and botanist of Seville, Spain. He published a botany book listing new plants called *Joyfull Newes of the newe founde Worlde* in 1569, 1571, and 1574 that was translated into English in 1577. The name *bergamot* was given to this plant because it is said to have much the same fragrance as the bergamot orange. *Beebalm* came into use because of the passionate way bees swarm *Monarda*'s flowers in search of nectar. *Oswego tea* was used (perhaps in derision by Europeans) because of *Monarda*'s use by North Americans as a tea drink. If you read the list of ingredients in Earl Grey tea now, you'll see *Monarda* listed on the packaging.

Bloom time: Midsummer to late summer
Height: 12″ to 36″ (30 cm to 90 cm)
Sun needed: Full sun
Bloom color: Reds, violets, pink-whites

Planting space: 24″ (60 cm) apart
Soil preferred: Open, sandy
Propagation method: Division and with cuttings

Recommended Varieties

Monarda x didyma

'Adam' has large, light red flowers.

'Beauty of Cobham' has a lilac-pink flower with a purplish tone to the foliage.

'Cambridge Scarlet' is an older variety with bright red flowers. It is not mildew-resistant.

'Croftway Pink' is bright pink and one of the showiest flowers in the garden.

'Gardenview Scarlet' has brilliant red flowers, with some tolerance to mildew.

'Jacob Kline' has bright red flowers and is mildew-resistant.

'Marshall's Delight' is a Canadian introduction. It has hot-pink flowers and is very mildew-resistant.

'Panorama Mix' is a seed strain with quite a wide range of colors. I've never liked it as it is too variable. It is normally quite cheap to purchase, but it is better to purchase named varieties and colors.

'Petite Delight' is another Canadian introduction. It has a dwarf growth habit, to 12″ (30 cm) tall, with lavender-pink flowers. It has good mildew resistance.

'Prairie Night' is a German introduction with dark purple flowers.

'Snow White' has white flowers that are smaller than the norm.

'Violet Queen' has a deep purple flower and is a vigorous grower. It is an older variety.

Growing *Monarda*

Monarda is an excellent clump-forming plant for the main herbaceous border and is one of those particularly useful plants because of its long blooming season. Give *Monarda* full sun and a well-drained soil. Good growth is encouraged

Monarda x didyma 'Adam'   DOUGLAS GREEN

Monarda x didyma 'Croftway Pink'   DOUGLAS GREEN

with a yearly topdressing of compost and a constant mulch to help keep the soil cool and evenly moist. The plant expands by creeping rhizomes under the ground and will require yearly digging to keep it within bounds. If you find that the center is dying out, dig up the dead areas and enrich the soil with compost in these areas. The outer shoots will quickly recolonize the well-composted soil.

Clean the debris up in the fall, as leftover leaves and stems can shelter mildew spores over the winter. Mildew is the only problem that sometimes bothers these plants.

Potions and Poisons

Monarda is a culinary herb.

Monarda x didyma 'Marshall's Delight'
DOUGLAS GREEN

NEPETA

Common names: catnip, catnep

The common names *catnip* and *catnep* are for all intents and purposes the same, and as anyone who has grown this plant will attest, it drives cats crazy. Interestingly enough, cats only tend to bother those plants that are already bruised in some way, as this tends to release the distinctive fragrance of this member of the mint family. The old garden saying, "If you set it, the cats will eat it; if you sow it, the cats won't know it," holds true.

Rather unromantically, *Nepeta* itself is the name used by the Roman Pliny for the plant. Historians think it may have been named after Nepi, Italy.

Bloom time: Midsummer

Height: 12″ to 36″ (30 cm to 90 cm)

Sun needed: Full sun

Bloom color: Blues, whites

Planting space: 18″ to 24″ (45 cm to 60 cm) apart

Soil preferred: Open, sandy, well-drained soils

Propagation method: Seed, cuttings, or division

Recommended Varieties

It wasn't all that long ago that many of the common garden varieties of *Nepeta* were classified as variations of *Nepeta x faassenii*. This always confused me because the original *Nepeta x faassenii* is a sterile hybrid, and it is this confusion that likely proves I am not a botanist. In the latest go-round of name classification, the varieties have been moved into different families, and it is this format that I present to you. No matter what species they are lumped under, the names will hold true as will their wonderful garden performance.

Nepeta cataria

'Citriodora' is a lemon-scented catnip that deserves a place in the garden for its fragrant leaves. The flowers are not overly spectacular, so grow it in the herb garden.

Nepeta x faassenii

Nepeta x faassenii is a sterile garden clone and is the classic pale lavender-blue garden plant of 18″ (45 cm).

Nepeta grandiflora

Nepeta grandiflora is my favorite in the family. It grows to 36″ (90 cm) tall in my garden and, with a bit of support from nearby plants, stands upright to give a truly wonderful display of blue-violet flowers.

'Bramdean' is a well shaped plant, not leggy. Lavender-blue flowers offer extended summer bloom time.

'Dawn to Dusk' has soft pink blooms with a darker calyx.

'Pool Bank' has rich blue flowers and darker calyces. They are long-blooming.

Nepeta x sintenisii 'Six Hills Giant'   DOUGLAS GREEN

Nepeta x hybrida

'Dropmore Blue' is an excellent Canadian introduction and is easily found. At 12″ (30 cm), it demands a place in the front of the border, and it has long-lasting bright blue flowers for an extended blooming season (one of the longest-blooming *Nepeta* varieties). Its long blooming season makes it ideal for perennial container growing.

Nepeta racemosa

Nepeta racemosa is 12″ to 18″ (30 cm to 45 cm) tall, and many varieties are worthy of garden space.

'Arctic Blue' has soft powdery blue flowers. It is long-blooming.

'Karen's Blue' has soft blue flowers and is quite compact as it grows.

'Little Titch' is mauve-blue and is quite ground-hugging.

'Snowflake' has small white flowers, but they are not too impressive (unless you happen to like white catnip).

'Superba' has mauve flowers with darker calyces.

'Walker's Low' is blue-mauve. It is very long-flowering in my zone 4 garden.

Nepeta sibirica

The species *Nepeta sibirica* grows upwards of 36″ (90 cm) tall.

'Blue Beauty' (known as 'Souvenir d'Andre Chaudron' in Europe) is shorter than the species at 18″ to 24″ (45 cm to 60 cm) tall but is a long-blooming variety. The flowers are a lovely deep lavender-blue and held upright over the plant with little need for support. This variety does tend to wander a bit, so a yearly shovel edging will be required.

Nepeta x sintenisii

Nepeta x sintenisii is the new botanic listing for one of the best garden hybrids.

U.K.-developed 'Six Hills Giant' should be in every perennial garden. Its deep violet-blue flowers are quite spectacular on plants 18″ to 24″ (45 cm to 60 cm) tall.

Nepeta subsessilis

Nepeta subsessilis is now listed in some garden catalogs. Up to a few years ago, it was found only in specialist seed catalogs. It has good glossy foliage and a mounding growth habit. The flowers are lavender-blue and quite large. It is well worth finding and growing, as it makes an excellent garden show. This species needs well-drained soils if it is to survive the winter in colder climates. It blooms a bit later than most of the other catnips, but while some authors call it a fall-blooming plant, it does not act that way in my garden.

Growing *Nepeta*

I love *Nepeta* and grow several different species and varieties. The deep blue of the flowers is welcome in midsummer, and on a still night, I enjoy wandering the garden and giving the plants a brush with my hand to release their fragrance. *Nepeta* wants full sunshine and gets rather floppy if shade is provided instead. The soil should be well-drained. Once established the plants will grow in drier ground, but they do best in average garden soil with regular watering. Several of the species will have to be kept in check with a yearly edging with shovels, and they do like to wander about the garden by self-sowing. Luckily, they are easily weeded and haven't become a nuisance. I note that more fertile soils will create bushier growth but reduce the flowering. A single application of compost in early spring or very late fall is all this plant requires for food.

This plant will rebloom if sheared after the original blooming is finished—but as soon as you shear it, the neighborhood cats will go berserk and likely invade and flatten the remaining plant in their all-consuming desire to cover themselves with the catnip fragrance.

Potions and Poisons

There are no special concerns with this culinary herb. *Nepeta* has been used for years for calming and for curing headaches as well as inducing sweating.

Stachys byzantina 'Sheila McQueen'   DOUGLAS GREEN

'Superba' is a deep rose pink and an excellent garden grower. It is one of my favorites.

Growing *Stachys*

The silvery-leaved varieties prefer full sun, while the others will tolerate some light shade. It also grows better in moderately fertile soils with good drainage. This is not a plant for clay. Cut off the flowers immediately after blooming to encourage leaf growth.

Potions and Poisons

This plant has a long and storied use in herbal medicine. At one time it was the most widely used of all plants for general tonics, teas, and remedies for problems associated with the head. *Stachys* is not considered poisonous, although fresh leaves are mentioned in one account as having stimulant properties. It was one of the principal ingredients in snuff—and snuff products containing it were reputed to be a cure for headaches.

VERBASCUM

Common names: mullein, Jacob's staff, Jacob's rod

Verbascum is the original Latin name for this plant used by the Romans and is thought to be a corruption of *barbascum*, which in turn is a form of *barba*, or "beard." If you're still with me, the plant was given this name because the silvery gray foliage looks like a beard. Blame it all on Linnaeus. *Mullein* comes from *moleyn* in Anglo-Saxon and *malen* in the Old French, both of which were derived from the Latin *malandrium*, meaning "the malanders of leprosy." The plant was used in the treatment of leprosy. It was also used in the treatment of lung diseases in cattle. *Jacob's staff* and *Jacob's rod* refer to the stafflike nature of the woody, upright flower stem that shoots up from the velvety leaves.

Bloom time: Midsummer

Height: 24″ to 72″ (60 cm to 180 cm)

Sun needed: Full sun

Bloom color: White, yellow shades, pinks

Planting space: 12″ to 18″ (30 cm to 45 cm) apart

Soil preferred: Well-drained

Propagation method: Seed or root cuttings of hybrids

Recommended Varieties

Verbascum bombyciferum

Verbascum bombyciferum is a biennial species. The leaves are quite white and hairy. The flowers easily reach 5′ to 6′ (150 cm to 180 cm) with their multicluster flowers.

'Polarsommer' (also sold as 'Arctic Summer') has bright yellow flowers.

'Silver Lining' is a lemon yellow.

Verbascum chaixii

Verbascum chaixii is a perennial species that reaches 24″ to 30″ (60 cm to 75 cm) tall with yellow flowers.

'Album' is a white flowering variety. It is 24″ (60 cm) tall and quite attractive.

Verbascum x hybrida

An increasing number of hybrids are coming onto the market. Some of the best are as follows:

'Helen Johnson' is 24″ (60 cm) tall with coppery peach blooms. It is quite spectacular.

'Jackie' is 24″ (60 cm) tall, and the flowers are peach-pink with a darker violet eye.

'Jolly Eyes' is 24″ (60 cm) tall with cream-white flowers for an extended bloom time.

'Letitia' is 24″ (60 cm) tall with gray-green leaves and bright yellow flowers for an extended bloom time. This plant does not do well where the winters are wet rather than cold.

Verbascum nigrum

Verbascum nigrum is a dark-leaved species. The flowers reach 48″ to 60″ (120 cm to 180 cm) and are medium yellow.

Verbascum thapsus

Verbascum thapsus is a biennial, growing to 72″ (180 cm) with yellow flowers. It's one of the more ancient of plants growing in association with man.

Verbascum nigrum   Douglas Green

Verbascum chaixii 'Album'   Douglas Green

Verbascum phoeniceum

Verbascum phoeniceum is a plant that has been hybridized and whose offspring can act as perennials or biennials.

'Candy Spires' is 24″ to 36″ (60 cm to 90 cm) tall. The color varies, as it is a seed mix and includes whites, mauves, and pinks. If you purchase it from a garden center, they won't guarantee the color.

'Flush of White' is 24″ to 30″ (60 cm to 75 cm) tall with white flowers.

Growing *Verbascum*

Verbascum is for the most part, a plant of full sun and gravelly or very well-drained soils. It is grown as much for its feltlike gray foliage as it is for its towering flower spikes. These spikes, you'll be pleased to know, do not require any staking. Do note that many of the species plants are biennial and not truly perennial.

Potions and Poisons

The entire plant—flowers, leaves, and roots—is said to contain a mild sedative and narcotic effect. The leaves have been used as tobacco and in other medicinal salves and treatments. The leaves have also been used as poultices and for the treatment of diarrhea. It comes with mixed messages in the old herbals, and while it probably isn't a problem—better safe than sorry. Avoid letting small children consume any part of this plant.

Verbascum thapsus   Douglas Green

YUCCA

Common names: Spanish bayonet, dagger plant

The herbalist Gerard named this plant. Well, actually he named it, but he thought he was naming a relative of *Manihot esculenta*, known in the native Carib tongue by the name of *yuca*. As it turns out, they weren't related but the name stuck anyway. *Spanish bayonet* and *dagger plant* refer to the erect, sharp-tipped leaves.

Bloom time: Midsummer to late summer
Height: 24″ (60 cm) for foliage and 60″ (150 cm) for flower
Sun needed: Full sun
Bloom color: White

Planting space: 24″ (60 cm) apart
Soil preferred: Well-drained, rich, organic soils
Propagation method: Division or seed

Recommended Varieties

Yucca filamentosa

The species *Yucca filamentosa* is commonly available in garden centers. Its leaves grow to 24″ to 30″ (60 cm to 75 cm) tall and the white flowers spike to 60″ (150 cm).

'Variegata' has white-edged leaves.

Yucca smalliana

Yucca smalliana resembles *Yucca filamentosa* except that the leaves are narrower. The variety named 'Variegata' is often sold as *Yucca filamentosa*. It has yellow variegations and white flowers.

Growing Yucca

Most gardeners think that *Yucca* grows best on poor ground. Quite the opposite is true. If given a rich soil high in organic matter, the plant will thrive. It doesn't like wet, boggy soil, poor drainage, or winter-wet soils. Because the plant is an evergreen, keeping it out of drying winter winds is a necessity if you want the plant to get large enough to produce flowers. Winter winds will burn the leaves off, making them resprout from the roots the following spring.

This plant is like a bank account. When you put enough sunlight and energy into it, the plant will produce a tall white flower stalk.

Yucca   MICK HALES

9

Fall Bloomers

Fall can be a frustrating time in the garden. The threat of upcoming winter looms as summer retreats, taking with it all the glorious blooms and fragrances. As blooms disappear, so does your enthusiasm for maintaining the garden. Yet fall doesn't have to be a time of decline—quite the contrary. If you choose your plants carefully, fall is a perfect time to create a bright, beautiful garden that defies the coming of winter and brings a last delicious gulp of color.

Fall gardens are not for the faint of heart. They scream in bright yellows, large flowering violets, and bold, tall plants that have spent the summer biding their time. These plants are ready to make a statement with their size and shout it across the garden. Of course, what that statement is depends on the gardener and how many of these fall glories are grown. Personally, I would grow as many as I had room for. I love the cool nights and crisp days of fall, and my color sense delights in the explosion of bright yellow and orange flowers. I truly enjoy the counterpoint of the blue asters and gentians, which tries to tone down this explosion of color, but my heart belongs to the really big garden plants, the fall bloomers.

Solidago rugosa 'Fireworks'/*Sedum spectabile*
DOUGLAS GREEN

ANEMONE

Common name: windflower

The name *Anemone* is rooted in Greek. *An* means "to blow," and a derivative of this is *anila*, which means "the wind." Hence the common name *windflower*. For a more detailed description of the name, see Chapter 6.

Bloom time: Mid to late fall
Height: 24″ to 36″ (60 cm to 90 cm)
Sun needed: Full sun to part shade
Bloom color: Pinks, rose, white
Planting space: 18″ to 24″ (45 cm to 60 cm) apart

Soil preferred: Evenly moist but very well-drained
Propagation method: Division

Recommended Varieties

Anemone hupehensis

Anemone hupehensis is a late-summer- or early-fall-blooming *Anemone* that is native to Chinese meadows and woodland edges. Light shade produces the best blooms in North American gardens, as the high summer heat shortens the bloom time. It grows to 24″ to 30″ (60 cm to 75 cm) tall.

'Bowles Pink' is medium to deep purple-violet at 24″ (60 cm) tall. And just for the record, A. E. Bowles, the famous plantsman, did select and name this plant 'Bowles Pink' even though it is a purple-violet.

'Hadspen Abundance' is deep rose-pink and has semidouble flowers. It grows to 24″ (60 cm) tall.

Anemone x hybrida

These hybrids bloom in late summer and early fall.

'Alice' has semidouble blooms in light pink and grows to 24″ (60 cm) tall.

'Honorine Jobert' is pure white and grows to 36″ (90 cm) tall.

'Margarete' is pure pink and has double flowers. It grows to 36″ (90 cm) tall.

'Pamina' has a single, deep rose-pink flower and grows to 30″ (75 cm) tall.

'Prince Henry' has small, deep rose-pink, semidouble flowers and grows to 36″ (90 cm) tall.

'Queen Charlotte' has pink semidouble flowers and grows to 36″ (90 cm) tall.

'September Charm' is light pink and grows to 24″ to 36″ (60 cm to 90 cm) tall. It is one of the latest *Anemone* plants to bloom.

'Whirlwind' has white, semidouble flowers and grows to 36″ to 48″ (90 cm to 120 cm) tall.

Growing Anemone

The autumn-flowering *Anemone* plants are mostly plants of damp, open woodland or meadows. This means they like sun or dappled shade and moist but not waterlogged soils. They will grow quite nicely on average garden soils but do not like heavy clays. I've grown them in medium

Anemone 'September Charm'   Douglas Green

Anemone 'Honorine Jobert'   Douglas Green

shade under a crabapple tree, and they continue to spread and make a nuisance of themselves under there. They require regular edging to keep them in bounds, as they do like to spread.

These plants are one of the must-have plants for the fall gardens. I simply cannot imagine my garden without them. They provide a late-season shot of pink and rose in the middle of the yellows and reds of autumn and if for no other reason than that should be on your shopping list. Their ease of growth and disease-free growth habit also endears them to my gardening heart.

Potions and Poisons

This plant has a long history of medicinal use and legend associated with it. The root is an irritant and somewhat poisonous, although older herbals recommended it be chewed as a purgative. In other words, chew it and you'll throw up. The leaves are acrid, and vinegar has been made from them; there are also reports of cattle being poisoned by eating them. This taste would probably deter any child from eating it, so it is not likely to be a problem. Of course, it is wise to keep children away from roots if you are transplanting.

ASTER

Common names: aster, Michaelmas daisy

*A*ster is "star" in Latin, and this is an allusion to the shape of the flower. *Michaelmas daisy* is a reference to the time of flowering.

Bloom time: Mid to late fall
Height: 24″ to 48″ (60 cm to 120 cm)
Sun needed: Full sun
Bloom color: Red, violets

Planting space: 18″ to 24″ (45 cm to 60 cm) apart
Soil preferred: Sandy, well-drained
Propagation method: Division or cuttings

Recommended Varieties

Aster amellus

Aster amellus is a European species averaging 18″ to 24″ (45 cm to 60 cm) tall. It is easily grown and hardy into zone 4 with no difficulty.

'Violet Queen' has large flowers of violet-purple with a yellow eye.

Aster coloradoensis

'Coombe Fishacre' is a 36″ (90 cm) tall and strong-growing plant with pretty lavender-rose blossoms.

Aster divaricatus

Aster divaricatus is a North American native, excellent for part shade or naturalizing. It is more tolerant of dry soils than other asters. It has white blossoms that resemble small stars on well-branched plants. The plant grows to 18″ (45 cm) tall.

Aster x frikartii

Aster x frikartii is an excellent hybrid group, and the flowers within it share several important characteristics. The first is that they are the longest-blooming, starting in midsummer to late summer and lasting well into fall. The second is

that they are quite disease-resistant. The key to growing them is well-drained soil (no clay for this plant), preferably in zone 5 or warmer. They do not grow reliably for me in zone 4 even though I have great soil for them; I'm not giving up yet, though.

'Flora's Delight' has lilac-mauve flowers with a yellow eye. It is a bit shorter than others at 18″ (45 cm) tall.

'Monch,' the classic *Aster x frikartii*, has lavender-blue flowers over an extended time and a height of 30″ (75 cm), making this an excellent plant for the fall garden.

'Wunder von Stafa' (also sold as 'Wonder of Stafa') is 24″ (60 cm) tall with delightful sky blue flowers in midsummer to late summer throughout the fall.

Aster lateriflorus

Aster lateriflorus is a North American species that has naturalized itself in Europe. In the wild, it can grow to 36″ (90 cm) tall, but the cultivated varieties vary in their height. It seldom needs staking owing to its strong, woody stem.

'Prince' has white flowers on interesting plum-colored foliage, making this a good plant for garden interest. The flower is small and white with a red eye and is quite distinctively attrac-

Aster amellus 'Violet Queen'

Aster x frikartii 'Flora's Delight'

tive in the profusion each plant produces. The good compact growth habit makes this plant a winner.

Aster novae-angliae

Also known as New England Aster, *Aster novae-angliae* is a North American native. Normally, it is one of the taller species, reaching upwards of 4′ to 5′ (120 cm to 150 cm) in the wild. It is hardy well into zone 3 and rarely needs staking owing to the stiff, woody stems. This species also provides some of the best cut flowers.

'Andenken an Alma Potschke' (also sold as 'Alma Potschke') is a salmon-pink and grows to just under 48″ (120 cm). It is one of the best and is well deserving of a place in the garden.

'Pink Winner' is medium pink and has quite an upright form, even though it is short, at 36″ (90 cm), for the species.

'Purple Dome' is an introduction from the Mt. Cuba Center in Delaware. It is deep purple and only 18″ to 24″ (45 cm to 60 cm) tall.

'Rudelsburg' is 36″ (90 cm) tall and a strong grower. Bright red blossoms cover this plant in the fall.

Aster novi-blegii

Species *Aster novi-blegii* is 48″ (120 cm) tall with woody stems that require no staking in its native North America. Now widely naturalized in Europe and hybridized for gardens, it comes in a variety of colors and heights. All are quite hardy into zone 2 and are delights in the fall garden. The shorter forms were bred as hybrids using *Aster dumosus* as the other parent. There are hundreds of available varieties in this species.

'Audrey' is 12″ (30 cm) tall and mauve-blue. It is a good garden performer.

'Coombe Rosemary' is a double-flowering violet-purple and grows to 36″ (90 cm) tall.

'Diana' is a clear rose-pink on plants 24″ (60 cm) tall.

'Lady in Blue' is a semidouble flower on plants 12″ (30 cm) tall. It has mid-blue coloring.

'Little Pink Beauty' is a semidouble, bright pink flower on plants 18″ (45 cm) tall.

'Professor Kippenburg' is a semidouble, bright blue flower on plants 12″ to 18″ (30 cm to 18 cm) tall.

'Royal Ruby' is a deep red, semidouble flower on plants 18″ to 24″ (45 cm to 60 cm) tall.

Aster novae-angliae 'Rudelsburg'   Douglas Green

Aster divaricatus   Douglas Green

'Winston Churchill' is a bright red single flower on plants 18″ (45 cm) tall.

Growing *Aster*

Aster is an easy plant to grow. It thrives in almost any garden soil that is well-drained and moderately fertile. It loves the full sun and will survive in light shade, although the taller forms will get a bit floppy if given too much shade. Some plants will require an annual edging, as they are good spreaders. Many of the taller varieties benefit from staking or planting next to something (plant or garden structure) that is sturdy to prevent flopping over in windy weather.

Aster coloradoensis 'Coombe Fishacre'
Douglas Green

BOLTONIA

Common names: Bolton's aster, false chamomile

*B*oltonia is named after James Bolton (died 1799), a weaver in Halifax, West Yorkshire, England, who as a self-taught botanist and botanical artist became an expert on British ferns. *Bolton's aster* is fairly simple—the plant is a member of the *Aster* genus, and it was named after Mr. Bolton. *False chamomile* is perhaps a bit more obtuse. It takes a stretch of imagination to picture this tall, larger-flowered, daisylike plant as a chamomile, but stranger things have happened in the plant world.

Bloom time: Early fall
Height: 36″ (90 cm)
Sun needed: Full sun to light shade
Bloom color: White, pink

Planting space: 18″ to 24″ (45 cm to 60 cm) apart
Soil preferred: Rich, evenly moist soils
Propagation method: Division or cuttings

Recommended Varieties

Boltonia asteroides

Boltonia asteroides can reach 6′ (180 cm) tall in the wild when found on its preferred moist and fertile soils. The species has white flowers.

'Pink Beauty' has pale pink flowers on a rather loose open plant that grows to 36″ (90 cm) tall.

'Snowbank' has white daisies on a compact-growing plant that is up to 36″ (90 cm) tall.

Boltonia asteroides 'Latisquama'

This variety of the species is well worth growing no matter what name you find it under in the garden center. It has mauve to violet flowers and should reach 48″ (120 cm) or taller in the back of your perennial border.

Growing Boltonia

Boltonia is a plant that is most often found in evenly moist but not boggy ground in the full sunlight. If given moist garden soil and good fertility, it will respond with huge displays of daisy blooms for most of the fall. It will survive in part shade even though it will not thrive there. Excessive shade produces floppy plants, and as this plant does not require staking in the full sunshine, move it into more sunlight if it starts to flop.

Boltonia asteroides 'Latisquama'   Douglas Green

CHELONE

Common name: turtlehead

The proper name *Chelone* and the common name *turtlehead* both come from the flower shape, which as you might imagine resembles the head of a turtle. *Chelone* is Greek for "turtle."

Bloom time: Mid fall
Height: 36″ (90 cm)
Sun needed: Sun to light shade
Bloom color: Pink, white

Planting space: 18″ (45 cm) apart
Soil preferred: Moist, fertile soils
Propagation method: Cuttings, division, or seed

Recommended Varieties

Chelone glabra

Chelone glabra is seldom found in garden centers, but sometimes you'll find it in seed catalogs. It is an excellent plant with more white tones in the flower than other species.

Chelone obliqua

Chelone obliqua is a wonderful pink-blooming plant for the fall garden.

Chelone obliqua DOUGLAS GREEN

'Alba' is a white-flowering variety.
'Rosea' is a clear pink but rarely available.

Growing *Chelone*

In the wild, *Chelone* is found in moist, even swampy, but well-lit woodland areas. Grow it in damp soils in part shade for best results. I have grown it quite successfully in regular garden soils in full sun, but it never reaches its full potential compared to when it's grown in a shadier site. This plant will tolerate heavy clay soils. The single best thing you can do to encourage the growth of this plant is to feed it heavily with compost; it responds very well to soils that are high in organic matter and fertile. This is an easy plant to grow as long as you keep it away from dry, sandy soils.

Potions and Poisons

The leaves of *Chelone* are quite bitter and were used by North American aboriginal people as a purgative and worm medicine. It was also used as a general tonic. It is not likely to be a problem in the garden because of the taste of the leaves.

CHRYSANTHEMUM

Common names: chrysanthemum, mum, pellitory

*C*hrysanthemum is a derivative of two Greek words, *chrysos*, or "gold," and *anthemon*, or "flower." *Pellitory* comes from the Latin *parietarus*, meaning "belonging to the walls." Some old forms of *Chrysanthemum* were typically found growing in cracks in rocks and in the cracks of stone walls. See Chapter 7 for a complete description.

Bloom time: Early to late fall

Height: 24″ to 36″ (60 cm to 90 cm)

Sun needed: Full sun

Bloom color: Yellows, pinks, whites, oranges, reds

Planting space: 18″ to 24″ (45 cm to 60 cm) apart

Soil preferred: Well-drained and fertile

Propagation method: Cuttings or division

Recommended Varieties

Ajania pacifica

Formerly *Chrysanthemum pacificum*, *Ajania pacifica* is a plant for the zone 5 garden. I've killed it here in zone 4 more often than I want to admit. It needs a long, warm fall season and full sunshine to really come into bloom, and my garden doesn't fill that order. The foliage is quite attractive, dark green and edged in silver, and the small, yellow buttonlike flowers come in the fall if the season is warm.

'Pink Ice' is a new variety with yellow flowers surrounded by a row of pale pink petals.

Chrysanthemum x hybrida

Chrysanthemum hybrids, whose name briefly changed to *Dendrathema x hybrida* or *Dendrathema indica*, are what we call *fall mums*. And there are literally hundreds of varieties on the market for you to choose from. Those living in colder climates might well search for two specific series— the Morden series developed by Agriculture Canada for cold climates and the Minnesota mums, a similar cold-hardy series developed at

the University of Minnesota. The Morden series is easily recognized because all plants include the name *Morden*, as in 'Morden Red.' The Minnesota mums are famous for their hardiness, and there are quite a few of them. Any mum name starting with a *Minn* is one of their series. 'Sesquicentennial Sun,' 'Rose Blush,' 'Peach Centerpiece,' and 'Inca' are more recent releases. In 1996, a new series was released called *Maxi Mums*, which is a departure in mum breeding in that the plants are huge and heavily flowered. 'Betty Lou' is the variety most common in this series. Mums normally found in garden centers other than the Morden and Minnesota series will not reliably survive the winter in zones 4 or colder. Grow fall mums in the full sun and feed regularly with compost or liquid food all season for huge bloom production.

Chrysanthemum x rubellum

Known just recently and mercifully briefly as *Dendrathema zawadskii*, *Chrysanthemum x rubellum* is a single-flowering garden mum that deserves a place in more gardens. This is an easy and hardy single-flowered, fragrant form.

Fall chrysanthemum   DOUGLAS GREEN

'Clara Curtis' is the most commonly available variety, and its deep-pink single flowers make it an excellent garden plant.

'Mary Stoker' is also available and has a golden-orange blossom that fades to a light pink. Both make a more attractive plant if pinched back by half their height in late June. If left unpinched, they tend to become quite sprawling. This plant is the antithesis of the cultured garden mum. It looks much more natural and is well suited for the cottage-garden look.

Nipponanthemum nipponicum

Formerly *Chrysanthemum nipponicum* or *Japanese daisy*, *Nipponanthemum nipponicum* is a wonderful white-flowered daisy with a heavy glaucous leaf. It blooms quite late in the season, and for this reason, it bloomed in my garden only every few years when we had an extremely late frost. Because it blooms late, it no longer exists in my zone 4 garden, but if you have a warmer garden you will find this an excellent bloomer and well suited for the back of a rock garden. Grow it in full sun.

Growing *Chrysanthemum*

Chrysanthemum plants love full sunshine and fertile soils. Greedy feeders, they do best when provided with a soil that is high in organic matter and kept evenly moist. They prefer a well-drained soil over the winter, and heavy clay soils will tend to kill them.

Potions and Poisons

In his herbal, Culpepper tells us that this plant is a fine purge for the brain (whatever that means). It has also been used for toothache and as a snuff to clear the head, and when used as a gargle, it is reputed to ease the partial paralysis of the tongue. This is not likely going to hurt you, but it is not recommended for use without a physician's supervision.

COREOPSIS TRIPTERIS

Common name: butter daisy

*C*oreopsis comes from the Greek *koris*, "bug," and *opsis*, "like"—buglike. This refers to the shape of the seedhead. *Butter daisy* comes to us from the butter-yellow flower color.

Bloom time: Mid to late fall

Height: 6′ to 8′ (180 cm to 240 cm)

Sun needed: Full sun

Bloom color: Yellow

Planting space: 24″ to 30″ (60 cm to 75 cm) apart

Soil preferred: Fertile and well-drained

Propagation method: Seed or cuttings

Recommended Varieties

Coreopsis tripteris

Only the one species, *Coreopsis tripteris*, is available (no hybrids) and if you can find it, grow it. It is a tall, heavy-blooming monster of a plant and well worth a place in the back of the large perennial border.

Growing *Coreopsis tripteris*

Coreopsis tripteris is a plant of open, sunny meadows in North America ranging from Michigan down to Louisiana. Do not worry about deadheading this plant, as the flowers are produced late in the season. Simply chop it down to the ground after it has finished blooming as part of your garden cleanup for fall.

Coreopsis tripteris   Douglas Green

EUPATORIUM

Common names: joe-pye weed, boneset, purple boneset

The King of Pontus (an ancient country in Asia Minor), Mithridates Eupator, is reputed to have discovered the use of this plant as a medicinal tonic, and it was named after him. *Joe-pye* apparently comes from the name of an Indian named Jopi who used it medicinally. *Boneset* is used for the ornamental plant as well as *Eupatorium perfoliatum* (the herbal boneset), which was used to combat influenza. I'm told that the name came from the relief of pain of the fever—break-bone fever—and was shortened to *boneset*. The ornamental form is called *purple boneset*.

Bloom time: Fall
Height: 36″ to 72″ (90 cm to 180 cm)
Sun needed: Full sun
Bloom color: White, rose-purple

Planting space: 24″ (60 cm) apart
Soil preferred: Moisture-retaining but well-drained
Propagation method: Seed or division

Recommended Varieties

Eupatorium maculatum

Known as joe-pye weed, *Eupatorium maculatum* grows to 6′ (180 cm) or taller if happy in its location. It forms huge flower heads the size of small umbrellas in the late summer and fall. It is very showy when combined with yellow-flowering fall bloomers.

'Gateway' is slightly more compact, growing only as tall as 6′ (180 cm) but with extremely large flower heads.

'Atropurpureum' is a darker rose-purple than the species. It has the same growth habit with slightly larger flowers.

Eupatorium rugosum

Eupatorium rugosum is sometimes found in garden centers. It is much more civilized and compact than *Eupatorium maculatum*. It grows to only 3′ (90 cm) tall and has clusters of pure white flowers. Some catalogs describe it as resembling a huge annual white *Ageratum* plant.

Eupatorium coelestinum   Douglas Green

Eupatorium maculatum   Douglas Green

'Chocolate' has dark bronze foliage in the spring that turns green at flowering. It is later-blooming than the species.

Growing *Eupatorium*

Eupatorium is a plant for the back of the larger border. With the exception of *Eupatorium rugosum*, *Eupatorium* is imposing in the late fall garden. It generally does better on moist soils that are not waterlogged or boggy during the winter. Moderate fertility is enough to feed this garden performer in the full sun or part shade. If it gets floppy, move it to a sunnier site. The better the site, the taller this plant will grow, and specimens upwards of 10′ to 12′ (300 cm to 360 cm) are not impossible if the plant is happy.

Potions and Poisons

The roots are used as a diuretic and stimulant and taste quite bitter. North American aboriginal people used *Eupatorium* to fight typhus. All parts of *Eupatorium perfoliatum* are active, but *Eupatorium maculatum* provides primarily a root-based tonic. Even though the constituent parts are so bitter, caution is recommended with small children.

GENTIANA

The name *Gentiana* was given to the plant by Gentius, a King of ancient Illyria (180–167 B.C.) who was reputed to have discovered the medicinal uses of this plant.

Bloom time: Early fall
Height: 6″ to 24″ (15 cm to 60 cm)
Sun needed: Shade
Bloom color: Blue
Planting space: 6″ to 12″ (15 cm to 30 cm) apart

Soil preferred: Damp, high in organic matter
Propagation method: Seed

Recommended Varieties

Gentiana asclepiadea

Known as *willow gentian*, *Gentiana asclepiadea* grows to 24″ to 30″ (60 cm to 75 cm) tall and has bright blue flowers. It blooms in late summer and early fall. There are some hybrids of this species in Europe, and we can only wait for them to cross the Atlantic.

Gentiana autumnalis

Known as *pine barrens gentian*, *Gentiana autumnalis* is a gentian for the more southerly of us. Grow it in well-drained soils but those that are constantly moist from streams or nearby ponds. I'm currently experimenting with this species myself, but I'm likely too far north. It grows 18″ to 24″ (45 cm to 60 cm) tall.

Gentiana x hybrida

An increasing number of hybrid forms of *Gentiana* are in Europe, but these are not available yet in North America. When you do see them in your garden center, the only thing you'll have to do is ensure the height and bloom time is acceptable to your garden design. Their growth needs are the same as the species.

Gentiana makinoi

At 24″ to 30″ (60 cm to 75 cm) tall, *Gentiana makinoi* has a good, strong blue color. It is native to Japan and flowers in late summer and early fall.

'Royal Blue' has very bright blue flowers. It is an outstanding plant.

Gentiana scabra

Gentiana scabra is 18″ (45 cm) tall and a good, bright blue.

Gentiana paradoxa

Gentiana paradoxa is a fall-blooming dwarf species best suited for the rock garden. It is more readily available than other species but is not really suited for the general garden.

Gentiana villosa

Gentiana villosa is 18″ to 24″ (45 cm to 60 cm) tall and violet-blue. This plant is native to North America.

Gentiana asclepiadea   © JUDYWHITE/GARDENPHOTOS.COM

Growing *Gentiana*

If you start with taller species of *Gentiana* and give them cool, shady spots with good soil moisture, you'll be able to grow gentians very easily. I have several species in my garden that come back year after year with no fuss. They are plants of damp woodland soils, so use lots of organic matter and mulch. Plant fresh seed in the spring, and they will bloom in their second year.

Potions and Poisons

Gentiana has a long history of herbal medicinal use. In medieval times, it was a commonly used antidote for poison. It is a bitter vegetable tonic, used to combat exhaustion or weakness in the general immune system. As the root is the active part, there should be no concerns with growing this plant in the garden. Do not let children eat the root.

HELENIUM

Common name: sneezeweed

This is another case of one plant getting named and then passing that name along. The Greek word *helenion* refers to another old-world plant, possibly *Inula helenium. Inula helenium* is said to refer to Helen of Troy. How it happened we are not sure, but we now have a plant named *Helenium. Sneezeweed* comes from the plant's use as snuff.

Bloom time: Early fall
Height: 36″ to 60″ (90 cm to 150 cm)
Sun needed: Full sun
Bloom color: Shades of yellow

Planting space: 24″ (60 cm) apart
Soil preferred: Moist soils
Propagation method: Division or seed

Recommended Varieties

Helenium autumnale

Helenium autumnale is less available than even a few years ago; the newer breeding of other hybrids has replaced the species in my garden.

Helenium x hybrida

'Bruno' is 48″ (120 cm) tall with yellow blooms and unusual mahogany-bronze leaves. It blooms in early fall.

'Butterpat' is 48″ (120 cm) tall and its flowers are light yellow with darker centers. It blooms in early fall.

'Coppelia' is 48″ (120 cm) tall and its flowers are coppery orange with warm yellow tones. It blooms in early fall.

Growing *Helenium*

Helenium is a North American native plant that enjoys an evenly moist soil and one that is high in organic matter. Grow it in this soil, and you'll have a long-blooming, low-maintenance plant with few pests or problems. Divide the clumps every three to five years to encourage strong growth. After blooming, deadhead the stems back to halfway, and then clean up completely after frost has killed all top growth. If you try to grow this plant in dry soils, you'll have a short-lived plant on your hands, or more likely in your compost pile.

Helenium 'Butterpat'
BLOOMS OF BRESSINGHAM NORTH AMERICA, BARBERTON OH

248

HELIOPSIS

Common names: ox-eye, false sunflower

*H*eliopsis shows off its Greek naming with *helios*, "sun," and *opsis*, "appearance," referring to the showy blooms. *Ox-eye* has also referred to *Bupthalmum* and *Chrysanthemum* family plants, and I suspect that applying it to *Heliopsis* is simply painting a yellow flower with the same brush. If it looks like a tall yellow daisy, it must be an ox-eye. Also, the plant superficially resembles a sunflower in that it has a tall, yellow, daisylike bloom—but it isn't a sunflower, so it's false. Plant names can be simple sometimes.

Bloom time: Early fall
Height: 36″ to 60″ (90 cm to 150 cm)
Sun needed: Full sun
Bloom color: Yellow shades

Planting space: 18″ to 24″ (45 cm to 60 cm) apart
Soil preferred: Poor, dry soils
Propagation method: Division or seed

Recommended Varieties

Heliopsis helianthoides

The species *Heliopsis helianthoides* is a North American native. It is easily grown and quite hardy in all but the coldest of gardens. The species is seldom grown except in naturalized gardens.

'Bressingham Doubloon' is 48″ to 60″ (120 cm to 150 cm) tall and has a double-flowering golden-yellow bloom.

'Summer Sun' is 36″ (90 cm) tall and is gold-yellow. It is commonly available in seed catalogs.

Heliopsis x hybrida

'Lorraine Sunshine' has variegated leaves that make it a winner. It is 30″ (75 cm) tall and 18″ (45 cm) wide. It blooms for a long time, and its large, golden-yellow blooms will grace your garden from the end of July till frost.

Growing *Heliopsis*

Heliopsis naturally occurs in areas of full sun and well-drained, dry soils. If you grow it in moder-ately fertile soils, you will be pleased with the lovely fall blooms. Most *Heliopsis* plants make good cut flowers. If they get too tall, treat them like a chrysanthemum and prune them back to half their height when they reach approximately 18″ (45 cm) in height.

Heliopsis helianthoides 'Lorraine Sunshine'
Blooms of Bressingham North America, Barberton OH

249

PEROVSKIA

Common name: Russian sage

*P*erovskia was named for the Turkestani general-statesman V. A. Perovski (1794–1857). *Russian sage* is fairly clear because of the fragrance of the leaves and the plant's origin in Asia.

Bloom time: Early to late fall
Height: 24″ to 36″ (60 cm to 90 cm)
Sun needed: Full, hot sun
Bloom color: Purple

Planting space: 18″ (45 cm) apart
Soil preferred: Well-drained, sandy soils
Propagation method: Cuttings or seed

Recommended Varieties

Perovskia atriplicifolia

The species *Perovskia atriplicifolia* is the one most often found in garden centers, and at 36″ (90 cm) tall, it is a wonderful addition to the late-summer and fall garden.

'Filigran' is a new introduction from Germany that has finer-cut foliage than the species, and the plants are more bushy and upright.

Growing *Perovskia*

Perovskia is a plant that demands good drainage and sandy soils. You will not overwinter this plant on clay or wet soils. It also loves the full, hot sunshine, and shade reduces it to a mere shadow of its potential. Certainly in my garden, it produces flowers that last well into the fall and complement other late bloomers. It does tend to be a bit floppy, but if planted next to *Rudbeckia* and late-blooming yellow goldenrod to hold it upright, it can be part of a stunning combination.

Perovskia atriplicifolia DOUGLAS GREEN

RUDBECKIA

Common name: black-eyed Susan

The plant *Rudbeckia* was named after Olaus Olai Rudbeck (1660–1740), a Swedish physician and botanist. *Black-eyed* is simple—the plants have a black eye. None of my resources tell me who Susan was.

Bloom time: Early to late fall
Height: 24″ to 72″ (60 cm to 180 cm)
Sun needed: Full sun
Bloom color: Shades of yellow and gold
Planting space: 18″ to 24″ (45 cm to 60 cm) apart

Soil preferred: Moderately fertile, well-drained
Propagation method: Division or seed

Recommended Varieties

Rudbeckia fulgida

Rudbeckia fulgida is a species 24″ to 36″ (60 cm to 90 cm) tall that is an excellent and long-lived perennial plant in my garden.

'Goldsturm' is 24″ (60 cm) tall and makes an excellent plant for massing or for naturalizing. Its golden flowers shout across the fall garden to capture the attention of all visitors.

'Viette's Little Suzy' is 12″ to 18″ (30 cm to 18 cm) tall with yellow flowers. It blooms in midsummer to late summer and right through fall. Its foliage turns deep mahogany in fall.

Rudbeckia hirta

All of the plants in species *Rudbeckia hirta* are either biennials or short-lived perennials.

'Indian Summer' is an award-winning plant, and its massive flowers make it clear why. It makes a wonderful display in the garden and provides excellent cut flowers. My only regret is that it does not live for very long in my garden.

Rudbeckia laciniata hortensia

Known as 'Golden Glow,' old-fashioned favorite *Rudbeckia laciniata hortensia*, also became known as *outhouse plant* in pioneer times because that

Rudbeckia fulgida 'Goldsturm'   DOUGLAS GREEN

Rudbeckia maxima   Douglas Green

Rudbeckia laciniata hortensia   Douglas Green

was usually the place it was found. It is a large, strong, relatively fast-spreading plant, and this was one place it could grow with impunity. The plant does require edging every few years to keep it in bounds. It easily hits 8′(240 cm) tall each year and has beautiful double golden-yellow flowers for the late summer and throughout the fall season.

Rudbeckia maxima

Rudbeckia maxima is a hardy perennial that grows to 6′(180 cm) tall with clear golden flowers in the fall. This little-known plant is one of my favorite family members.

Rudbeckia triloba

Rudbeckia triloba is another tall favorite that reaches 5′to 6′(150 cm to 180 cm) with yellow to orange blooms.

Growing *Rudbeckia*

Grow *Rudbeckia* for its amazing displays of golden-yellow daisies throughout the late summer and fall. They'll grow well in the full sun as well as in light shade. Regular garden soil is fine, but the biennial types do better on lighter, well-drained ground. The entire family makes a good cut flower for the fall dinner table display.

SEDUM SPECTABILE

Common name: stonecrop

*S*edum comes from the Latin word *sedere*, meaning "to sit." This is a reference to the way in which some members of this family attach themselves to rocks, seemingly to sit on the rock. *Spectabile* means spectacular or extremely showy in horticultural Latin. *Stonecrop* is a similarly descriptive name—the plant is commonly found in stony areas—a crop of the stone. Note that some catalogs might be selling this plant under the name *Hylotelephium spectabile*. This was a botany change of a few years ago, but the plant has been moved back to *Sedum* in the latest revisions.

Bloom time: Early fall
Height: 18″ to 24″ (45 cm to 60 cm)
Sun needed: Full sun
Bloom color: Whites, shades of red, pinks

Planting space: 18″ (45 cm) apart
Soil preferred: Well-drained, sandy soils
Propagation method: Division or cuttings

Recommended Varieties

Sedum alboroseum

'Mediovariegatum' is a green-and-white leaved plant with a pale pink bloom. It is an easy grower and its variegated foliage makes it quite attractive. It is often sold as *Sedum spectabile*.

Sedum spectabile

This is the classic fall-flowering sedum that grows so well in mixed perennial borders.

'Autumn Joy' is the classic form found in most garden centers. It has very large flower heads of salmon pink that age to a bronzed-red tone atop this sturdy plant.

'Brilliant' is a mid-mauve-pink bloom at 18″ to 24″ (45 cm to 60 cm) tall.

'Iceberg' is a white flowering form at 18″ (45 cm) tall.

'Indian Chief' is one of the brightest reds.

'Matrona' is 18″ to 24″ (45 cm to 60 cm) tall with a pinkish bloom. It is an excellent plant.

Sedum spectabile 'Indian Chief'   Douglas Green

Sedum spectabile 'Matrona'   DOUGLAS GREEN

Sedum spectabile 'Autumn Joy'   DOUGLAS GREEN

Growing *Sedum*

All you really need to remember about this plant is that it loves the full hot sun and fertile ground. If you give it these two requirements, you can hardly kill this plant. It prefers soils that are well-drained to clay but will survive in anything but standing water. I have seen many gardeners try to grow this plant in shade conditions and it always amazes me that they do so. In shade, the plant tends to flop over and lie down just as it develops its flower heads; this creates an ugly display of poor gardening technique.

Potions and Poisons

This plant has been used medicinally for centuries, and the herbalists couldn't seem to agree on what it was good for. There are no concerns about growing it in the garden.

Sedum spectabile   DOUGLAS GREEN

SOLIDAGO

Common name: goldenrod

*S*olidago comes to us from the Latin word *solido*, meaning "to make whole." This is in reference to its use in medicine and its apparent effectiveness. *Goldenrod* is a reference to the golden yellow of the flowers and the upright way in which they are carried.

Bloom time: Early to late fall
Height: 18″ to 48″ (45 cm to 120 cm)
Sun needed: Full sun to part shade
Bloom color: Shades of yellow
Planting space: 18″ to 24″ (45 cm to 60 cm) apart

Soil preferred: Well-drained, fertile
Propagation method: Division, seed, or cuttings

Recommended Varieties

There will be more and more new varieties of *Solidago* coming onto the market and in my opinion, deservedly so. This is a hardy plant with wonderful fall color, and the newer hybrids are spectacular in the flower border.

Solidago canadensis

'Crown of Rays' has golden-yellow blooms that grow horizontally from the stems, giving the plant a rather mop-top look. It grows to 24″ to 30″ (60 cm to 75 cm) tall.

Solidago glomerata

'Golden Wings' is 48″ (120 cm) tall and is one of the older hybrids but still one of the heavier-blooming forms in bright yellow.

Solidago rugosa

'Fireworks' is 36″ to 48″ (90 cm to 120 cm) tall. It has massive sprays of bright yellow flowers.

Solidago rugosa 'Fireworks'   DOUGLAS GREEN

Solidago sphacelata

'Golden Fleece' has spreading branches of gold flowers in early fall and at 12″ to 18″ (30 cm to 45 cm) tall makes a good ground cover.

Solidago virgaurea

'Praecox' is gold-yellow with upright flowers growing to 24″ to 30″ (60 cm to 75 cm).

Growing *Solidago*

Grow *Solidago* in almost any soil but heavy clay. It grows best in full sun in a fertile soil without water stress. This is a plant well suited for the back of herbaceous borders where it can be allowed to grow to its full majesty. Rogue out seedlings, as they will not breed true to their hybrid parentage. Expand the collection by division of the mature plant in early spring.

You might want to identify the plants with a large label. The first time I installed one of these plants in my gardens, I forgot about it. Without a large label to remind me, the next summer when I saw a goldenrod starting to grow in the garden, I assumed it was a weed and popped it out. It was only that fall that I remembered about the new goldenrod and wondered what had hap-pened to it. I said I was a gardener; I didn't say I had a good memory. I now insert a really big stake label every time I put one of these plants in my garden.

Potions and Poisons

Solidago has been used as a stimulant and an aromatic. Apparently it is excellent when used for bladder stones, according to the older herbals. When made into tea, it apparently is also excellent for diphtheria. The tea has been given to infants as a diuretic and is also used for headaches, so it should not be a problem in the garden. As with all plants, though, children should not be allowed to consume it unattended.

Goldenrods have been given a bad bit of press when it comes to symptoms. Their bright yellow blooms stand out across the country just as the hay-fever symptoms strike, so naturally they were blamed. The fact of the matter is that their pollen is quite heavy and sinks to the ground when knocked off the plant. The pollen doing the damage is from the ragweed plant; its green flowers are inconspicuous, and the clouds of pollen it releases can float for miles in gentle breezes.

TRICYRTIS

Common name: toad lily

*T*ricyrtis comes from the Greek *treis*, "three," and *kyrtos*, "convex," referring to the three outer petals, which are convex, or swollen, at their base. It is possible that *toad* is Anglo-Saxon and the word is not well translated: possibly having the meaning of "father" (from Welsh), or the reptile, "toad" (from Frisian), or even "dough" (from German). While these all make a good story, don't put any money on the source of the name *toad lily*.

Bloom time: Mid to late fall
Height: 24″ to 36″ (60 cm to 90 cm)
Sun needed: Part shade
Bloom color: Yellow, green

Planting space: 12″ (30 cm) apart
Soil preferred: Well-drained but moisture-retentive, acidic soils
Propagation method: Seed or division

Recommended Varieties

Tricyrtis is another plant where the species are seldom grown except by collectors. The named varieties are the better bloomers.

Tricyrtis formosana

'Empress' is 30″ (75 cm) tall and flowers in late fall. The flowers have pink tones with dark spots.

Tricyrtis hirta

'Hatatogisa' is 30″ (75 cm) tall with pale blue flowers.

'Shirohotogisu' is 30″ (75 cm) tall with white flowers.

'Togen' is 30″ (75 cm) tall and has lavender flowers with white centers.

Growing *Tricyrtis*

Grow *Tricyrtis* in part shade in an excellent woodland soil. The soil should be high in organic matter and an even moisture level. Excess moisture should drain away, and clay is not recommended, as the plant will rot. A per-manent mulch is an excellent method of keeping the soil cool and damp as well as holding down weeds. Acidic soils are preferred, although I grow *Tricyrtis* on a sandier, more neutral soil. Alkaline soils are not recommended. *Tricyrtis* also makes excellent cut flowers.

Tricyrtis formosana 'Empress'   TERRA NOVA NURSERIES

VERNONIA

Common name: ironweed

Vernonia was named after the English botanist William Vernon (died 1711) who traveled extensively in the northern United States. Apparently the stem on *Vernonia* is so tough that it has been likened to iron, hence *ironweed*. There is another plant called *ironwort*, supposedly so named for its ability to heal wounds created by iron (war wounds). *Vernonia* is not that plant.

Bloom time: Early to late fall
Height: 72″ (180 cm)
Sun needed: Full sun
Bloom color: Purple
Planting space: 18″ to 24″ (45 cm to 60 cm) apart

Soil preferred: Well-drained, dryish once established
Propagation method: Division or seed

Recommended Varieties

Vernonia noveboracensis

Vernonia noveboracensis is 6′ (180 cm) tall with huge numbers of purple flowers in mid to late fall.

'Albiflora' is a white-flowering variety.

Growing *Vernonia*

Vernonia is not a plant that you'll swoon over and demand to have in your garden. But it is a fall bloomer and it is purple—two characteristics that make it worth searching out to put at the back of the border so the hot yellows of the rest of the fall plants have something to be contrasted with. Grow *Vernonia* in the full sun, on drier soils. Do deadhead the flowers, or you might find yourself knee-deep in them in a good garden soil.

Vernonia gigantea Douglas Green

VERONICASTRUM

Common names: Culver's root, Bowman's root

The name *Veronicastrum* comes from the joining of *Veronica*, referring to the *Veronica* family of plants, and the Latin suffix *astrum*, meaning "incomplete resemblance." So, this plant almost resembles *Veronica*. *Culver* has been associated with the Latin word for "pigeon," so unless the root resembles a pigeon we have to assume that Mr. Culver and Mr. Bowman had some herbal uses for the plant and had their name attached to it.

Bloom time: Early to late fall
Height: 60″ to 72″ (150 cm to 180 cm)
Sun needed: Sun to light shade
Bloom color: White to light blue

Planting space: 24″ (60 cm) apart
Soil preferred: Moist and rich
Propagation method: Division or seed

Recommended Varieties

Veronicastrum virginicum

Veronicastrum virginicum is the species to grow (there is only one other, and it is seldom grown), and it makes an excellent garden performer. It is an elegant, erect plant that never requires staking.

'Alba' is a clear white and a good variety.

'Roseum' has a soft pink flower and is worth searching out.

Growing *Veronicastrum*

Veronicastrum is a plant of sunny, moist meadows or dappled shade in woodland openings. Grow it in an evenly moist soil that is high in organic matter for best results. If it is not allowed to dry out, it will give an incredibly tall fall display of flowers that will be a true showpiece for your fall garden.

Potions and Poisons:

The root of *Veronicastrum* is a cathartic (causing vomiting) if eaten. There is also some folklore about the root having abortifacient properties. This is a plant that should not be left lying about the garden surface if children are present. The dried root has been used medicinally in treating different diseases, including leprosy. There appears to be less of a problem with dried roots than with fresh roots.

Veronicastrum virginicum   Douglas Green

10

Foliage Perennials and Multiple-Season Bloomers

Despite seasonal variations from region to region and from year to year, choosing plants that will flower in spring, summer, and fall is really quite straightforward. Where I get into a problem is recommending plants that really don't fit a particular season—and some of these are the very best perennials for your garden. Every gardener wants to know about those wonderful plants that stay in bloom for weeks on end. Similarly, we all crave plants with excellent foliage color, no matter what the season of bloom.

Phalaris arundinacea/Sedum kamtschtium
DOUGLAS GREEN

Foliage Perennials

I've organized this chapter to describe plants that display wonderful foliage, whatever the season. So that you can appreciate the problem, consider one of the newer plant introductions like *Tiarella*. In the past, I would have had no hesitation putting *Tiarella* under spring-blooming plants. Now, however, with breeders introducing wonderfully colored foliage plants, it is tough to decide whether to list it for its spring blooms or for its fall foliage. I leave it as a blooming plant, and I made a similar decision about *Pulmonaria* and its new varieties. This is not to suggest that these plants do not have foliar design interest—far from it. Grow them—and the plants listed in the table below—for the foliage as well as flowers. The listing also includes plants that have varieties with variegated foliage. All these plants create tremendous foliage interest in the garden.

Euphorbia dulcis 'Chameleon'   DOUGLAS GREEN

The following plants have great foliage, but most gardeners tend to grow them primarily for their blooms. For full descriptions, see the chapters referenced.

Aquilegia	See Chapter 6	Gold-leaved varieties
Campanula 'Dickson's Gold'	See Chapter 8	Gold-leaved variety
Dicentra spectabilis 'Goldheart'	See Chapter 6	Gold-leaved variety
Epimedium	See Chapter 5	Good coloring in leaves
Euphorbia dulcis 'Chameleon'	See Chapter 6	Good dark leaves all summer long
Polemonium	See Chapter 7	Variegated variety
Pulmonaria	See Chapter 5	New patterns of leaf markings
Tiarella	See Chapter 7	New patterns of leaf markings

ARTEMISIA

Common names: wormwood, old man, old woman

*A*rtemisia was named after Artemis, the Greek goddess of chastity and, apparently, a few other things that are no longer remembered outside of the classics. Chiron the centaur (remember him, the great healer?) was given these plants by Artemis, and he named them after her. The term *wormwood* should not come as a surprise if you've ever tasted *Artemisia*, but I was unable to find any reference that described the origin of that name. *Old man* and *old woman* apparently come from the silvery appearance of the leaves, which resembles the gray hair of old folks.

Bloom time: Summer
Height: 12″ to 72″ (30 cm to 180 cm)
Sun needed: Full sun
Bloom color: White, inconspicuous
Planting space: 18″ to 24″ (45 cm to 60 cm) apart

Soil preferred: Well-drained, not overly fertile
Propagation method: Cuttings or division

Recommended Varieties

Artemisia abrotanum

Known as *southernwood, Artemis abrotanum* is 48″ (120 cm) tall with spicily fragrant leaves. It is not invasive in the garden but is a rather slow spreader.

Artemisia lactiflora

The species *Artemisia lactiflora* is interesting in that it might be the only one worth growing for flowers as well as the foliage. While the flowers are not outstanding, they do make excellent cut or dried material. This is one of the few *Artemisia* plants to prefer damp soils over well-drained sites.

'Guizhou' has blackish green leaves and mahogany stems that make this an interesting plant. It grows to 48″ (120 cm) tall and spreads out to 36″ (90 cm) wide.

Artemisia ludoviciana

Artemisia ludoviciana is 24″ to 30″ (60 cm to 75 cm) tall. It is leafy and does not have the fernlike, finely cut leaves of most of the family. This is a bushy upright plant that spreads quickly, requiring constant attention and edging to keep it under control. It has excellent heat and drought tolerance.

'Silver King' is 30″ to 36″ (75 cm to 90 cm) tall, with silvery leaves and a good upright growth habit. It is not floppy unless it is overfed.

'Valerie Finnis' is a compact sport of 'Silver King' and grows to 24″ (60 cm) tall. It is not as aggressive as 'Silver King.'

Artemisia pontica

Artemisia pontica is more of a ground-hugging species than many of the other family members. Growing 12″ to 18″ (30 cm to 45 cm) tall, it is fine at the front of the border. It can be invasive

64 PERENNIALS ALL SEASON

Artemisia ludoviciana 'Silver King'   DOUGLAS GREEN

if it likes where it grows. I had one of these plants in a sandy, miserable soil for four years, and it never moved past a foot of its original planting. When I moved it in anticipation of improving and renovating the garden, it took off and became a pest within two years.

'Powis Castle' is the best-known variety, and at 24″ (60 cm) tall, it has not been invasive at all in my gardens (even the ones with good soil). It has been a bit tender for me in zone 4, which may explain why it doesn't spread that much. A protected zone 5 garden should not have any trouble, and overwintering it in zone 6 is easy.

Artemisia schmidtiana

'Silver Mound' is most commonly known by its variety name. This is probably the most popular gray-leaved plant in the garden center trade. If it gets too leggy in midsummer, simply shear it back to the ground and it will resprout to form a nice mound again. It does get too leggy in fertile, moist garden soil. Treat it rough, and it stays bushier.

Artemisia stelleriana

At 12″ tall, 'Silver Brocade' resembles the annual dusty miller more than it does other perennials.

While it is evergreen in mild regions, here in zone 4 it dies to the ground in winter. If it gets a bit ratty looking in midsummer, do trim it back and let it resprout.

Growing *Artemisia*

Artemisia is a plant family that as a rule likes it hot and dry. Once established, these plants will take almost as much heat as a garden can deliver. Overfeeding leads to rank, unattractive growth, and in the case of the spreading species, you'll almost be able to see them throw new colonizing shoots to take over your garden, they'll expand so fast. They make excellent cut and dried flowers, and the fragrance of some of the species is quite powerful and spicy. As gray-leaved plants, they are deservedly among the most popular plants in the garden.

Potions and Poisons

Artemisia has a long history of medicinal and folk use. It is quite bitter, and it is unlikely that any person would willingly eat it directly from the garden. Its use was generally as a tonic and stimulant (not to mention a love potion).

Artemisia lactiflora 'Guizhou'

BLOOMS OF BRESSINGHAM NORTH AMERICA, BARBERTON OH

Artemisia pontica 'Powis Castle'

DOUGLAS GREEN

FERNS

The word *fern* comes to us from the Anglo-Saxon word *fepern*, meaning "feather."

Bloom time: Not applicable
Height: 8″ to 48″ (20 cm to 120 cm)
Sun needed: Part shade to shade
Bloom color: Insignificant
Planting space: 12″ to 18″ (30 cm to 45 cm) apart

Soil preferred: Rich, woodland soils high in organic matter and with even moisture
Propagation method: Division or spores

Recommended Varieties

Adiantum pedatum

Known as *maidenhair fern*, *Adiantum pedatum* grows to 18″ to 24″ (45 cm to 60 cm) tall. Delicate fronds with black stems and rock solid hardiness make this an excellent mid-height plant for the shade garden. The fronds turn a golden color in the fall after frost. It is an excellent plant.

Asplenium ebenoides

Known as *dragon's tail fern* or *Scott's spleenwort*, *Asplenium ebenoides* has shiny, triangular fronds and is only 12″ (30 cm) tall. It is often sold for shady rock gardens or for the front of the shady border. It forms a small, compact plant. It is marginally hardy in my zone 4 garden.

Athyrium filix-femina

Known as *lady fern*, *Athyrium filix-femina* is 18″ to 24″ (45 cm to 60 cm) tall with lacy, bright green foliage. It makes a dense clump. I've grown this species in the sunshine but found that it requires constantly damp soil. It's best in the shade.

Athyrium niponicum

Known as *Japanese painted fern*, the fronds of *Athyrium niponicum* 'Pictum' are a metallic green with red tones. This is a very popular fern and is extremely easy to grow. It grows 12″ to 18″ (30 cm to 45 cm) tall. I note that the more sunlight you give this fern, the less intense the coloring becomes.

Each leaf of 'Silver Falls' has a heavy silver coloring that increases as the plant ages. It has red veins on the leaves.

Dryopteris carthusiana

Known as *toothed wood fern*, *Dryopteris carthusiana* is 24″ to 36″ (60 cm to 90 cm) tall and is one of the easiest to grow. Its bright green fronds lighten up shady gardens well. It simply loves wet spots in the shade and is perfect for naturalizing.

Dryopteris x complexa

'Robusta' (robust male fern) is a vigorous grower, reaching 36″ (90 cm) tall. The fronds are lacy and arch well, giving a typical fern look to this plant.

Dryopteris cycadina

Known as *shield fern, Dryopteris cycadina* is 24″ (60 cm) tall and has light green fronds that appear to be leathery. This is marginally hardy in my zone 4 garden, and using a heavy layer of leaf mulch seems to work better than simply using bark chips to help it through the winter.

Dryopteris dilatata

Known as *broad buckler fern, Dryopteris dilatata* is an easy fern to grow, although zone 4 is pretty much its cold limit. It is 24″ (60 cm) tall, and if you search, you'll find varieties of it that have been imported from Europe, where it is a native species.

'Jimmy Dyce' grows to 24″ (60 cm) tall, but the fronds are stiff and upright with a blue-green coloring.

The fronds of 'Recurved Form' (recurved broad buckler fern) are very lacy, and each leaflet curls under to give it a distinctive garden look. Personally, I simply think it looks sick, but many fern fanciers love it.

Dryopteris filix-mas

Commonly known as *male fern, Dryopteris filix-mas* is 36″ to 48″ (90 cm to 120 cm) tall and is one of the easiest to grow and one of the tallest, most elegant ferns in the garden. It will tolerate sunshine if the soil is kept damp. There are numerous varieties being made available in specialty garden centers and mail-order catalogs.

'Barnesii' is more slender than the species and quite upright.

'Grandiceps' has long, arching fronds with forked crests on the ends of each frond.

'Linearis Polydactyla' has lacy fronds with "forks" or "tassels" on the ends of each frond. It is a fine-textured fern.

Matteuccia struthiopteris

Known as *ostrich fern, Matteuccia struthiopteris* is 36″ to 48″ (90 cm to 120 cm) tall and is one of the most popular ferns in the garden. Not only can you eat the young fiddleheads of this species, but also it produces an extremely attractive garden plant. Wide fronds and good-sized clumps combined with an upright growth habit and ease of growth make it an excellent first fern for your shade garden.

Osmunda cinnamonea

Known as *cinnamon fern, Osmunda cinnamonea* grows to 36″ to 48″ (90 cm to 120 cm) tall with wide triangular fronds that make it a stunning display plant. It does best in dampish, acidic soils.

Osmunda regalis

Known as *royal fern, Osmunda regalis* is 36″ to 48″ (90 cm to 120 cm) tall and unique. It throws its fronds from a ring-shaped central crown, creating a circular, arching mass of foliage.

Polystichum acrostichoides

Known as *Christmas fern, Polystichum acrostichoides* is 18″ (45 cm) tall with leathery-looking fronds that were once used as Christmas decorations, hence the name. The plant is easy to care for and grows to a medium-sized clump that is perfect for the front of the shade garden. It is an evergreen, so keep it out of the winter winds.

Thelypteris decursive-pinnata

Known as *beech fern, Thelypteris decursive-pinnata*'s fronds, 24″ (60 cm) tall, hold their bright green color all season, and this alone makes it worthy of a place in the darker garden to act as a source of light. The more light you give it, the lighter the color of the frond, until it becomes a lemony green color. It is a slow spreader.

Growing Ferns

Ferns thrive in part shade in evenly moist soils. For the most part, a soil that is high in organic matter is better than a sandy one, but as long as even moisture is present, the fern plant will be happy. I've grown them in full sunshine, and as

Athyrium niponicum 'Silver Falls'   TERRA NOVA NURSERIES

long as the soil moisture is high, the plants will live. The fronds can become quite tattered and brown as soon as the soil dries out or if strong, hot winds "burn" the foliage, sucking out its moisture. They are much happier out of the noonday sun and in damp soils.

If you purchase your fern as a root and not a growing plant, then the following tip will save you many transplant problems. Soak the root for twenty-four hours in warm water before planting or transplanting it. The root soaks up the water and revitalizes itself, but I confess I don't understand the chemistry. All I know is that when I learned and implemented this trick, my nursery-transplant survival rate dramatically improved.

Potions and Poisons

Ancient herbalists believed that if you collected the small and almost invisible spores of ferns and used them in drinks, you would become invisible. I have also read that fern spores would make you perpetually young. Neither has worked for me. Some reports say that the fronds are a mild laxative.

GRASSES

Common names: they are indicators of origin or descriptors of the plant and are listed under Recommended Varieties.

Most of the common names of ornamental grasses describe their geographic origin or some feature of their appearance. Each of the scientific names comes with a history that is similar to other plants listed in the book. For the sake of brevity and ensuring a common listing, I have omitted the descriptions for these grasses.

Bloom time: Fall

Height: 8″ to 72″ (20 cm to 180 cm)

Sun needed: Full sun

Bloom color: Silver, whites, pinks

Planting space: 8″ to 24″ (20 cm to 60 cm) apart

Soil preferred: Well-drained, average garden soil

Propagation method: Division or seed

Recommended Varieties

Acorus calamus 'Variegatus'

Known as *sweet flag*, native *Acorus calamus* 'Variegatus' has broadly striped green and yellow leaves. It doesn't flower spectacularly, but the foliage is wonderful, particularly if you grow it in damp soils next to ponds. It will tolerate a bit more shade than other grasses, but the slugs get busy on it if you grow it in shady gardens—at least they always did when I tried to grow it there.

Alopecurus pratentus 'Aureovariegatus'

The common name of *Alopecurus pratentus* 'Aureovariegatus' is *meadow foxtail*. Having tried to eliminate foxtail from my hay fields, I confess to having mixed feelings about inviting it to share my garden space. This variety, with its variegated leaves, may someday find itself there, but for the moment I am resisting the temptation to plant it.

Adropogon scoparious

Known as *blue stem*, *Adropogon scoparious* is a native prairie grass, and there are now varieties such as 'The Blues' that have a more pronounced blue tone to them than the species. This makes a good clump in the garden and isn't overly aggressive. The foliage turns a bronze-orange in the fall and is quite attractive.

Arrhenatherum bulbosum 'Variegatum'

Known as *bulbous oat grass*, *Arrhenatherum bulbosum* 'Variegatum' is a low-growing grass, 12″ to 18″ (30 cm to 45 cm) tall, that doesn't spread too quickly. The variegated variety has wonderful spring foliage, but by midsummer it starts to look quite brown and ratty. Shear it back to the ground (or close to it), and it will regrow and color up again to complement the fall garden.

Arundo donax

Known as *giant reed*, *Arundo donax* is technically not a grass but a reed, but it is surprisingly easy

Miscanthus sacchariflorus   Douglas Green

to grow if you live in a zone 6 garden. I have overwintered it in zone 4, but it was not happy about it. There is a variegated variety that is quite stunning. This plant grows to over 10′ (300 cm) tall and is not for the faint of heart in garden design, as it will quickly become a focal point in the garden.

Calamagrostis x acutiflora

Known as *feather reed grass, Calamagrostis x acutiflora* is a stiff, upright grass that grows to only 24″ (60 cm) tall and is beloved of designers because of this height restriction.

'Karl Foerster' is a common variety with white flowers that fade to pink and then to the tan seedheads. The blades are upright. The plant tends to clump rather than spread aggressively.

'Overdam' has variegated white-and-green leaves with a gold flower head.

Carex buchananii

Carex buchananii's common name is *leatherleaf sedge*. The sedges are interesting plants if you have a damp area or pondside area for them. They have never done all that well for me out in the full sunshine in the regular garden. The only problem with plants such as this one is trying to decide whether it is alive or dead. More than once I've poked and pulled at this plant to try to tell whether it was growing or just sitting there with dead-looking foliage. There are several species and varieties available through specialty nurseries. They are worth experimenting with in the damp garden.

Chasmanthium latifolium

Known as *sea oats*, *Chasmanthium latifolium* is 36″ (90 cm) tall and prefers a damp garden soil. With a bit of imagination, you could say it resembles bamboo, with its upright green shoots. It is also an excellent grass for a part-shade location. If happy, this plant will self-sow extensively and become a weed.

Festuca glauca

Known as *blue fescue*, *Festuca glauca* is a dwarf grass of 8″ to 12″ (20 cm to 30 cm) that makes an excellent clumping exclamation point in the front of the garden.

‘Elijah Blue’ is a good bright blue that holds its color all season.

‘Sea Urchin’ is a compact grower with metallic blue leaves.

‘Skinner’s Blue’ is a turquoise green color and extremely hardy but not as blue as other forms of the grass.

Hakonechloa macra ‘Aureola’

Hakonechloa macra ‘Aureola,’ known as *golden variegated Hakonechloa*, is an extremely showy grass at 24″ (60 cm) tall but is slow to establish. It is rated as a zone 5 grass and has been tender for me. I’m still trying, though. The leaves are bright golden-yellow with narrow green stripes. It is a very distinctive plant, and its arching growth habit makes it resemble a waterfall.

Helictotrichon sempervirens

Known as *blue oat grass*, *Helictotrichon sempervirens* is a popular grass, hardy to zone 3 and easily grown. It reaches 36″ (90 cm) in height and is not an aggressive spreader. The leaves are quite blue and make an excellent contrast with other foliage.

Imperata cylindrica

The common name of *Imperata cylindrica* is *Japanese blood grass*. It’s 18″ (45 cm) tall with reddish leaf tops (green at the bottom) and can be a bit of a pain to establish in the garden. It has so far resisted my attempts in zone 4 (it is rated for zone 5), but apparently I’m not alone, as it is reputed to be picky about where it grows even in warmer gardens. Avoid the extremes of hot and dry and damp; try to find a soil with medium fertility and good water-holding capacity.

Leymus arenarius

Leymus arenarius is known as *lyme grass*. It’s a 24″ (60 cm) tall, blue-leaved grass, and is sometimes sold in garden centers. More’s the pity. I was convinced once to plant it in my main perennial border, and while it sat still the first year, this thug was slowly building an underground network. The second spring it exploded and sent shoots reaching up to 8′ (240 cm) away from the mother plant. I quickly removed it before it took over the garden. Forewarned is forearmed.

Miscanthus

The *Miscanthus* family of grasses has produced some of the finest used in gardens. These are typically large, bold grasses with superior winter survival and spreading aggressiveness. Grow them, but keep an edging shovel handy.

Miscanthus sacchariflorus ‘Robustus’

Miscanthus sacchariflorus ‘Robustus’ grows to 48″ (120 cm) tall with wonderful silver plumes. Thin, bamboolike stems can be used like—well, thin bamboo. It is an aggressive spreader. The plant is excellent for cut flowers, and the fall foliage turns a reddish color. It is slowly taking over the field around my large farm pond, and the fall display is gorgeous.

Miscanthus sinensis

The common name of *Miscanthus sinensis* is *Japanese silver grass*. It can be a bit tender sometimes in my zone 4 garden. I’ve had some clumps for several years, while others seem to last only a few years before fading away. In general, *Miscanthus sinensis* is one of the last grasses to start in the spring. Some years I will almost dig it up, as I think it won't come, but procrastination has its rewards, as it then shoots up as one of the last plants in the garden to show life.

'Cosmopolitan' has a broadly striped, variegated green, wide leaf, which is taking over in the trade from the older 'Variegatus.' It grows 6' to 8' (180 cm to 240 cm) tall.

'Gracillimus,' or *maiden grass*, grows 6' (180 cm) tall and has graceful arching grass blades that make a wonderful fountain effect. Do not look for flowers every year if you live in zone 4, as it requires a long warm season to produce them. I never worried about the flowers, as this grass is not a spreader but a clumper and is wonderful in the perennial garden.

'Malepartus,' at 6' (180 cm) tall, is an interesting variety. It has green summer foliage that turns bronzy red in the fall, but the flowers are a purplish pink.

'Morning Light' is a variegated sport of 'Gracillimus,' with narrow white stripes along the leaf.

'Purpurascens' or *flame grass*, is a bit shorter than other *Miscanthus* plants at 4' to 5' (120 cm to 150 cm) but has rose-colored flowers in late summer. The leaves turn orange in the fall.

'Undine' has lower, more compact foliage, but the flower spikes still reach upwards of 4' to 5' (120 cm to 150 cm). This would be excellent for urban gardeners who would like grass but hesitate because of the size and aggressiveness of some species.

Molinia arundinacea

Known as *moor grass*, *Molinia arundinacea* is 6' (180 cm) tall and is a clumper with few tendencies to seed or spread itself with aggressive underground rhizomes. The flower stalks on this plant turn golden yellow and are wonderful as they wave about in the wind.

Panicum virgatum

The common name of *Panicum virgatum* is *red switch grass*. The green foliage is 2' to 3' (60 cm to 90 cm) tall, and this is an upright growing grass. Its claim to fame is the red seedheads that appear in late August. The foliage is a red and yellow as it dies off for the winter, and grass enthusiasts uniformly love this plant for those winter colors.

'Heavy Metal' has metallic blue foliage for the spring and summer turning to the typical red and yellow for fall.

A steel blue leaf color makes 'Prairie Sky' almost irresistible. It is one of the bushiest varieties, with arching leaves that turn yellow in the fall.

'Rotstrahlbusch' has undeniably the best red fall color of any *Panicum virgatum*.

Pennisetum alopecuroides

Known as *fountain grass*, *Pennisetum alopecuroides* is 4' (120 cm) tall and has arching stems of mid-green leaves. It is quite an architectural plant and somewhat tender here in zone 4.

'Hameln' is a semidwarf variety at 24" to 30" (60 cm to 75 cm) tall. I'm told this is hardier than the species.

Phalaris arundinacea

Known as *ribbon grass*, *Phalaris arundinacea* grows to 3' (90 cm) tall with green-and-white-striped leaves. It has invaded more gardens than all other grasses combined. Do not put it in a good garden. However, it is worth growing in damp spots where little else will grow and for naturalizing. I believe the catalogs call it *robust*; I call it downright thuglike—an Attila the Hun of the plant world.

Spartina pectinata 'Aureo-marginata'

The common name of *Spartina pectinata* 'Aureo-marginata' is *variegated cord grass*. The upright nature of and wide yellow stripe on this grass make it attractive for anyone needing a grass 6' to 7' (180 cm to 210 cm) tall. It does particularly well beside ponds in damp soils, but take note that it can be a trifle aggressive and will need regular edging to keep it in bounds. It is not a grass for a refined garden design because of its spreading nature.

Growing Grasses

Grasses are plants of open meadows and prairies. They prefer full sun and well-drained but average soils with adequate water. The best blooms come from soils that are not allowed to totally dry out nor allow standing water. There are too many species to list individually, and trying to list the varieties, to do this plant justice, would require an entire book. There are also many tender varieties suited for zones 8 to 9 that are not covered in this book.

Grasses are easily maintained and fashionable. My only warning comes from my experience that says that some of them are aggressive spreaders and if allowed into the good garden can quickly become a nuisance. They are wonderful when used in combinations in wilder gardens that give them the opportunity to spread and mingle with other plants. The smaller and less aggressive forms are wonderful accents at the front of the border.

HOSTA

Common name: plantain lily

Hosta was named after Nicholas Tomas Host (1761–1834), physician to the emperor of Austria. *Plantain* comes from the leaf's resemblance to the common plantain plant (*Plantago*) and *lily* from its flower's resemblance to a lily.

Bloom time: Midsummer
Height: Leaves to 6″ to 36″ (15 cm to 90 cm), flowers to 6′ (180 cm)
Sun needed: Part shade to shade
Bloom color: White, violet

Planting space: 12″ to 24″ (30 cm to 60 cm) apart
Soil preferred: Rich woodland
Propagation method: Division or seed

Recommended Varieties

It is almost as hard to give suggestions for *Hosta* varieties as it is for *Hemerocallis*. Thousands of varieties are available and more are pouring into garden centers every year. Here are some of the great old varieties and a few more modern hybrids to whet your appetite for this most popular of shade plants. I have not even listed all the plants I have in my own garden, but there's only one *Hosta* listed here that I would not have in my own garden. I wish I had room for more—both here and in my garden.

'Antioch' is 18″ to 24″ (45 cm to 60 cm) tall and has a good spreading form. The leaf is light green with a wide stripe of pale cream on the edge.

'August Moon' is 24″ (60 cm) tall and an award winner. Very large pale green (almost yellow) leaves with good crinkling make this an excellent plant for combining with blue-leaved hostas.

'Big Daddy' is 36″ (90 cm) tall and has very large, ribbed leaves in a deep blue color. It is slug-resistant because of the thickness of its leaves.

'Francee' is 24″ (60 cm) tall with very dark green leaves with a well-defined white edge. This is an award-winning plant.

'Ginko Craig' is only 12″ (30 cm) tall with narrow dark green leaves with white edges. It is an excellent ground cover or plant for the front of a shade border.

'Gold Edger' is 12″ (30 cm) tall and has a good heart-shaped gold leaf that holds its color for most of the gardening season.

'Gold Standard' is 24″ (60 cm) tall and truly the standard by which other gold varieties are measured. Leaves start out greenish but change to yellow as they emerge and mature. It has some green tones depending on how much sunlight it gets. A few hours a day will lighten up the leaves considerably.

'Golden Sunburst' is a gold sport of 'Frances Williams.' It grows best in shade.

'Hadspen Blue' is one of the classic blue-leaved varieties, and it holds its blue color longer than many others. There are heavily ribbed leaves (some called them *corrugated*) and light lavender flowers on this plant, which grows to 12″ to 18″ (30 cm to 45 cm) tall.

Hosta undulata 'Wolverine'
BLOOMS OF BRESSINGHAM NORTH AMERICA, BARBERTON OH

Hosta 'Potomac Pride'
BLOOMS OF BRESSINGHAM NORTH AMERICA, BARBERTON OH

'Hillbilly Blues' is a flat-growing hybrid—the leaves stay only 10″ to 12″ (25 cm to 30 cm) from the ground, while the plant expands to 36″ (90 cm) wide. The leaves are deeply ribbed and powdery blue in color. The plant has light lavender flowers in late summer.

'Honeybells' is 24″ (60 cm) tall and has light green, largish leaves. Grow it for the fragrant, pale mauve flowers.

'Janet' is 16″ (40 cm) tall with green-margined leaves with golden centers. The gold does fade during the summer to white, and this plant can tend to revert back to straight green leaves if divided or unhappy.

'Krossa Regal' is one of the classic standards in *Hosta* growing. Steel blue foliage and very upright growth to 36″ (90 cm) tall make a stunning garden statement. It has lavender flowers on 48″ to 60″ (120 cm to 150 cm) stalks.

'Patriot' is 24″ (60 cm) tall with wonderful heavily variegated leaves in green and white. I think this is one of the best green-and-white variegations, and I have several clumps of it in my garden.

'Potomac Pride' is an award winner. This dark black-green-leaved plant is 20″ (50 cm) tall and stunning when planted with gold-leaved varieties. The flowers are small and insignificant.

Hosta sieboldiana

'Elegans' is perhaps the original in blue-leaved *Hosta* plants and in my opinion still the best.

Hosta 'Hillbilly Blues'
BLOOMS OF BRESSINGHAM NORTH AMERICA, BARBERTON OH

Heavily ribbed leaves and good blue coloring make it a garden classic and a standout.

'Frances Williams' is a classic plant with a gold edge around heavily ribbed leaves. It is one of the most popular plants and deservedly so.

'Sum and Substance' is 30″ to 36″ (75 cm to 90 cm) tall with huge gold-green leaves (largest leaves of any *Hosta* I've ever seen). Give this one room, as it can spread upwards of 48″ (120 cm) across in a few years.

Hosta tokudama aureo-nebulosa

Hosta tokudama aureo-nebulosa is 12″ to 18″ (30 cm to 45 cm) tall. Its blue-green leaves have a center that's gold and light yellow-green. This is my favorite *Hosta* plant. It is slow-growing and usually expensive but worth the price. It has good slug resistance.

Hosta undulata

'Medio variegata' is my least favorite *Hosta* but the most commonly grown one. It's 12″ to 18″ (30 cm to 45 cm) tall, green-leaved with heavy white center variegations, and found in every garden center. It grows rapidly and handles full sunshine.

'Wolverine' has lance-shaped leaves with blue centers and gold-yellow edging on plants 14″ (35 cm) tall.

Growing Hosta

Hosta is a plant that loves a rich woodland soil in shade or part shade. If you give it this, you'll quickly find out how easy it is to grow and how hardy it is. Once planted, *Hosta* can be left alone for many years without touching it with a shovel—the clumps slowly expand into show-pieces but rarely become invasive. I do make a point of deadheading the flowers, otherwise unwanted seedlings quickly pop up all over the garden.

The only problem that *Hosta* has is that slugs consider it a delicacy, and you'll have to work on slug prevention devices and activities for summer-long control. Thicker-leaved plants are not as prone to damage as the thinner-leaved forms are.

Multiple-Season Bloomers

Most perennial flowers are quite ephemeral—they are with us for all too short a time. *Hemerocallis* blooms last only one day, hence the name *daylily*. If it were not for the fact that each plant produces so many blooms, this perennial would not be as popular as it is. The blooms of the double-flowering bloodroot last five to six days at most before the petals begin to drop. Do not take a spring holiday if you want to watch this flower bloom.

To complicate things further, the start of bloom time is a variable in the garden, controlled by both cultivation and weather factors. Also, the length of time that a flower is in bloom is largely controlled by environmental variables. Remember that hot weather shortens bloom life and cool weather extends it. So a cool spring will delay the onset of flowering and extend the flowering time of spring bloomers into the early-summer blooming period. Then, when summer finally arrives and the soil warms up, the summer flowers explode into bloom and the poor gardener is looking at a garden full of early- and late-spring

Leucanthemum x superbum 'Alaska'   Douglas Green

flowers as well as early-summer flowers. What really messes things up is when the summer then turns very hot; the heat brings the late-summer bloomers into bloom earlier than normal. When they bloom too soon, along with the early-summer bloomers, there is nothing left to ease the transition into the fall garden.

Campanula carpatica   Douglas Green

Fall chrysanthemum   Douglas Green

Geranium 'Bressingham's Delight'

BLOOMS OF BRESSINGHAM NORTH AMERICA, BARBERTON OH

Hemerocallis Lovely Lady™, 'Lady Florence'

BLOOMS OF BRESSINGHAM NORTH AMERICA, BARBERTON OH

Fall chrysanthemum

DOUGLAS GREEN

Geranium 'Rozanne'

BLOOMS OF BRESSINGHAM NORTH AMERICA, BARBERTON OH

Hemerocallis Lovely Lady™, 'Lady Rose'
BLOOMS OF BRESSINGHAM NORTH AMERICA, BARBERTON OH

Heucherella 'Burnished Bronze'
TERRA NOVA NURSERIES

Heucherella 'Viking Ship'
TERRA NOVA NURSERIES

Monarda 'Cambridge Scarlet' / *Gypsophila*
'Schneeflocke'   DOUGLAS GREEN

Phlox paniculata 'Norah Leigh' DOUGLAS GREEN

Phlox paniculata 'Prince of Orange' DOUGLAS GREEN

Nobody said that timing garden flowers was a science, nor should you expect the same results each and every year. Still, there is one thing you can do to mitigate the problem—you can select perennials that stay in bloom longer than most to extend the life of your garden. The average bloom time for perennials is four weeks. So if you can find a plant that blooms for a longer period or that you can convince to rebloom by shearing it, then this plant is a candidate for inclusion in the garden design.

The plants listed below are some of the better plants for long bloom times. Included are cross-references to the chapters where they are fully described.

Recommended Varieties

Allium

Choose *Allium* if you consider the seedheads attractive and part of the flowering season. I do. See Chapter 7.

Anemone

The fall-blooming varieties of *Anemone* such as 'September Charm' bloom for extended periods. See Chapter 9.

Arisaema

Arisaema species bloom for a surprisingly long time for shade plants. See Chapter 6.

Aster x frikartii

Aster x frikartii is one of the longest-blooming plants in the garden and worth trying even if you are a bit out of its growing range. Nothing ventured is nothing gained in the flower garden. See Chapter 9.

Campanula carpatica

Campanula carpatica is the longest summer-blooming blue flower. See Chapter 8.

Chrysanthemum

Leucanthemum x superbum, or *shasta daisy*, is a long bloomer, particularly if each dying flower is cut off before it sets seed (deadheading). Fall mums are also long-blooming, particularly if they are kept watered after transplanting into the garden. See Chapters 7 and 9.

Coreopsis

Summer-blooming *Coreopsis* plants are all long-blooming. Both *Coreopsis grandiflora* and *Coreopsis lanceolata* are good if they are deadheaded, while *Coreopsis verticillata* and *Coreopsis rosea* don't need any particular care to keep them flowering for a long time. See Chapter 8.

Corydalis

Corydalis is hard to beat, particularly the yellow *Corydalis lutea*, which flowers from early summer till hard frost. See Chapter 6.

Delphinium

Delphinium qualifies as a long bloomer because if you shear it after flowering, it'll rebloom in the fall. See Chapter 7.

Dianthus

The carnation or single-flowered *Dianthus* species are particularly long bloomers. The biennial forms are not. See Chapter 7.

Dicentra formosa

'Luxuriant' and other varieties are excellent for long-lasting blooms. See Chapter 6.

Echinacea

Echinacea is a good bloomer that requires little work except deadheading. See Chapter 8.

Gaillardia

Gaillardia is one of the easiest flowers to grow for multiple-season bloom. It does it all by itself but is better if deadheaded. See Chapter 8.

Geranium

While the first flower flush is reasonably long-lasting, *Geranium* qualifies as a multiseason plant because it reblooms if you shear it after its first flush is over. See Chapter 7.

Gypsophila

The masses of white *Gypsophila* flowers seem to hang on and on in my garden. See Chapter 7.

Hemerocallis

It is possible to achieve multiple-season *Hemerocallis* bloom in two ways. The first is by obtaining a variety that reblooms, like 'Stella d'Oro' or 'Lady Florence' and then growing it in a climate warmer than zone 4 to give it the ability to rebloom. The second is to purchase varieties that have early-, mid-, and late-season-blooming characteristics and create a longer season using different varieties. See Chapter 7.

Rudbeckia maxima   Douglas Green

Heucherella

Heucherella has always impressed me with its long-lasting flowers and should be well worth a try. See Chapter 7.

Hylomecon japonicum

Hylomecon japonicum produces small, yellow, poppylike flowers over an extended time. See Chapter 6.

Iris

Iris can be a long-lasting bloomer if you take care to choose remontant or reblooming varieties. See Chapter 6.

Lavandula

Lavender is one of the classic multiple-season flower producers, particularly if kept deadheaded or sheared after the first bloom. See Chapter 8.

Malva

Malva flowers for an extended time, continually producing new flowers from midsummer onward. This of course ensures it self-sows like mad to become a weed in your garden. See Chapter 8.

Monarda

Monarda flowers simply last for a very long time in my garden. See Chapter 8.

Phlox paniculata

Phlox paniculata is another of the classic backbone plants that last and last and last all season. See Chapter 8.

Primula japonica

Primula japonica is perhaps the longest-flowering *Primula* species, if only because it produces more flowers than most others. It keeps on growing and growing. See Chapter 7.

Rudbeckia

The individual flowers of *Rudbeckia* last for a long time, and the plant continues to produce them. See Chapter 9.

Scabiosa

Scabiosa flowers much the same way as *Rudbeckia*; I've seen it produce several flushes of flowers over the summer. See Chapter 8.

Tradescantia

Tradescantia is an excellent multiple-season bloomer but only if you keep the soil moist. If you allow it to dry out, then the blooms will stop. See Chapter 7.

Viola

Some varieties of *Viola* bloom for extended periods, particularly biennial forms.

Afterword

I may be repeating myself, as gardeners tend to do, but I think it is important to leave you with a simple thought to ponder as you work in your garden: perfection is fleeting.

Now at first that might sound harsh, but I have found that it is a reason to celebrate. Since I know that the perfect perennial garden depends as much on weather conditions and the plants themselves as it does on my mastery of design, I console myself when I see something in the garden that doesn't quite reflect the picture I held in my mind's eye all winter long. My garden is not ever likely to be perfect, but that's fine with me. It means I have next year to get it right.

There's always next year. How many times have I said those words? When the chipmunks get the lily buds, when the rabbit eats the lavender to the ground, when the deer destroy the daylilies? When the rainstorm knocks over those almost-perfect delphiniums? I've said them so often that I now accept that *next year* is part of my gardening toolbox.

And this is how it should be. We gardeners need to look toward the future; we don't belong in the past. Perennials, by nature, are just not intended for instant effect; we nurture them for the long term. We plant them to interact with each other, the soil, the weather, and ourselves. And sometimes we discover that they have minds of their own about how and when they'll bloom. We find that plants are a life form unto themselves, and if we want them to give us their best, we have to take their needs into consideration in our planning. After all, being a gardener does not mean putting plants in the ground; it means helping those plants grow and bloom.

And so we plan and we dig and we struggle to create that delightful image we started out with of a garden that is ever in bloom. We choose flowers and colors, we arrange and rearrange, we plant and replant. This process is the essence of perennial gardening—it is a continual and absorbing challenge to create something unique and lovely. And for a fleeting moment, early in the morning, dew sitting gently atop newly opened blooms, we catch a glimpse of the miracles we have made in our gardens. This is when I treasure my garden. I suspect it is the same for you.

Resources

Plant Names

All plant names have been identified by referring to the Royal Horticultural Society's (RHS) *Plant Finder*. This is the most up-to-date botanical listing available to home gardeners. You can order your own copy from the Royal Horticultural Society, 80 Vincent Square, London, SW1P 2PE, UK, or you can order it online at www.grogro.com. I normally order a copy every two to three years just to see what changes there are and what plants are newly available in Europe. If you want to check out only a few plants rather than order the book, use the online sources at the RHS site, www.rhs.org.uk. For more than a few plants, the book is easier.

Internet Resources

I write from my own gardening experience, and my website is at www.simplegiftsfarm.com. Quite a few gardening articles are also online at that site that may help answer your questions.

While many gardeners use the major search directories such as Yahoo, I almost exclusively use www.google.com. It has one of the most extensive collections of archived Web pages, and you can find most plants or sources for plants right there. If you want to find a specific plant, simply type the name and variety of that plant into the search box and you'll quickly find nurseries that sell it via mail order. Google is arguably the largest and certainly one of the fastest search engines on the Internet. Other plant people use www.alltheweb.com and swear by its results.

Dr. Len Perry at the University of Vermont has Perry's Perennial Pages at http://www.uvm.edu/~pass/perry. It is an excellent starting point for creating perennial plant overload—always assuming, of course, that such a condition is possible.

You can't buy plants at www.terranovanurseries.com because it is wholesale only, but you can dream and drool along with me over their new introductions. Let me point you to the similar Blooms of Bressingham North America website at www.bobna.com for great plants and information. It is not necessarily about growing the plants—it *is* about dreaming about them, and these are two sites worthy of dreams.

Plant Societies

Visit the North American Rock Garden Society (NARGS) pages at www.nargs.org to discover where the local chapter of the society meets, and attend those meetings. The people who belong to NARGS's local chapters are some of your best garden resources for obtaining wonderful plants and the locations of the best nurseries. You'll find that the majority of these people grow a wide variety of plants beyond alpine plants. There are also local and national seed exchanges that are easily worth the membership costs.

The Hardy Plant Society (HPS), whose website is at www.hardy-plant.org.uk, is also a good resource for perennial plants. It is based in the United Kingdom, and their idea of a hardy plant doesn't necessarily conform to ours. That being said, they do have a good seed exchange and provide an opportunity to meet other perennial plant addicts.

Mail-Order Resources

This list only scratches the tip of the trade, but these are good places to start if you are looking for something other than what you find locally.

Asiatica, Box 270, Lewisberry, PA 17339, USA, www.asiatica-pa.com. This nursery probably has the finest collection of Asian rare plants—mostly for the shade—in North America. The catalog is $4.00 and if you can resist purchasing something, you're a better person than I.

Chiltern Seeds, Bortree Stile, Ulverston, Cumbria, England LA12 7PB. This nursery carries a wide assortment of seeds, some rare, some obscenely interesting. The catalog is a must-read if you like plants of all kinds. It offers a bit of eccentricity in the midst of an increasingly commercial world.

Cusheon Creek Nursery, 175 Stewart Rd., Salt Spring, BC, Canada, V8K 2C4. This nursery, which ships to the United States, has a wide range of rare plants—from *Acanthus* and arums through to *Trichodiadema* and *Trillium*. The catalog is $2.00.

Dowdeswell Delphiniums, www.delphinium.co.nz/, is a small breeder's site, and they have some of the finest new delphiniums you can imagine. If you don't use the Internet, contact them at 692 Brunswick Rd., R D 1, Wanganui, New Zealand. They sell out quickly, so check with them and order as soon as their seed is ready for shipping, or sign up for their newsletter that tells you when seed is ready.

Fraser's Thimble Farm, 175 Arbutus Rd., Salt Spring Island, BC, Canada, V8K 1A3, is a nursery with a very wide range of rare and unusual perennial plants. It's well worth checking these folks out. I love getting their catalog and finding plants I haven't grown.

Gardens North, 5984 Third Line Rd., RR#3, North Gower, ON, Canada, K0A 2T0, offers a wide variety of hardy perennial seeds, most collected from their own gardens. The catalog is $4.00.

Karmic Exotix Nursery, Box 146, Shelburne, ON, Canada, L0N 1S0. This seed company is a project of well-known alpine plantsman Andrew Osyany, for the purpose of giving European seed explorers and collectors a window into the North American market. He distributes these rare seeds for several Czech collectors. The catalog is well worth the $2.00. Many of these seeds are not available elsewhere.

Plant Delights Nursery, 9241 Sauls Rd., Raleigh, NC 27603, USA, www.plantdelights.com, offers one of the most famous plant catalogs—you can get it by sending ten stamps or a box of chocolates. Many of the plants in this catalog are from owner Tony Avent's hybridizing efforts. They are excellent plants to dream on.

Whitehouse Perennials, RR#2, Almonte, ON, Canada, K0A 1A0, www.whitehouseperennials.com. These folks send one of the biggest divisions of any company I order from. They offer good plants and a fine selection of *Hosta* and daylilies.

Index